BOOKS BY

REYNOLDS PRICE

CONTENTS

FOR

ERIK BENSON

THREE GOSPELS

A GENERAL PREFACE

I AM HARDLY alone in the world in saying that the central narratives of the Old and New Testaments—especially the four life stories called Matthew, Mark, Luke, and John—drew early at my mind and have kept their magnetism for me. In my case, their hold has lasted undiminished nearly six decades. Before I could read I often turned the profusely illustrated pages of *Hurlbut's Story of the Bible*, imagining what tales had produced such swarming pictures. By the age of eight, I had begun making drawings of my own from the knowledge I gained in reading the tales with my new-won literacy and yielding to the pull of their fresh unnerving actions—Abraham bent on butchering his Isaac, the boy David with the hacked-off head of a monstrous Goliath, or (strangest and most riveting of all) the birth of a unique glistening child in a strawy stable with attendant angels, shepherds, and Wise Men.

By then, in the countryside near my parents' home, I had also undergone solitary apprehensions of a vibrant unity among all visible things and the thing I guessed was hid beneath the visible world—the reachable world of trees, rocks, water, clouds, snakes, foxes, myself, and (beneath them) all I loved and feared. Even that early I sensed the world's unity as a vast kinship far past the bond of any root I shared with other creatures in evolutionary time, and the Bible stories had begun to engage me steadily in silence and to draw me toward the singular claim at their burning heart—*Your life is willed and watched with care by a god who once lived here.*

Soon I was hoping to spend a good part of my coming life in making pictures and stories of my own. That hope arose partly in emulation of the row of secular books I had come to prize, partly because I had spent hundreds of hours of my childhood in dark movie houses consuming the great filmed stories of the 1930s and forties (some of which told Biblical tales) but also because I meant to learn to exert a power as nearly strong and awful, as irresistible and fertile, as those old stories of ancient Jews and their endless trials. Mine would be stories that felt as near to the truthful ground as the ones I had learned in Genesis, Exodus, Judges, Samuel, Kings, or Matthew, Mark, Luke, and John. I wanted, over all else, to make new stories that might somehow share in those old stories' radiant will to change whole lives and alter the sun in its course if need be.

By the time I was broiling in adolescence, I could see especially that the four gospels' successful accounts of a single life, a life that was tortured and then transfigured by the dark hand of the source of creation, had not only shaped the actual Earth and the lives of its creatures through two thousand years, those brief accounts had also produced—as sparks from their core—the work of my early models and masters: Dante, Michelangelo, Milton, Bach, Handel, the late poems of Eliot, those stories of Ernest Hemingway that also ache for sublime transcendence, and a good many more of the props of life for millions at least as curious and needful as I. My own hopes for work began to take a big share of heat from what I thought was that same core, the life of a man who apparently refused to die (or to be precise, the *acts* of a man who could rise from death; for the gospels are more nearly records of a chain of acts and a few indispensable words than of a single consecutively examined life).

Given the gospels' continuing force on the lives around me, in the years to come I began to sense that any subsequent secular writer—even Shakespeare or Tolstoy—was hardly likely to equal the pull those brief works exert on human minds with no resources but words and an invisible architecture as severe as the desert their hero frequents. Though I have yet to concede entire defeat in my own stories, still—here after decades of emulation—I have paused in the usual work I do and attempted to pay in this book a partial install-ment on my old debt to a pair of tales that have counted as much in my life—for hope and long-range grounding on Earth—as the primal tales of my parents' love and its sorrows, the memories of my own first loves and pleasures.

That payment takes the form of close and thoroughly plain translations of the two entirely original gospels—Mark and John, with prefatory essays—and a modern gospel writ-ten by me on the basis of the classic ancient four, on my knowledge of other early documents pertaining to Jesus, and on what I have gained in reading widely in the recently re-vived attempt by scholars to provide a minimally reliable his-tory of Jesus' life and work (the original gospels are accurately described, not so much as histories but as histories perceived through the lenses of a sober yet unquestioning trust in the supernatural roots of their hero).

Though I have always tried to make my private narra-tives—novels, poems, short stories, plays—useful beyond my own mind and place, I think I can partly discern why the tales of the ancient gospels, which are one joined tale, have kept their steady heat for any witness who is at least half ready to watch the news that they press toward us and to face, with the guts to answer Yes or No, their imperious claim on our lives. Those partial findings are laid out in my prefaces to the gospels—Mark's, John's, and my own—and the findings are open to any reader's judgment once he or she has read the translated texts in my literal English.

*

The English word *gospel* is a descendant of the Anglo-Saxon word *godspel* or *good news*. *Godspel* was an accurate equivalent of the original Greek word *euaggelion*, literally a *good message* or *good tidings*. And the oldest surviving Greek manuscript copies of the four canonical gospels bear only the headings According to Matthew, Mark, Luke, or John (the four books together comprise the whole of the single *gospel*; and the word *canonical* derives from the Greek *kanon* or *measuring rod* and indicates, in this case, those few gospels that were approved as holy scripture by the orthodox church of the late second century).

Those first available complete manuscripts date from the fourth century AD and are copies made more than two centuries after the completion of their originals and well over three centuries after the death and resurgence of their subject. That subject was the scarcely known man Jesus, an itinerant Jewish healer and teacher who worked briefly in an obscure corner of the Roman empire, who moved his mission south from rural Galilee to the Judean capital of his people's theocracy, who incurred there (perhaps intentionally) the lethal opposition of the Temple hierarchy, was executed at the pleasure of the Roman prefect, was thought by his colleagues to have risen bodily from death three days thereafter, to have appeared to them unmistakably, then ascended to Heaven, and proved deserving of their subsequent proclamation that he had been the anointed Son of God who would soon come again to judge humankind and transform the Earth into the reign of God.

Whatever their roots in Aramaic, which was the Semitic language of Jesus and his pupils, the four gospels were written and first circulated in an evolved form of classical Greek, a form called *Koine* or *common language*. Anyone writing in the Roman empire in the first century with hopes for the widest possible audience outside Italy itself would have been virtually compelled to write in Koine Greek since Koine was not only the vernacular of Greece itself but also of the Roman Middle East from the fourth century BC until at least the mid–sixth century AD. Yet it was not long after the gospels' slow dissemination in handwritten copies throughout the Roman world that the four texts began to be translated into other languages—first Latin and Aramaic; then the other languages of Asia, Africa, and Europe. As a result of sustained activity by the Jesus sect, from the first century till now, the gospels are presently available in some 2,018 languages and dialects—an unparalleled magnitude of communication whose breadth conceals the complex difficulties of the project. For each of the four texts confronts any would-be translator with a number of both common and individual challenges.

Mark—the earliest, for instance—is written in an extremely plain, abrupt, often unidiomatic and dogged Koine which has generally been made to seem falsely natural, even eloquent, in English translations (Mark was anciently called "Stump-fingered," perhaps from the unusual size of his digits or more aptly in the sense of *maladroit* or *all thumbs*). Admittedly, Mark's final effect in Greek is one of a great and spare eloquence; but that strength is seldom owing to the actual words or structure of his sentences and never to calculated effects of mellifluous rhetoric. If his eloquence has primarily linguistic origins, that power rises from the struggle between Mark's headlong intent and his gravely hobbled command of his medium. Yet a strong argument can easily be made that Mark—whoever he may have been (and we have no other sure work from his hand)—is the most original narrative writer in history, an apparently effortless sovereign of all the skills and arts of durably convincing storytelling. He is, above all, the first great master of ideal narrative distance—he stands his reader in the ideal position before his subject: the reader sees precisely enough at any moment to induce in him or her a further hunger to see more; and to the very end, that hunger is never surfeited, perhaps never sated.

My translation of Mark is based on a version I published,

with other translations from the Old and New Testaments, in *A Palpable God* in 1978. In ensuing years I have often read through that aging version; and while I have also continued to study the Greek and to read widely in both new and old studies of Mark's original text—especially those studies by the almost unimaginably well prepared scholars of the late nineteenth and early twentieth centuries before the mainstream of German, British, and American scholarship succumbed to its present obsession with a punitively unreasonable degree of historical doubt—I feel no need to start again from scratch.

I have, however, introduced a number of changes in word, idiom, and word order. All my revisions are intended to match the tone of Mark's original more nearly than before. Throughout, for instance, the Greek word which I previously translated as *sin* or its cognates *sinners* and *sinning* is now translated as *wrong* or *error* and their cognates—the word *hamartia* means at bottom *a failure of aim, a missing of the mark* and appears to have fewer connotations of the fleshpot than the English word *sin*, so long ago hijacked by the puritan and the hypocrite. I have also, when the Greek allows me and because the change seems to me more than trivial, extended the implications of gender in Mark's nouns—*men* has become *people*, for instance, where mixed groups seem indicated. Again as before, throughout the breathless pages, I hope to let the reader feel the invisible but startlingly rude force of Mark's thrust and the all but perfect efficiency of his hobbled Greek. I discuss the concealed richness of his complex results in the preface below.

The writer of The Good News According to John is likewise fluent in moving an action steadily forward through his Greek; and he is also rough handed, though in quite a different way from Mark. From the opening sentences of John, a reader of Greek can see that this writer is working with immense self-confidence both in what he has to tell and in how he is going to tell it. For a modern reader of his Koine original, John seems like nothing so much as a hugely skilled and intelligent expatriate (which early tradition in fact claims he was)—an Einstein or a Thomas Mann, a Conrad or a Nabokov: one who is able to express himself readily and powerfully on most of the difficult matters he encounters but in a homemade and eccentric patois. No one can for a moment believe that Vladimir Nabokov was born writing English; but the English of his later novels is, to say the least, imposing in the bizarre strength with which it insists on oaring upstream against the whole natural flow of English. John likewise is always pushing hard uphill in what is clearly an acquired vehicle, a medium that requires him often to work outside and against the thought processes of his native tongue, which Semitic scholars can tell us is Aramaic.

And while John narrates with unadorned speed, in the several metaphysically complex discourses set in the voice of Jesus (especially in Jesus' almost maddeningly looping and repetitive farewell address to the disciples), John is even more gravely impaired than Mark by his entrapment in an alien tongue. Seemingly undeterred however—like an intelligent but not entirely communicative guide who offers to lead us through the remains of, say, old Palmyra—John readily resorts to the circling and numbing reiterations of a very small vocabulary of Greek words and idioms in the hope of conveying his unprecedented meaning. So a modern translator, especially one with religious preconceptions, is constantly tempted to convert John's flat-footed and sometimes droning monologues into an English that is too lucid, too idiomatic, and resourceful. I have tried to give the reader some sense of John's dilemma and his Pyrrhic victory.

My own translations then are aimed at giving a Greekless contemporary reader the truest possible sense of the narrative and discursive atmosphere of my originals. Though I have studied it for more than twenty years, my own command of Koine Greek is not that of a professional scholar. But since the gospels are, by a long stretch, the most written about and minutely commented upon texts in the history of literature, even an imperfect student like me can resort to mountains of helpful guidance on the meaning of virtually every word and phrase of Mark's or John's original. The problem often becomes one not of too little available help but too much.

Still, through more than two decades of work, I have availed myself of a wide assortment of the more serious aids—the United Bible Societies' edition of the Greek New Testament, Arndt and Gingrich's magnificent edition of Bauer's lexicon of Koine Greek, numerous individual commentaries on Mark and John, several word-by-word interlinear translations (which are fascinating to read for their own sake—naked English words in the original order of the Greek); histories of Rome and Israel, of Judaism in its numerous sects, of the mystery religions of Hellenistic cultures, of the early life of the Jesus sect, and any other reliable source that has come to hand as relevant. My constant aim has been to suppress any tendency to think that I know precisely and unmistakably, here toward the end of the twentieth century, what my originals "meant to say"—linguistically or theologically—to variously constituted audiences in the first-century Mediterranean world.

Despite such a likably humane doctrine as what might be called *the universality of the human heart in all times and places,* it remains beyond doubt that human beings alive on the same day in the same city block—not to speak of different countries and centuries—will witness, reflect on, and respond to equal stimuli in ways as divergent as an infant's and a leopard's. Can any of us claim seriously to feel at all confident of sharing the feelings of a poor Roman Jew—or a Roman senator's well-heeled wife—as they sat together in a threatened *domus ecclesia* (a house church) in the mid-sixties AD and listened as Mark or some literate friend read the agony scene in Mark's gospel—Jesus terrified in the lonely hours before his arrest—while, a few yards away, Nero's or Galba's police combed the streets for bodies to feed an imperial craving for scapegoats? Or try imagining the contrary pulls on a young Greek sailor as he paused near the harbor in Ephesus, by the great temple of Artemis with its many-breasted statue of the goddess, and then chose to follow a gently importunate man from the Jesus sect up a blind alley into a dim room to hear the ancient Beloved Disciple recount Jesus' fourth and last appearance after death. Now try to convey your imagined experience to others less resourceful than you.

Such exercises are both entirely legitimate and also laughable; they smack more of the ludicrous Hollywood fumblings in *Quo Vadis* or *Ben Hur*. In fact, we have no firm notion of how it felt to exist in Rome, Palestine, or Asia Minor some two thousand years ago—burdened with all the assumptions and hopes of our past lives; then confronted in words by the flaming demands of a recently dead, maybe resurrected Jew named Jesus with a ravenous will to change us and the Earth. Neither do we know something so initially obvious sounding as how the emperor Nero felt when he kicked his consort, the pregnant Poppea, to bloody death—no more, in all candor, than Cecil B. DeMille comprehended in his Biblical and historical epics the tone and unconscious principles of daily life on the Palatine Hill or in pharaonic Egypt.

Archaeology has often made it possible for us to imagine clearly enough the look of ancient life. What is certain to be lost forever is the feel and the tone of specific moments in prior centuries—the million unexamined assumptions that underlie the thoughts and actions of a particular human being at a given moment. Especially irrecoverable are the thoughts and choices, the fears of and reliance on the realms of angels and demons, of that large majority of people who never read or wrote a word but were sure that they lived at the momentary mercy of overlords, goblins, not to speak of an unimagined world of microbes. Nonetheless, in an understandable effort to bridge the chasms between our minds and those of the gospel writers—as well as the minds of their subjects and their audiences—translators who convince themselves of possessing access to the psychic atmospheres of the first century have frequently lurched into slangy or loose-mouthed approximations that ring suspiciously wrong and pretend to strip from their subjects the immovable screens of age and distance.

Attempts to find, for instance, what some leading students of modern translation have called a *dynamic equivalence* for first-century Greek are logically suspect in the extreme but have been pursued so often by individuals and groups that we now have in English several popular versions of the gospels that constitute what are well-intended but almost certainly major distortions of their originals. Among gospel versions that have most frequently stumbled in their efforts to make the originals contemporary, I note especially J. B. Phillips's single-handed effort (often lively but very approximate); the American Bible Society's immensely widespread committee translation called *The Good News Bible* (so committed to oversimplifying paraphrase as to lose itself often on errands of its own), long stretches of *The New English Bible*, *The Amplified Bible* (which is honest in admitting its expansive method), *The New Revised Standard* version, and the several editions of the Polebridge Press versions (Polebridge editions result from the work of the notorious Jesus Seminar, a group of American scholars which has recently—and with a straight face apparently—announced that 80-odd percent of the sayings attributed to Jesus in the gospels are later inventions and that the resurrection, of course, never occurred except as a psychic phenomenon).

By contrast, I have tried to work in much the same manner as the forty-seven committee members who worked at the most successful English version of all—the Authorized Version of 1611, commonly known as the King James. Though its translators express, in their preface, the same hope that enlivens even the most egregious of paraphrasers—"we desire that the Scripture may speake like it selfe, as in the language of *Canaan*, that it may bee understood even of the very vulgar"—and though their result derives heavily from older English versions by Wyclif, Tyndale, and others, in general King James's translators proceeded under a single guiding principle (one word of the original in the fewest equivalent words of English, with the preservation when possible of at least some suggestion of the Greek word order), it is debatable how much "the very vulgar" in Canaan or elsewhere in western Asia would have understood some of the more archaic language of the Hebrew scriptures or of Mark's and John's later Greek gospels.

Five minutes spent even today in the Bible section of an ordinary bookstore will show that no later version has equaled the King James in popularity; and in many conservative churches still, it is the only version consulted, as it is in a thousand college courses on "The Bible as Literature." And while it is customary to say that such enduring popularity derives from the King James's sonorous diction and stately syntax—the diction of Shakespeare and Ben Jonson—a close comparison of its language to that of the originals will very often show that the power and memorability of the King James is an almost automatic result of its loyal adherence to principles of literalness and the avoidance of paraphrase. Nearly four centuries of Greekless readers have sensed, unconsciously perhaps but with considerable accuracy, that the very strangeness—the sober exoticism—of the language of the King James is truer to its strange originals than any of its successors. Unfortunately for its present readers, the passage of time has made it inevitable that much of the diction of the King James is now obscure; and the subsequent discovery of new and better manuscripts has made its text occasionally unreliable.

Nonetheless a straightforward conversion of one word of Koine into the scholar's best estimate of its contemporary match is likely to come, in the hands of a watchful craftsman, as near as we can get to a sense of the weight and tone of such ancient texts. The rest is left to our personal reaction—the resources, or lack of resource, that an individual reader brings to the task. Reading the gospels, in whatever language or era, is the same perilous and incessantly demanding transaction that we conduct by the moment with our nearest kin and loved ones. *What do you mean? How have I failed you? What do you demand of me?*

Whatever my own translations may offer by way of legitimate freshness, then, derives from a working fidelity to the by no means simple or always possible aim of word-for-word conversion. Such a method hardly makes for idiomatic modern English, but again neither of my originals is written in a suavely idiomatic nor always lucid Greek. A *lingua franca* like Koine Greek or twentieth-century English acknowledges no authoritative standard for the measurement of idiomatic ease. Alexandrian Jews, Roman prefects, tribal chieftains in Macedonia, merchants in Galilee, and priests in Jerusalem all employed a Greek that could look to no particular dialect as "correct." Likewise, the English of educated London, New York, or Washington is hardly a standard against which we judge, say, the English of a U.N. diplomat not born to the language. So the pursuit of idiomatic translations of ancient texts is illusory on yet another score.

And in fact, since my attempts on Mark and John have developed over a stretch of twenty years, they show minor differences of approach from one another. In the hope of conveying the supreme originality and strangeness of Mark, my version of him is the more earnestly literal of the two. With the more fluent John—alien to Greek and idiosyncratic as he is—I have taken a very little more liberty in diversifying his small vocabulary, though I have awarded myself nowhere near the license taken by such recent and church-endorsed translations as *The New English* or *The New Revised Standard* versions that, again, resort to loose paraphrase and occasionally conceal instances of gendered language which, as evidence of the kinds of energy that moved the gospel writers, should not be concealed. In the discourses which John attributes to Jesus, I have hewn close to the original's relentlessly limited battery of words and to the original order of the Greek when feasible (it is, after all, the order in which an early reader or listener encountered the writer's images and ideas). In that respect at least I think my translation gives the reader perhaps the fairest sense of any modern version of the stern limitations John strained against to express his complexity.

But why Mark and John without Matthew and Luke? I have already mentioned the conclusion of most modern scholars that Mark is the oldest of the gospels, the one that stands closest in date to the lifetime of its subject. It is also the most striking in its rude but functional language and structure and—above all—it is the surprisingly brief document (a pamphlet really) that single-handedly invents a literary form which has only three other successful companions in history and which constitutes, with them, the most successful known form of narrative (if we measure success by the ability of a story, over long arcs of time, to elicit belief from the largest number of human beings in the fidelity of its representations to observable nature or to some alleged transcendent reality). So, however a reader may value the additional episodes and considerable stretches of teaching that are advanced in the gospels of Matthew and Luke, there can be no question that Mark is primary and indispensable both to any attempt at comprehending the acts and intentions of the man Jesus and to any full reflection on the aims and possibilities of narrative art.

John is the one gospel—whatever we make of the long and apparently endless debate on the identity of its writer—

which makes an explicit claim to come from an intimate eye-witness of Jesus' life and which gives steady and convincing narrative support to that singular claim. When members of the Jesus sect were choosing characteristic visual emblems for the four gospel writers, they cannot have chosen arbitrarily in assigning the emblem of an eagle to John (who was also early designated as John the Divine, or John the Theologian, in deference to the probing and soaring thought implicit in his curious words). No other gospel writer, even Mark, climbs above the limits of language and the closely knit spine of his story with a comparable ferocity of focus and intent. And any translator choosing among the gospels would be punitive indeed to deny him- or herself the high challenge and rewards of John. Whatever the virtues and riches of Matthew and Luke, they remain secondary to their briefer but weightier companions.

*

I have made clear above that my own translations attempt as faithful a conversion as is possible of my Greek originals into modern English. By *modern English* I do not mean that I have sought an English that is more idiomatic or eloquent than I can perceive my originals to be in their time-locked Koine. Again, we do not know how Mark and John sounded to their authors or to any members of their original audiences. Above all, we have little sense of what constituted verbal decorum for the various audiences who would have heard the gospels in the years immediately after their composition. To have Mark's Jesus turn to the leper who asks for healing and tell him "O.K., you're healed!" (as he does in a translation sponsored by the Jesus Seminar) suggests Woody Allen far more nearly than the agonized and self-doubting thaumaturge of Mark's early pages.

Rather than repel modern readers, however, with an unjustifiably obstructive literalism, I have introduced a few consistent revisions of the Greek. Chief among them are these.

1. The King James version has conditioned us to expect that the narrative prose of the New Testament, as in the Old, moves by a progression of subject-verb clauses joined by the word *and*. And in fact the Greek of both Mark and John often proceeds in that manner. But we have come to understand that the Greek word *kai*, which the King James translates fairly invariably as *and*, has implications not conveyed by our English word *and*—meanings that range through such connotations as *also*, *but*, *even*, *so*, *likewise*, and *next*. I have therefore tried to translate *kai* by the appropriate English conjunction when necessary; otherwise I generally omit it.

2. Where the Greek frequently says "He answered and said to them," I generally translate only the more appropriate verb, *answered* or *said*. The double verb sounds excessively liturgical in modern English.

3. A more difficult decision concerns matters of verb tense. Mark especially, but John as well, often shift verb tenses from various levels of the past to the historical present—"Jesus turned to the woman and says to her." Though tenses in modern English oral narrative shift with equal frequency and arbitrariness, and though I experimented in preserving tense shifts in my early drafts, I have finally abandoned the attempt to reproduce my originals in this respect. Inconsistent tenses in written English are frequently misleading to the passive reader who is out of the presence of a controlling narrator (a good storyteller can sweep a bodily present *listener* along in his shifts of tense; a written author has no such access to his silent distant reader).

4. Since the earliest surviving manuscripts of my originals are not divided into chapter, verse, or paragraph—in fact, there is no space between their individual words—and since the originals are devoid of marks of punctuation, I have arranged the prose in standard modern narrative form without the distraction of the chapter and verse numbers, which were added by the printer Estienne only as recently as 1551; and I have severely pruned my punctuation wherever possible. These texts were not written for, nor can they be successfully read by, the inattentive.

5. Single words—or occasional short phrases—when set in italics, are generally transliterations of Hebrew, Aramaic, or Greek words. Longer italic passages represent translated quotations from the Hebrew scriptures of the Old Testament.

6. In the prefaces and the gospel texts, I indulge only once in a footnote. Otherwise I follow my Greek originals in assuming the reader's native wit and the availability of a few standard reference works.

But why provide a gospel of my own? The preface which accompanies *An Honest Account of a Memorable Life* explains its origin, but I can add here that in no sense have I entertained a hope of rivaling the authority of the canonical gospels. My own attempt arose from a desire to study the ancient originals so closely that I could extract from them at least one feasible chronology of Jesus' career, a very few guesses at the turns of his private thought and self-understanding, and a possibly representative choice from his teaching and dialogues. None of my narrative or theological choices is intended to imply a silent suppression or condemnation of any elements in my sources. Those sources consisted of the four gospels themselves with occasional hints from other early Jewish and Roman history, from the earliest apocryphal gospels; and the canonical letters of Paul, Peter, James, Jude, and John. Like most storytellers I have attempted both the reader's spellbound pleasure and some degree of challenge to his or her assumptions about Jesus' life and to the reader's own choices in the world of thought and action. My gospel's title is meant to describe both its contents and its conscious purpose—the word *honest* means of course, not *infallible* but *void of deceit*.

In my preface to The Good News According to John, I mention the problem presented to translators and to modern readers by John's characterization of Jesus' opponents as the *Ioudaioi*, a Greek adjective or plural noun that has generally been rendered in English as the *Jews*. Since John's word seems often deployed with a negative connotation, there is more to say here on the problem. Despite a virtual certainty that the author of John was himself a Jew and that Jesus the Jew went to his death as a man profoundly loyal to the faith and law of his people, it is worth repeating that—by the time John wrote—some sixty years had apparently passed since Jesus' death. From the crucifixion onward, a gulf had deep-ened inexorably between the all-Jewish members of the early Jesus sect and those members of the Pharisee and Sadducee establishments who maintained the Temple and its sacrificial worship in Jerusalem and who exerted a considerable degree of civil power under the watchful eye of Rome. Though the destruction of Jerusalem and its resplendent sanctuary occurred in AD 70, with a subsequent dispersion and exile of those powerful groups, the antagonism between subsequent synagogue Judaism and the Jesus sect only compounded fraternal bitterness on all sides; and the author of John was candid in his rancor.

Mark, who wrote—probably in Rome—some twenty-five years before John, employed the plural noun *Ioudaioi* only a few times and without an apparent negative charge; but by about the year 90 that chasm between the Jesus sect and the religious authorities of Judaism had widened sufficiently to permit the insertion into mainstream synagogue worship of a prayer that effectively cursed all members of the Jesus sect and thereby precluded their synagogue attendance. John seems to reflect that historical situation with a baffled and bitter sorrow, though alas he employs a generic noun for a limited group of his own blood kin.

Though John does not repeat the terrible words of the crowd in Matthew as they harangue Pilate for Jesus' death—"His blood be on us and on our children"—he nonetheless leaves a modern translator with a troubled wish that the English language provided some word with a less tragic history than *Jew* as an equivalent for the Greek *Ioudaios* and its plural *Ioudaioi*. Recent versions by members of the Jesus Seminar have offered the translation *Judean* as a substitute for the traditional *Jew*. The translators argue with some initial cogency that, since *Israelites* denotes those who worshiped Yahweh in the time of the first Temple, so we might identify those who worshiped at, and especially those who administered, the second Temple as *Judeans*.

I have tried to convince myself that this substitute provides an accurate solution to a dilemma with grave implications beyond the linguistic. But after close examination, *Judean* seems little more than a quixotic gesture and one that stands no chance of wide acceptance. Two major objections to its use are the facts that many devout first-century Jews did not live in nor were natives of the region strictly defined as Judea and that we cannot, after all, know precisely who John means by the word *Ioudaioi* nor can we gauge the shades of meaning in each of his sixty-two uses of the plural noun. Granted, in the majority of cases John seems to indicate the Temple hierarchy alone—the allied aristocratic enemies of Jesus. But in a few instances (as when John mentions "the Passover of the *Ioudaioi*"), he seems to mean *all the Jewish people*—all the family, friends, and enemies of Jesus; and at such points the version of the Jesus Seminar is forced to abandon *Judeans* for *Jewish*. So despite the initial attractiveness of *Judeans*—and the fact that it is a near transliteration of John's Greek noun—I cannot see that it mitigates the huge dilemma.

In any case I have worked throughout in the strong hope that every reader will consider how far from the recoverable thoughts of Jesus are those wastes of destruction that have poured, and still pour, from the savage pit of a wide crevasse which yawned so tragically and so soon within a single family—the children of Abraham and Sarah and of their father Yahweh, some of whom came to see the man Jesus as a unique aspect of God in the world of flesh and time. Try as we may to comprehend the atmosphere of familial discord in which John wrote, we can only lament the two millennia of genocide that have partly grounded themselves on words he would almost surely revise could he know of their subsequent career.

*

The reader may legitimately wonder, by now, at the entire reason for my own work in these tangled matters. Do I have a purpose that extends beyond a narrative writer's desire to comprehend the structure and strategy of two remarkable ancient narrations? In short, and fairly enough, do I participate in that state of mind which John's Jesus calls "trusting" in him? And if I share that trust, even sporadically, do I share it because of the gospels of Mark and John, with their important companions Matthew and Luke?

The answers to both halves of that question are complicated forms of Yes. The man Jesus of Nazareth, a Jew of first-century Galilee whose life affected very few of his contemporaries, seems to me to have stood in a demonstrably but inexplicably intimate relation to the creator of our world and all that we see and don't see beyond our world in this one universe (one of perhaps many). The intensity of that relation and its resultant climax in Jesus' execution, resurrection, and abiding influence convince me that the relation was unique among all such relations known to me in human history—unique to the point of some degree of identity, an identity comprehended first in that astonishing moment in The Good News According to John when Jesus himself, with a kind of blazing glee, rounds on his detractors in the Temple and claims in fact to be one with the sole God of all: "Amen amen I tell you before Abraham was I am."

A trust in that fact and its implicit promises for my life have been crucial for me in both the joy and devastation of more than fifty conscious years. That trust is braced above all for me by the patently honest, if ultimately immeasurable, testimony of those first terrified followers who saw Jesus alive and palpable after undoubted death—an honesty that soon made them into fearless bearers of his unprecedented news and that, launched from an unthinkably insignificant fishing village in a backwater province of imperial Rome, transformed all subsequent history. I have come to that trust through years of reading and watching the probing efforts of other times and peoples at the comprehension of mystery in their own cultures, through the unimplored early arrival of an uncanny sense of the rightness of one man's claim, but above all from the overwhelming impression of both an emblematic truth and an honest effort at accuracy conveyed to me in the hit-or-miss words and domestic wonders explicit in both Mark's and John's stories.

If their slender documents say anything to a human being at the end of the twentieth century, it is surely that—by the end of his career among Jews, Greeks, Romans, and other Gentiles—Jesus of Nazareth was a man, above all else, merciful and welcoming. He was as well a man who knew himself to be, by birth and choice, one of the central aspects of pure reality (whatever that reality is, wherever it resides, whatever hopes it holds for my fellow creatures and for me,

32

who am after all a creature as much like Jesus and his pupils as are the great balance of humankind) but who made no crushing demand of any other creature rapt in the struggle for decent existence or blind in innocence to the depths of reality.

I don't however assert for an instant that my private convictions in any of these matters, beyond verbal translation, are worth the unthinking trust of anyone else alive. I clearly believe that the gospels deliver what they claim to contain — excellent news for anyone with ears to guess at the tone of its naked first-century voice, with eyes to pierce its local dress and gait — but I cannot believe that even such excellent news excludes any member of the human race. Though much of what we can glimpse of the historical Jesus seems immensely far from our modern selves, though he announced God's coming justice and scalded the hypocrites and the self-pleased pious of his time, Jesus the Jew also dined — by free conviction and desire — with the furthest outcasts of his time and place, Jew and Gentile, the sheep despaired of by all other shepherds; and he did not apparently exhort them to shame but pledged them first entry rights into God's kingdom.

Orthodox Christianity, the church in most of its past and present forms, has defaced and even reversed whole broad aspects of Jesus' teaching; but in no case has the church turned more culpably from his aim and his practice than in its hateful rejection of what it sees as outcasts: the whores and cheats, the traitors and killers, the baffled and stunned, the social outlaw, the maimed and hideous and contagious. If it is possible to discern, in the gospel documents of Mark and John, a conscious goal that sent the man Jesus — himself an urgent function of the Maker of all — to his agonized death, can we detect a surer aim than his first and last announced intent to sweep the lost with him into God's coming reign?

*

33

Two last observations. First, any reader who does not possess prior acquaintance with the ancient gospels may well gain by reading the texts of the gospels here before reading the prefaces I have added to them—those fairly loaded essays may well serve better as afterwords; and since they are meant to provide independently useful companions to the texts they accompany, a watchful reader will notice some necessary repetitions in their contents. It is fair to inform the reader, as well, that my approach to Mark and John is a generally conservative (though by no means hidebound) one. Despite wide reading in the radical wing of contemporary gospel studies, I am led by my own long experience of the texts to find a mostly reliable basis for speculation and understanding in the oldest surviving traditions about their sources, their composition, and their intentions. As with all ancient documents, my originals demand a powerfully attentive intelligent reader and—above all—a reader with an acknowledged personal share of humankind's old fears and hungers.

Second, I have often described early Christianity as *the Jesus sect*. The phrase is devoid of praise or blame and is meant only to suggest the threatened and marginal atmosphere of that small and often clandestine group who persevered in loyalty for three bloody centuries after Jesus' death and resurrection until the emperor Constantine made their faith acceptable to Rome. The name provides, as well, at least one accurate alternative to the word *Christianity*, a word which continues to evoke, for millions throughout the world, a history of murderous intolerance so foreign to Jesus' apparent hopes, and worse, of a violence that has gone on issuing from institutions and individuals still immensely potent among us who hope to conceal their viciousness beneath words that form themselves from a single hapless Greek word *Christos*, a word which was meant by its first Jewish users to mean no more nor less than God's *Anointed*.

A NEW THING ENTIRELY

A PREFACE TO

THE GOOD NEWS ACCORDING TO MARK

MARK can be read through in less than an hour; and whether you read its original Greek or a later translation, you will quickly scent its pawky roughness of language and movement—*Jesus came here and did this; then at once he turned elsewhere and did that.* It reels out its jerky, very peculiar story at full-tilt speed and with what seem the first words at hand—a small and modest vocabulary. Yet Mark's words, in their energy and efficiency, have proved surprisingly ready through the past two thousand years to spring into vivid action in a watchful reader's mind. And the images of that action have proved to be literally seismic in the history of the world.

As if more than half aware of that power, Mark feels no need to explain its characters' motives or aims—its few explanations concern Jewish law and custom of the first century AD—and it flatly declines to clarify the terms of its own discourse for any reader who has not previously learned a good deal about Jesus and the world of his time. What, for instance, does Mark mean by *the reign of God* or *the Son of Man* or the one word *Abba*? Who are the *Pharisees* and *elders* and *scholars*? What is the *Sanhedrin*? Who is *Pilate* and who gave Pilate the right of life and death over common creatures from a country apparently alien to his own? And among dozens of other unexplored mysteries—even more crucially, for most of its length—Mark the writer will tell us no more of the mind and nature of his central figure than a modern cub reporter of average intelligence might deduce on a two-day visit to the hectic periphery of a briefly magnetic and momentarily popular preacher-magician with a gift for healing the psychically afflicted.

With all those refusals to satisfy the curiosity of any but the previously prepared reader, however, the pamphlet which is commonly called The Gospel of Mark is generally thought to be the first-written of the four canonical or church-approved gospels. As such—despite centuries of neglect when it was thought to be a mere summary of the longer and fuller Matthew and Luke—Mark has proved the most influential of human books. All other books from four thousand years of epics, plays, lyrics, and biographies have touched human life less potently.

Mark has weighed that heavily on its immediate gospel successors and thus on subsequent Western literature, on a good deal of Eastern literature, and on the art and worship of countless millions. The audacious claims it makes for the single life and the career it describes have pressed more heavily on two millennia of geopolitical history, for good and ill, than even the lunatic call to action of Hitler's *Mein Kampf* (which is unimaginable without the prior existence of Mark) or the immense and passionate bellow for justice in the lifework of Karl Marx, its only visible rival for attention.

*

It will take awhile to lay out a summary of Mark's action; but if we attempt to divest ourselves of all that we've previously heard, believed, or doubted about the existence and career of a man named Jesus in the first century (that is, *Anno Domini* or AD), then what is the action that a keen-eyed modern reader is likely to witness in its pages? Grant for a start that we readers possess little or no knowledge of Jewish history, literature, theology, or worship and that we have slim sense of the power of Rome through the Mediterranean world of the time. Then a mysterious action is laid out for us by Mark in his forced march along these broad lines.

A man named Jesus, of uncertain age and with no

known past or companions, comes south from Galilee to Judea—wherever those places are. There the man undergoes a ritual cleansing "of repentance for pardon of sins" in the Jordan river at the hands of someone called John the Baptizer, whom Mark also later calls *the Baptist*. At the moment Jesus rises from the water, he experiences a literal event or a vision in which the spirit of God descends upon him and the voice of God informs him that he has been chosen as God's beloved Son. Whether God's choice is made at this instant or was made at some prior time, we are not told. Neither does Mark tell us whether anyone but Jesus experiences the phenomenon. The sights and sounds may be entirely private to Jesus, or be shared with John, or with John and all or some of the bystanders.

After a long and solitary withdrawal to a nameless desert, where Jesus is subjected to unspecified temptations by Satan, and after John has been "handed over" (to some civil authority?), Jesus returns to his home region. There in Galilee he proclaims to all listeners that something called "the reign of God" is approaching and that they must "turn" or "change" (the Greek word generally translated *repent* means literally to *change one's mind*) "and trust the good news"—the news of God's impending reign presumably. By now the Greek reader has registered the fact that the word *euaggelion* is both the theme of Mark's pamphlet and of Jesus' first teaching—crucial news is impending and will prove good for those who believe in its coming. How the reign of God will come to Earth and in what form it will arrive, Jesus does not say.

Passing the shores of a lake in Galilee, Jesus calls four professional fishermen to follow him. They are apparent strangers to him; and again we are told almost nothing of their past, only that he will make them "fishers for humans." With no apparent pause for thought, the men follow Jesus; and at once in a town called Capernaum, with swift drama of word and act, Jesus begins to expel evil demons from the afflicted, to heal the gravely ill, and soon thereafter to forgive the sins of the common men, women, and the social outcasts who seem to be his favorite companions and whom he does not condemn or (it appears) further urge to change. One of the expelled demons loudly identifies Jesus as "the Holy One of God," and Jesus commands the demon to silence—our first hint that this strange man possesses a secret he means, for his own unstated reasons, to keep.

Those initial actions are centered on or in a synagogue and then in the house of one of the four fishermen, Simon (whom Jesus will nickname *Kepha*, which means *Rock* in Aramaic and whom we know in English as *Peter*, after the Greek *Petros* or *Rock*). The swift early deeds are both so loaded with wonders and so apparently revolutionary in some unstated way that they win Jesus a fervent crowd of followers— including "tax collectors and sinners"—as well as the immediate enmity of others who are called "Pharisees and scholars," persons whom we deduce to be especially concerned with the tribal requirements of Jewish diet, worship, and Sabbath observance. Even this early in the story, triggered perhaps by Jesus' mysterious reference to himself as "the Son of Man"—a figure whom he seems to identify with himself and who has the power to forgive sin—these enemies lie in wait to kill Jesus. And Jesus' own mother and brothers, thinking him deranged or demon possessed, attempt to stop him. He refuses to hear them; his followers are his family now.

Jesus is apparently of two minds about the diverse crowd of spectators—he is shown responding in pity to their genuine suffering and also in several unsuccessful attempts to flee from their attentions. But he chooses eight more male followers—bringing the total to twelve—and continues his healing, accompanied now by public speeches in which he encodes messages about the reign of God in brief and often puzzling poetic stories. When his followers are as puzzled as the crowd, Jesus confides to his inner circle that the full meaning of his stories is intentionally concealed from the crowd and kept for the followers only.

In explaining that withholding, Jesus admits to a dauntingly hard motive that appears to contradict his earlier public call for change. If the crowd learns the full mystery of God's coming reign, he says, they will "turn and be forgiven." At no point does Mark tell us who the crowd consists of nor that the Galilee of Jesus' time was by no means an exclusively Jewish province; nor does he explain that Galilee was ruled, under long-distance Roman control, by a puppet king Herod Antipas. In fact, Mark never tells us what a *Jew* or a *Gentile* is or how Jews differ from their neighbors and overlords—especially how they differ from the plainly Gentile audience for whom Mark is initially writing.

In a visit to Jesus' hometown, Jesus is spoken of by his townsmen at last as a *tektōn*, traditionally a *carpenter* but more accurately a *builder* or *craftsman*. They also identify him as "the son of Mary." Mark fails to tell us that a Jewish man of the time was generally spoken of as the son of his father; and in fact no human father for Jesus is mentioned in Mark, though the omission gives us no explicit information about the facts of his paternity, least of all that the phrase necessarily implies Jesus' illegitimacy as in later rabbinical tradition. The truculent doubts of his old townsmen leave him powerless to work wonders among them. But once on the move again, he continues to perform ever more impressive acts of personal power or at least of intimate access to God's might. He stills a violent storm on the lake, and he raises from apparent death a twelve-year-old girl (her family believes her dead; Jesus himself says only that she "sleeps"). Then he sends his inner circle of twelve disciples out into the countryside and villages to exorcise demons and to announce that people must change.

Still—and the expectation is growing very odd for a modern reader—we are given no clear information about the nature of God's coming reign or about the alterations that individual Galileans are to make in their lives when they make the *change* Jesus demands of them. Is Jesus concerned with the spiritual and physical health of all Galileans or only his fellow Jews? Are we, as modern readers, to feel that we are among those whom Jesus exempted from his proclamatory mission and left unsolicited; or are we included in his broadest aim, in the random crowds Jesus taught and healed? Did any sizable portion of Mark's original audience share our sense of exclusion from the world of his story? To this point in the story at least, such questions are not even acknowledged by Mark, much less answered.

And while the disciples are away on their own teaching and healing travels, the reader is told nothing of Jesus' movements or choices—where he goes, whom he sees; what he thinks about the events of recent days, weeks, or months; and we are given no calendar. Instead our attention is pulled aside and directed to Mark's ominous account of the contemporaneous murder of John the Baptizer at the hands of Herod and his illicit wife Herodias, whose union John had denounced (she was Herod's brother's wife). Mark's implicit question is *Will Jesus soon suffer a like fate?*

When the disciples return from their mission, Jesus tries to withdraw with them for a private rest; but again a huge crowd finds them late in the day in a lonely place. Sympathetic to their lack of direction and their hunger, Jesus first teaches them. We are not told what he teaches or what he withholds for the inner group only. Then with a mere five loaves of bread and two fish, he manages to satisfy the hunger of five thousand people.

Jesus continues his restless wandering, healing, and teaching through Galilee; this oncoming *reign of God* has got him on fire. There is no detectable burgeoning of wonder in his public acts—as before, all his acts are benign; indeed nowhere in Mark does Jesus employ his power directly against a human being (even his later violence in the Temple appears to be focused on the money changers' furniture, not their persons). But despite the lack of novelty, crowds persist; and now the still-unexplained "Pharisees and scholars" are increasingly offended by Jesus' insistence on the inner nature of purity and by his continued flouting of Jewish ritual law and custom—a rejection that seems to imply his contempt for whatever religious and civil authority the Pharisees and scholars claim for themselves.

Here at last, nearly halfway through Mark's story, we eavesdrop on a passage of ethical instruction as Jesus privately explains to his disciples that certain evils proceed entirely from within the individual human heart—"bad thoughts . . . fornications, thefts, murders, adulteries, greeds, malice, deceits, lust, evil eye, slander, pride, folly." Since the catalogue is one that virtually all world religions have deplored, we may wonder why Mark has bothered to repeat such worn advice. Is moral rectitude an implicit requirement for membership in the coming reign? In fact, it is legitimate to wonder by now whether this Jesus is anything more than an attractive healer of psychosomatic ailments, a purveyor of moral truisms seasoned with a persistent but vague and unfulfilled threat about God's coming reign, and a sideline of secret knowledge for his cronies.

Just as that skepticism nags at us—as if to forestall further doubt—for the first time since his baptism and desert withdrawal, Jesus ventures well outside the boundaries of his familiar Galilee. This time he goes, seemingly without the disciples, into the region of Tyre and Sidon—in fact north to what is now Lebanon, though at no point are we told the distances involved in Jesus' movements, nor in which compass directions they take him, nor the Jewish/Gentile ratio of the new towns. Likewise for the first clear time, we hear his response to a specifically Gentile request.

A Greek woman begs him to expel a demon from her

daughter. His initial response is startlingly harsh—"It's not right to take the children's bread and throw it to the pups" (his Greek noun is the diminutive of *dog*). Neither Jesus nor Mark pauses to tell us who the *children* are—is it the Jews or only the Twelve or some other limited group?—but the Greek woman's feisty wit saves her daughter. She politely but pointedly tells Jesus that even the pups may eat what falls from the table; and for her resilience, Jesus heals the daughter.

He goes next, with the disciples again, to towns east of the Galilean lake. There he continues healing, though he warns a deaf-mute to keep his cure secret—what, again, is his sporadic concern for secrecy? But the enthusiasm of by-standers compels them to spread the miraculous news; and soon a crowd of four thousand gathers and is fed mysteriously, this time from seven loaves and a few fish. Mark plainly suggests that there were two miraculous feedings, not just the same feeding described in slightly different ways in his tradition; the fact that Jesus was a source of nourishment to people hungry in many ways was crucial to both Mark and John. Yet when Jesus has moved on, Pharisees confront him, demanding "a sign from Heaven"—presumably a sign more valid than any he has yet shown, a sign that will validate the audacity of Jesus' procedures and his cavalier dismissal of religious custom with its implication of special access to the mind and will of God.

It is interesting to note here that nowhere in Mark, or in any of the other three gospels, do the enemies of Jesus deny the reality of his healings nor his triumphs over the normal laws of nature; and the few surviving records from his Jewish and Roman adversaries likewise make no such denials. Though Mark never tells us, magicians and other healers were not uncommon in Jesus' place and time; and some of their feats seem to have been impressive, especially their ability to calm the disturbed. Yet when Jesus has talked privately with his disciples, just after the Pharisees' demand for a sign, the disciples reveal their own appallingly obtuse response to the facts and signs they have been watching for some time now.

Near a pitch of frustration at his failure to reach them—and very near the physical center of Mark's story—alone with the disciples in a boat on the lake, Jesus says to the twelve men he has chosen as confidants, "You still don't understand?" And they offer him no answer. What do we readers understand at this moment in the arc of Mark's action? If we imagine ourselves with no further sources than a copy of Mark's pamphlet and a skeleton knowledge of ancient Mediterranean history, could we respond more resourcefully—or even more loyally—than the intimate disciples, who were undoubted eyewitnesses? However feckless their motives, they are continuing to accompany Jesus after all, on his hectic and besieged itinerary; they are offering at least their dumb presence, as Peter will soon and heatedly remind Jesus.

That awful moment of Jesus' realization of failure—a moment that Mark presents in quiet isolation but that rivals in power the initial descent of the Spirit on Jesus some weeks or months back—is the start of the first great climax of the story. When Jesus and the baffled, spiritually obdurate disciples land at Bethsaida, Jesus conducts a single peculiarly detailed and apparently difficult healing. He lays his own spittle on the eyes of a blind man. When Jesus questions the man at that first stage of the process, the man says that he can now see dimly—"I see men that look like trees walking." So Jesus lays on his hands again; and the cure is complete, though again Jesus cautions the man against discussing his luck.

Having restored sight to one human being at least, Jesus leads the even more culpably blind disciples toward the villages round Caesarea Philippi. Mark does not tell us that Jesus has again moved north out of Galilee, apparently to the foot of the Mount Hermon range. No cures or public teaching are described; instead in deep privacy, as they are on the road, Jesus asks the disciples "Who do men say I am?"

When they respond variously that people think he is John the Baptist or Elijah or one of the prophets, Jesus turns to Peter (and despite numerous earlier moments that may or may not have come directly to Mark from Peter's own memories, we now enter a crucial stretch of narrative that can have come from almost no one but Peter or from Mark's own invention). Peter answers Jesus' question simply but thunderously "You are Messiah." Mark offers us no further word, from here through the end, about who *Messiah* is or is expected to be. The pagan Greek reader would have noted, however, that the Greek word for Messiah, *Christos*, means *Anointed*. Jesus does not correct Peter's identification—does he tacitly accept it?—but he repeats his familiar warning that no one be told the growing secret about him. Then he proceeds at once to a new and mysterious prophecy—that "the Son of Man," with whom he has previously identified as the forgiver of sin, must be killed by the authorities and then rise on the third day. Mark only adds "He said the thing plainly." Peter—perhaps thinking better of his own fervor—takes Jesus aside and warns him presumably of the danger in claiming Messianic status, though we are not told the terms of the warning. Jesus rebukes Peter strongly, even calling him "Satan"; but the meaning of that rebuke is not given—does Jesus feel that Peter is tempting him with the prospect of a Messianic identity which Jesus is mentally rejecting or is, at least, ambivalent about?

There is one further meeting with a crowd, at which Jesus announces that anyone who follows him must "lift his cross"—*cross* is not defined—and that anyone who is ashamed of Jesus in this life will be shamed by the Son of Man when "he comes in the glory of his Father with the holy angels." Are Jesus and the Son of Man absolutely one person or, in some sense, two persons—or is the Son who will come in glory to be in some sense the human Jesus transformed supernaturally? If the disciples or the crowd are baffled by this new turn, they say nothing.

An even deeper strangeness is to come; and as if to signal our keenest attention, Mark begins the account with one of his rare indications of a precise time for an action. "After six days" Jesus took the inner core of disciples—Peter, James, and John—and led them up an unspecified mountain alone. The remainder of the inexplicable outcome is described with Mark's usual unadorned particularity. Indeed, among Mark's most convincing credentials is his refusal to heighten wonders with the easy details of legend; a glance at the runaway fancy in much of the apocryphal Christian storytelling of the second and third centuries will show at once how chaste Mark is in his narrative claims. At this critical moment, having brought us up the mountain with Jesus' three most intimate followers, Mark tells us only that Jesus "was changed in shape before them." Note that Jesus does not effect the change himself but is literally *transfigured*—the Greek word is *metemorphōthē, is changed in form.*

We learn only that Jesus' clothes become an unearthly shade of white and that Elijah and Moses appear beside him. The three disciples are terrified, and Peter literally babbles incoherently about erecting tents or bush arbors for the three apparitions. Then a cloud obscures the sight, and a disembodied voice repeats the essence of what Jesus himself had heard at his baptism—"This is my Son, the loved one. Hear him." Exorcised demons have howled their own version of the news in the intervening time, but at last some human being other than Jesus himself has heard a pure repetition of God's declaration at the moment when John the Baptizer lifted Jesus from the Jordan.

In an apparent instant Peter, James, and John find themselves alone again on the mountain with Jesus, who tells them as they descend that no one must know of the experience till the Son of Man shall rise from the dead. And though Mark does not tell us, it is clear in retrospect that here—at the literal center of his story—he has brought us to the awful hinge of the door in Jesus' life. Like Peter, by now (if never before), Jesus knows beyond doubt that he is the Anointed Son of God, the long-delayed Messiah; but he knows a further terrible thing—that same Son must be killed (is the Son of God also the Son of Man?) and then be raised from the dead. The dice are firmly cast.

As Jesus and the three disciples reach lower ground, there is not a moment's breathing space. Jesus is faced immediately with a healing petition from the father of a young man possessed by a powerful demon. True to their seamless incompetence, the nine remaining disciples have tried to master the demon but have failed. With no hint of his recent exaltation on the mountain, Jesus turns to the human task at hand; and the ensuing encounter with demoniac misery— with its terrible picture of the young man's foaming seizure, the father's touching but fragile faith, the rushed healing, and the healed boy's exhaustion—is described with a clarity rivaled only in the prior healing of a Gerasene demoniac, the man possessed by a "legion" of demons. By now, whatever a reader's doubts, it is time to conclude that—if Jesus is God's son in some unique way—then God the Creator apparently yearns toward his human creatures with a mercy prepared to visit the humblest among us. What diverts that mercy from us is apparently demonic possession—our voluntary or, as in the case of this young man perhaps, our helpless surrender to some malign force. To the end of his story, Mark will decline to guess whether that force reaches us with God's direction or assent.

From the foot of the mountain, Jesus and the disciples return to Galilee where, for the third time, Jesus predicts that the Son of Man will be killed and on the third day will rise. Next, and for only the second time in his story, Mark provides a substantial section of Jesus' teaching—first, in his private instruction of the disciples; then in dialogue with the Philistines and before a crowd. The attentive reader of Greek will perhaps have noted that the blocks of teaching seem to be connected, not by logical progression but as the sentences were presumably recalled by similar catch words in the written or oral tradition available to Mark.

In light of what Mark has already shown us of Jesus' teaching, there is nothing especially surprising in the content of his more fully revealed ethic. It is generally cast in compact and vivid language; its rhythms, even in a relatively literal English translation, are striking. But, again, virtually no single injunction or opinion is without its parallel in earlier religious lore—whether Jewish, Greco-Roman, Hindu, Confucian, or Buddhist. What is most striking in Mark's account of Jesus' public voice—on first contact at least—is Jesus' high level of eloquent authority. He maintains, throughout, a much higher level of verbally striking discourse than the level and self-effacing tenor of Mark's own prose narrative, as any edition of the gospels which prints Jesus' words in red ink will instantly demonstrate.

Jesus' striking and verbally memorable presumption of immense personal privilege, as well as his fearless self-confidence, continue to generate an intense extremity of feeling and hope in his nonprofessional listeners, those who are not "Pharisees and scholars." Especially imposing are his absolute forbidding of divorce on any grounds, for instance; his demand that a certain young rich man must sell what he has and give all proceeds to the poor, his warning of the near fatality of personal wealth, his powerful protection of the sanctity of childhood. What I have never seen noticed is the silent and astonishing fact that virtually no one in Mark's tale appears, before our eyes, to obey one of Jesus' solemn moral injunctions or to heed one of his admonitions. In fact, we are shown several instances in which the exact opposite occurs— the petty quarrels and general oblivion of Jesus' disciples and the immediate proclamations of healed persons whom Jesus has warned to silence.

As Mark ends this final block of Galilean teaching with Peter's moving and justified rebuke to Jesus for not acknowledging that the disciples "left everything and followed" him, we are surprised to learn simply that "They were on the road now going up to Jerusalem and Jesus was preceding them. They [the disciples] were stunned and the followers were afraid." Neither Mark nor the reader, nor any player in the tale, knows why the move comes now, nor what Jesus can mean to do by forging ahead with this first-mentioned visit to what the reader can assume is at least a large city. Neither do we know specifically that Jesus thinks of Jerusalem as both the spiritual center of his people and the nexus of his enemies—both the site of their ancient and ongoing rendezvous with the God who has so mysteriously chosen them from all the Earth to do his will or pay the appalling toll and the seat of the human power which longs to stop Jesus.

Yet even on that ominous journey, two of the inner circle of disciples—James and John—ask Jesus to give them the thrones on his right and left when he comes in his glory (the glory presumably of the coming reign of God, though we have yet to be told what that reign will involve and when it may occur). Jesus warns the brothers ruefully of the blindness of their request. Then having cured one more blind man in Jericho, and halting short of Jerusalem at Bethany, he sends the disciples ahead with detailed if puzzling instructions. They are to find a particular tethered colt and bring it to Jesus. Mark gives no notice to the question of whether Jesus' instructions are based on supernatural knowledge or on normal, but secret, prior arrangements.

When they have managed that small uncomplicated chore, Jesus mounts the colt and enters the city to the shouts of the disciples and a crowd—" '*Blessed he who comes in the Lord's name!*' Blessed the coming reign of David our father!" Only a prior reader of the Hebrew prophet Zechariah will recognize that, by entering the city ceremoniously and on such a mount, Jesus has silently assumed the role of Messiah in the eyes of all who are capable of understanding. The eerily quiet, even anticlimactic end of the scene—with Jesus looking in silence round the Temple precincts, then returning to Bethany with the disciples—suggests that few in the crowd and perhaps even few of the disciples are capable of understanding such a peaceful Messiah. They misconstrue his mildness.

For on the following day Jesus enters the Temple again, but this time in violence. He overturns the tables and chairs of various merchants installed there, then explains his action as an apparently symbolic cleansing—the money changers and peddlers of sacrificial animals have turned a "house of prayer" into a "bandits' cave." When Jesus has departed from the uproar, more than ever the priests and scholars are eager to destroy him. After a brief passage of instruction to the disciples on the subject of forgiveness, human and divine, Jesus returns next day and—with no further notice of Temple commerce—he readily enters into debate with the chief priests, scholars, and elders. This is apparently his first encounter with the priests who will actually accomplish his death.

In these exchanges, which Mark seems to spread over several consecutive days, Jesus' antagonists pose numerous trick questions in the hope of trapping him in blasphemy or in treason against Rome, a power whose relation to Jews Mark has still not explained. Generally with a crowd of spectators at hand, Jesus deftly evades these snares, though in one of his most elaborate parables—the tale of the murderous vineyard keepers and its avenging owner—he seems publicly to encode again his uniquely filial relation to God and his approaching execution, with God's ensuing wrath on the killers. And in a prediction to the disciples of the coming destruction of the Temple, Jesus speaks words that will somehow be reported to the authorities and used against him in his trial.

In a scene that appears to include only the inner circle of disciples, Mark provides his single substantial report of a clearly apocalyptic prophecy from Jesus—a final accounting of the coming reign of God. We may well wonder if the present dire account is the same that Jesus might have given at the start of his career. At the start, did he expect such a calamitous arrival of the reign? Sitting on the Mount of Olives, opposite the Temple yet in sight of it, he delivers a forecast of ruin and agony, not only for the Temple but the entire nation. Jesus warns the disciples that many false Messiahs will clamor for attention in the course of the coming troubles but that only when the Son of Man himself comes "on clouds with great power and glory" will the angels gather "his chosen" from the entire Earth; then presumably the reign of God can begin. He specifically tells them that neither the angels nor the Son himself knows the time of that coming, only the Father. And though the reader shares with Peter, James, and John the prior experience of the unexplained mountaintop transfiguration, Jesus still does not explicitly equate himself with the Son.

Meanwhile the Jewish feast of Passover is nearing, though Mark offers no reminder of the feast's commemoration of a substitute blood sacrifice far back in Jewish history. The priests and scholars hope to trap and kill Jesus before the sympathetic holiday crowd reaches a peak. When Jesus continues to elude them, one of the Twelve—Judas Iscariot, about whom Mark has told us only that he will be Jesus' betrayer—goes to the authorities in secret and offers "to hand him over to them." Mark never explains what that betrayal will consist of. It had to consist of more than a revelation of Jesus' whereabouts. Surely he and twelve other men, not to mention assorted other followers including some women, could not have kept their lodging place secret for long in the vicinity of a festival-crowded city. The priests accept Judas's offer, promising to pay him for his deed.

Jesus sends two of the disciples into Jerusalem on another mysterious errand—to find "a man carrying a water jug" and then to arrange for a big upstairs room where Jesus may eat the Passover feast with them. Again they succeed in the chore. The room and the meal are prepared; in the evening Jesus and the Twelve recline to share it. Quickly he tells them the alarming news that he has somehow learned, guessed, or divined—one of them will betray him. In the face of their consternation, he breaks the bread, blesses the communal cup of wine, and passes that food and drink to all. The bread and wine are, Jesus says, signs of his body and blood that are to be given and "poured out for many" in "the covenant." The old covenant is never described by Mark. Presumably it was God's promise to Abraham that he would give Abraham's progeny, God's chosen people, a home and would dwell among them. If so, then what is the new covenant? Is it God's renewed promise, to all humanity now, that through the coming sacrificial death of his Son he will forgive all sin and establish his reign on Earth?

At the end of the shared bread and wine, Jesus and the Twelve sing a final hymn. (Or is it the eleven now? Has Judas already left on his errand? The Good News According to John says that he has; Mark ignores Judas's interim acts.) Then they depart from the upstairs room for the Mount of Olives. On the way Jesus tells the disciples that tonight all of them will stumble and be scattered from him—even presumably James and John who, in their recent grandiose request for adjacent thrones in Jesus' reign, have nonetheless vowed their willingness to share all his trials.

Only Peter impulsively vows that, even if the others stumble, he will not. Jesus says, terribly, that Peter will deny him three times before the morning cock has crowed twice. Mark does not tell us; but any reader familiar with Passover custom and the hours of Palestinian daylight will know that now we move in deep darkness, well after sundown; and anyone familiar with hilly Jerusalem in the spring will know that the nights are often cold.

They stop at an undescribed place called Gethsemane. Mark does not tell us that it lies at the western foot of the Mount of Olives, a few hundred yards east of the Temple, nor that there is still a cave on the site in which Jesus and the Twelve may have slept earlier—John will tell us that the place is a garden. Jesus takes Peter, James, and John and moves apart from the others. He tells the inner three to stay near and watch for him—Jesus is, in Mark's intensest moment of portrayed emotion, "deeply appalled and harrowed."

Jesus moves on a little, falls to the ground, and prays to the Father that the "hour might turn away," that the cup might be taken from him—the cup of the Father's will, that Jesus seems nonetheless to know he must drink. Initially Jesus addresses God by the word *Abba*, which Mark does not tell us is the Aramaic familiar name for *Father*. Twice Jesus breaks off, goes back to the inner three, finds them dozing, and returns to his solitary prayer. Mark makes no effort to explain how the sleeping disciples can have heard Jesus' prayers—did one or more of them rouse briefly and listen, did the mysterious young man who will soon be mentioned report Jesus' prayer, or did Mark invent a scene which (after all) shows Jesus at a moment of terrible doubt, however poignant?

When Jesus comes the third time and wakes the sleepers, he says only that "It's paid. The hour came. Look, the Son of Man is handed into wrongdoers' hands"; and he adds that even now the traitor is approaching. The sentence translated "It's paid" represents the single Greek word *apechei*, a verb that generally denotes the completion of a business transaction—*it's done* or *the debt is paid*. Jesus' dying words in John—*it's finished* or *accomplished*—will sound a strange echo.

At that, Judas arrives with an armed cohort from the

priests and scholars. With a kiss of greeting, the treacherous pupil indicates his master to them. They seize their prey and the eleven other disciples scatter—no word of where Judas goes nor of his later fate. In a moment so strange that many readers miss it entirely, one unidentified young man flees the scene naked; and Jesus is led off to appear before a council of the chief priests, elders, and scholars. Though Mark later describes Peter's following Jesus at a distance, he will likewise relate unflinchingly the specific conditions under which—before the cock crows twice—Peter three times denies any knowledge of Jesus.

In the course of the interrogation, Jesus is confronted by false witnesses who accuse him of threatening to destroy the Temple and rebuild it in three days; other witnesses testify inconsistently. Jesus remains silent. At what Mark implies is the critical moment, the High Priest himself demands to know— "You are Messiah, the son of the Blessed?" And while an individual's claim to be Messiah does not seem to have been a capital offense in the first century, Jesus answers in what Mark implies is the most inflammatory way—"I am and you will see the Son of Man sitting at the right of Power and coming with clouds of Heaven." Not only does Jesus' phrase "I am" repeat the divine name which God reveals to Moses in the book of Exodus—"I am what I am"—but the remainder of the answer reinforces Jesus' claim of participation in the nature of God by an apparent threat to come with supernatural power and, by implication, to assume control of the temporal world. We may continue to wonder now whether Jesus the man always referred to the Son of Man as his supernatural counterpart—Jesus transformed again, this time in the ultimate glory of the reign of God—but Mark works to allow the reader no such ambiguity.

The High Priest knows what he has heard—not merely a claim to Messianic status but, above all, Jesus' stark claim to a unique filial or even co-existential relation with God. The

High Priest tears his robes in ritual revulsion from the sacrilege; then he defines Jesus' claim as blasphemy and asks for advice from the assembly. They at once condemn Jesus "worthy of death" and begin to revile him physically, with spittle and blows. Mark gives us no explanation of his source for describing the events of the trial; we must wait for John's gospel to glimpse at least one source—an unnamed disciple who had free entrance at the High Priest's gate. The trial is not entirely finished, but it is worth remarking at this point that only Mark and John, in their quite different ways, make it clear why the Temple authorities were compelled to demand Jesus' death. His claim—at its simplest in Mark, at its most unthinkable in John—was literally intolerable to any conceivable human establishment.

A second quasi-judicial assembly gathers in the morning, this time with the whole Sanhedrin (which Mark does not define—it was the presiding council for religious, political, and legal considerations); and Jesus is led off, bound, to Pilate. The usual brisk pace of the narrative increases to avalanche haste. Mark does not pause to tell us the source of Pilate's superior authority and power, only that Pilate is more interested in temporal than divine pretensions. He phrases, differently from the High Priest, the ultimate question put to Jesus—"You're the king of the Jews?" Jesus replies only "You say." The priests continue to charge him; and the crowd cries out "Crucify him" (given the presence of a crowd, we are presumably now out of doors, near Pilate's headquarters). So Pilate concurs. Jesus is led off by soldiers to be flogged and mocked as a king; "then they led him out to crucify him."

Mark gives no description of the process of crucifixion; if we are reading his Greek, we see only that the verb *crucify* means *to stake* or *stake up*. Jesus is staked up then at nine in the morning, and the charge against him is set above his head—"The King of the Jews." The soldiers, who are still not specified as Roman, divide his clothes by casting lots; and the spectators, including the chief priests and scholars, taunt Jesus with his absurd claims and evident failure. Six hours later, at three in the afternoon, the sky darkens; and Jesus cries out in Aramaic a dreadful last time—"My God, my God, why did you forsake me?" Mark does not tell us that the cry is a quotation from Psalm 22, a poem which ends in affirmation of God's goodness; Jesus can hardly be thinking affirmatively now. He only cries out once more and dies.

At that, the centurion in charge of the execution party affirms Mark's own contention—"Surely this man was son of God." In Mark's Greek the centurion does not use an article before the word *son* (neither *a* son nor *the* son), and Mark has still never told us in what sense Jesus is that son. What may be most important is the realization that no colleague or countryman of Jesus has made that statement before now, a statement which corroborates the words perceived at Jesus' baptism and later confirmed by demons. With no further comment by Mark or any participant, last rites begin on the corpse. In haste, since the Jewish Sabbath will begin at sunset, Joseph of Arimathea, an important member of the council "who was himself expecting the reign of God," asks Pilate's permission to take down the corpse and bury it. Joseph has made no prior appearance in the story, and no explanation is given of his apparent closeness to Jesus.

Pilate summons the centurion and confirms the death—apparently, after only six hours on the cross, it has taken less than the expected time for death by crucifixion. Joseph is then allowed to wrap the corpse in new linen and place it in a rock tomb, the entrance to which is sealed by a stone. With his usual brevity, Mark records only that the burial was witnessed by Mary the Magdalene, Mary the mother of the younger James and Joses (an alternate Greek form of the name usually transliterated as Joseph), and Salome—three women alone of all Jesus' followers. Considering the imminent discovery to be made by the women, Mark does not tell us of the low esteem in which the testimony of women was held in first-century Judea.

Mark records nothing of the next thirty-odd hours—the Sabbath and its succeeding night when presumably all Jerusalem, including the fled disciples if they are still in the city, is observing the hours in silence and relative immobility. Mark likewise avoids all speculation about the state or the actions of Jesus' body through those hours—dead or alive, divinely resuscitated or stolen. Of the major surviving early documents, only Matthew and the fragmentary apocryphal Gospel of Peter indulge in such speculation with a visionary fantasy. Instead Mark moves directly to the hours of dawn on the first day of the new week—the day we call Sunday—and shows us a group of women again. This time, Mary the Magdalene, Mary the mother of James, and Salome come to Jesus' tomb with spices to anoint his hastily buried corpse. Again, nothing more is told us about the women's relation to Jesus or his known followers.

As the women wonder who will roll away the presumably heavy door stone, they see that the stone has already been removed; and in the tomb, on the right side, sits a young man "dressed in a white robe." Mark does not remark that, in Hebrew scripture, angels are more than once described similarly. The women are stunned; the young man attempts to calm them and says that Jesus was raised and is gone. He instructs the women to tell the disciples and, specifically, Peter that "He's going ahead of you to Galilee. There you'll see him as he told you" (Mark has recorded only a vague earlier prediction). The women flee the tomb "wild and shuddering"; and in their fear, for an unspecified interval, they tell no one anything. The oldest surviving complete manuscripts of Mark, which come from the fourth century AD, end at that moment with a grinding abruptness. The summary endings to Mark that are found in modern Bibles are easily identifiable as the work of other anonymous early hands, not Mark's own. Students differ in their sense of whether Mark himself chose to end the story at such an abrupt juncture or whether his original manuscript (or a unique surviving copy) somehow lost its final page or final lines at a vulnerable time in the first few years of its life, a time when full copies had not been widely distributed. My own sense, which I shall expand on later—and it seems to be the conclusion of a majority of modern students—is that Mark intended to end his story as we have it, in literal midair while the women flee the tomb in terror. Such an apparently reckless last-minute abandonment by an author of his reader's keenest final expectation is thoroughly characteristic of the kind of narrator Mark has been throughout his book. *This is my story, suddenly told—you tell it from here.*

*

We cannot know how many available facts and traditions about Jesus Mark has omitted from his account. In such a brief frame, he can hardly have told us half of what he had seen or learned. In fact, while modern New Testament scholars frequently speak of such and such a piece of information as being *unknown* to a given writer, they can only mean *undivulged* by the writer—and undivulged for any number of tacit reasons, from ignorance or carelessness, up or downward in importance. Mark, after all, was almost surely available in the flesh to his original audience and could have answered their questions about many details and meanings omitted from his written narrative. In any case we can certainly deduce, from his boldly elliptical written voice, that Mark is committed to at least two guiding assumptions. First, he assumes a great deal of prior knowledge by his reader of the geographic, sociological, and psychic background of his story. Second, he trusts implicitly that his story *in itself*—in its headlong plunge through quickly registered personal acts by a single man—is so compelling and so ultimately convincing as to eliminate the need for a full authorial account of the personality, physical, psychic, spiritual, and historical details of Jesus, his colleagues, and their actions.

What matters to Mark—quite aside from the resources he has at hand—is what mattered to the great J writer in the Hebrew Bible and to the towering protohistorian of the lives of Samuel, Saul, and David. Their central concern, first and last, is with the literal line which human action makes on the surface of time and place, and with the degree to which we can infer from those writers' words alone that the frail human line is echoing the movement of God's magnetic call or is fleeing from it. Those older writers give us more of the grit of individual human nature—Saul's melancholia and his sudden rages; David's physical beauty, his winning moral inconsistency, and the tragic self-made ruins that lie about him in old age. But like Mark (far more than like Matthew, Luke, or John), the older authors share the ancient trust of all those who bet their entire hand on *story*, whether oral or written: the thin compelling thread of an action that is worth our attention.

Like his great predecessors and the masterly Western narrators who have succeeded him as his pupils, Mark knows that the first thing a listener or reader craves from the teller is clean-lined portrayal of mighty, or at least magnetic, acts—an apparently magical summoning up through mental pictures of memorable acts achieved by actual human beings, however heroic, against the overwhelming force of years and enemies. And with his Hebrew forebears, Mark alone among Christian narrators stands with a very few narrators from Asia as supremely successful in the two prime aims of storytelling. Surely those aims are the capturing and holding of an audience (readers from many times and cultures) and the compulsion from that audience of literal belief as the story unfolds. In short, Mark commands a degree of attention in the reader—an attention which soon becomes a conviction that what he or she is reading or hearing is in fact a possible tale, a possible figure made by humans against the background sight of the Earth and the distant sky, pregnant with meaning for every soul.

*

Who was Mark, what did he know; when, where, and for whom did he write his gospel? The oldest surviving answer comes from Papias, bishop of Hierapolis, writing in what is now Turkey some hundred years after the death of Jesus, a death which (from other historical parameters) we can calculate as occurring most probably in AD 30 or 33. Papias's whole book seems no longer to survive, though copies were present in medieval libraries; but Eusebius—the first systematic historian of Christianity and himself a native of Palestine, writing in about 300—quotes the following two statements from Papias. Far from suggesting the possibility that Papias independently deduced the names of authors from anonymously circulated gospel texts, the passages quoted by Eusebius claim a direct transmission from disciples of Jesus to Papias.

> If ever someone arrived who had followed the elders [*those who had known Jesus*] I inquired as to the words of the elders, what Andrew or Peter or Philip or Thomas or James or John or Matthew said and what Aristion and the Elder John, the Lord's disciples, say. . . . [*Note that Papias apparently refers to two Johns—the first seems to be John son of Zebedee, one of Jesus' inner circle with his brother James; the second John is distinguished by Papias only as the Elder, a figure not mentioned by name in any gospel, though the author of the canonical Second and Third Letters of John does refer to himself as the Elder.*]

And the Elder said this too — Mark, becoming Peter's interpreter, wrote down correctly all he recalled of things done and said by the Lord but not in order. For he neither heard the Lord nor followed him but afterward Peter who adapted his teachings to the needs [*of his audience*] yet not as if making a connected account of the Lord's sayings. So Mark did nothing wrong in writing some things just as he recalled them since he was scrupulous of one thing — to leave out nothing he had heard and to make no untrue statement therein.

Eusebius, a careful and honest if not infallible scholar, also records that Jesus' disciple Philip (or perhaps Philip the evangelist, another early member of the Jesus sect) and Philip's daughters had settled in Hierapolis; and their location in the same city with Papias suggests the possibility that some further information was transmitted firsthand from them to him. There is other mid–second-century testimony from Irenaeus, a native of Asia Minor and later bishop of Lyon in France. In about 180 Irenaeus writes that in his youth — a time that may have been anywhere between twenty and fifty years earlier — he himself had known Polycarp of Smyrna, who was a pupil of the disciple John, meaning apparently John son of Zebedee. In that case, both Papias and Irenaeus would have been in direct touch with at least one person who had studied with Jesus or was anyhow an eyewitness of Jesus' life and work (how accurately they may have recalled such contacts is another matter; but on the face of their evidence, neither of them can be shown to be lying or confused).

While it is demonstrable that these early witnesses were capable of error, the chances are excellent that Irenaeus, like Papias, possessed more than a single line of contact with traditions older than himself. We know for instance that Irenaeus's predecessor in Lyon—a man with whom Irenaeus was apparently acquainted—was Pothinus. Pothinus seems to have been a pupil of those who knew the original apostles; and he seems to have lived past the age of ninety, dying in the persecution of Christians at Lyon in the year 177, very near the time of Irenaeus's written testimony. Such spans of time—stretched across no more than two or three contiguous lives—are not necessarily fatal to an oral tradition that has urgent reasons for renewing itself, even in a country as stunned by violence as first-century Palestine.

Yet in recent years, as Christian scholars have grown more and more punitively self-limiting in the strictures they set round their work—strictures that amount to degrees of suspicion unfamiliar in sober historians of other fields—such unimpeachable-sounding traditions have been severely questioned and often rejected with striking degrees of misrepresentation. Numerous recent scholars contend for instance, against tradition and quantities of internal evidence to the contrary, that the canonical gospels arose in some such manner as this—multiple anonymous narratives of Jesus' life and teaching were developed in various early and relatively isolated Christian groups of the Middle East, the Roman province of Asia. In fact, the writer Luke himself says nearly as much in the preface to his gospel—"many took in hand to arrange a narrative of the matters accomplished among us, as delivered to us from the beginning by eyewitnesses and caretakers of the word" (but note what may be an important difference between Luke's claim and those of the modern scholars—Luke does not specify that those narratives which preceded him were all anonymous; in fact, he specifies the role of eyewitnesses in the process).

Most scholars contend also, and with a good deal more evidence behind them, that the canonical gospels were only accepted gradually throughout the Jesus sect toward the end of the second century, when other full narratives of Jesus' life had disappeared for whatever reasons, been rejected on grounds of literary inferiority, or judged heretical in doctrine. We know that early bishops sometimes destroyed manuscripts that they thought pernicious in teaching or erroneous in narrative; and certainly the sizable surviving body of fragments from such apocryphal documents makes for almost uniformly desolate reading—harum-scarum wonder stories and bizarre clandestine teachings that yield little sense to a modern reader.

Granted—that in the wake of a four-year cataclysmic war in Palestine, culminating in the Roman destruction in AD 70 of Jerusalem and its Temple with the forced exile of many Jews and Jewish Christians, early students of the Jesus sect may have speculated on the origins of their founding documents with more hope than precision in the face of slim and unconfirmable information. Granted—that, as eyewitnesses to Jesus began to die, there would have been a powerful desire in the late first and early second centuries for some guaranteed written survivals of that trustworthy testimony. And granted that we possess no complete manuscript copy of any canonical gospel which can be dated to the first or second generation, still extensive reading in the works of those early scholars will show that the second-century scholars often seem as wary of error as a sober modern historian should be.

The question of authorship of the gospels, both for readers in search of evidence about a figure in whom they invest urgent interest and for those who only hope for the most reliable accounts of an influential career, is immensely important and is never likely to be resolved, barring the always possible discovery of fresh documentary evidence. My own sense however—from long reading of the gospels, from the intimacy with their language and strategy which translation requires, from my own experience as a veteran of an oral culture, and as a writer of prose narrative—is that there is a good deal to be said for the claims of tradition. Those claims at least make sound human and literary sense; in fact they re-peat a pattern of narrative transmission which is virtually the rule in secular history.

That gospel tradition, as it has reached us, may rely solely on the known testimony from Papias and Irenaeus, whatever those two men knew; and they can hardly have told us all they knew. There are later second-century voices which re-peat and offer suspiciously elaborate expansions of that older tradition; but almost no student now questions Papias's asser-tion that he had talked with men who had known Jesus, or Irenaeus's claim that he had heard Polycarp, who had known the disciple John, though it is just conceivable that the young Irenaeus was mistaken in his understanding of which John had been Polycarp's master.

It is reasonable likewise to interpret Papias and Irenaeus, taken together, as saying further that Matthew compiled the sayings of Jesus (the sayings as opposed to an entire gospel—Papias actually says that Matthew compiled the *logia* of Jesus, that is, the *sayings* or *oracles*)—that Mark produced a personally arranged narrative from his recall of Peter's first-hand memories, that Luke wrote both his own gospel and The Acts of the Apostles after traveling with Paul who had known Peter, John, and Jesus' own brother James; and that the gospel of John preserves the firsthand memories seasoned by a long life's reflection of the disciple John bar Zebedee, again a member of the inner circle of Jesus' twelve disciples. True or false or part-false, those claims are hardly outlandish on their face; they imply no impossibilities or supernatural interventions. And long acquaintance on the part of a watch-ful reader with the evidence and the legitimate objections to it may leave the reader at relative ease with several possible responses.

1. The contention, by some scholars, that the iden-tity of the gospel writers is not only unknown but

also irrelevant is absurd. Whether we hope to establish historical accuracy or to find firm ground for personal belief, then the degree of closeness of a given author to firsthand experience of his subject is of the greatest importance.

2. If we allow for later editing of the texts by other hands, however close those hands may have been to the original writers, it seems entirely possible that (despite real problems) the tradition in respect to Mark and John is at heart correct.

3. The more extensively one explores modern conjectures about the authorship and editing of the gospels, the more one discovers an all but infinite proliferation of theories—from the relatively simple to the hilariously complex. If the gospels did not concern the life of someone with alleged divine origins, most students would have long since accepted the early testimony. The reader may wonder how four documents as consistently atmospheric in their individual ways—and offering so many different aspects of a remarkable hero—as Matthew, Mark, Luke, and John could have come into existence in a period of thirty-odd years under conditions as complicated as those posed by scholars. We may likewise wonder how four such accomplished artists and editors sprang up, invented their own genre (with their intense focus on consecutive action, significant speech, and the life-transforming urgency of the claims they make for their human subject, the gospels are fundamentally unlike earlier forms of narrative), performed their literally world-altering work within the first six decades of the life of a small and threatened, largely working-class movement, and then vanished without leaving behind so much as the accurate memory of their names.

4. If on no other ground than that of Ockham's razor, and especially when confronting documents whose internal tone and consistency are as striking as those in the four gospels, the leanest explanation is likely to be the safest. Each of the four gospels is, in the majority of its parts, the work of a single author as he or she deploys a considerable quantity of sources and skills—from first- or secondhand memory, from prior written matter, and from invention and other personal strategies for the achievement of an honest and convincing narrative logic.

5. In the absence of a certainty that may never arrive, it is consistent with scholarly, artistic, and human intelligence to assume that the sanest and most rewarding view of the problem is that "Matthew," "Mark," "Luke," and "John" were four individual authors subject to later editing and that the oldest available tradition as transmitted by Papias and Irenaeus—in the absence of any evidence of deceit on their parts—constitutes an imposing if not infallible guide to the identity of those authors and the depth of their authority as reporters.

Despite the almost incredible fact that none of the four gospels bears an inarguable reference to the destruction of Jerusalem and the Temple in AD 70—indeed, no other book of the New Testament bears an inarguable reference to that catastrophe—the dates of the gospels are nearly as contested as the identities of their authors. The earliest available tradition maintains that Matthew wrote first, even if his work involved only the compilation of Jesus' oral teaching; but it has been recognized by a majority of scholars since early in the nineteenth century that the gospels of Matthew and Luke both lean so heavily on the narrative order, the specific language, and the theology of Mark that they seem inevitably to have copied directly from Mark, though perhaps from an earlier version than the one we now possess.

Mark is therefore almost surely the first-written of the three (the question of John's date is explored below in the preface to John). Since we know that Peter likely died in Rome during Nero's persecution of Christians in 64–65, the general estimate is that Mark wrote at least his original draft between 64 and 70, some thirty to forty years after Jesus' death—the length of a single generation. But that fragile consensus could be easily disrupted by the discovery and confirmation of a single substantial manuscript fragment.* For years there have been serious modern scholars who argue, from scattered early evidence, that Peter and Mark were in Rome as early as 42 and that Mark may well have written at least his first draft before Peter's death—perhaps as much as twenty years earlier than the current general dating. Again, even if Mark wrote and published thirty years after Jesus' death, three decades is hardly a long stretch in a culture committed to the oral preservation of facts and impressions, though the four gospels' many inconsistencies of chronology, story, and theology warn us against excessive trust in the ability of oral transmission to preserve complex bodies of memory without varying degrees of accidental or intentional rearrangement and recasting.

It has often been pointed out that significant portions of Mark's narrative seem to derive from personal memories of the disciple Peter. Passages like the two feedings of the multitudes, the Transfiguration, and above all Peter's bitterly humiliating three denials of Jesus can be converted into convincing first-person narratives with a simple change of

*As recently as 21 January 1995, *The New York Times* reported that a German scholar had just dated three papyrus fragments, found in Egypt and bearing passages from The Good News According to Matthew, to the middle of the first century. If such a date is confirmable, the publication of Matthew may be moved back to within a few years of Jesus' death; and new questions will be posed about the date and priority of Mark.

pronouns from third person to first. With no other important character in the whole of Mark's story can that conversion be performed. A skeptic might of course contend that Mark possessed an unparalleled power of narrative invention and that he created single-handed and out of whole cloth a kind of clandestine first-person point of view that would not be fully exploited again until the twentieth-century novel. A further consideration weighs heavily in favor of Peter's potent force at some distance behind Mark. To state the matter in the simplest terms, the stupidity and obtuseness of the disciples as portrayed in Mark could be a natural result of strong reliance on the memories of the most humiliated and perhaps guiltiest of them, Peter. What other reason would there be for a mainline early Christian's giving such an unflattering picture of those "pillars of the church"? Even an unorthodox believer could hardly have assailed the pillars without considerable risk of his own severance from the community.

Given Mark's many other contradictory signs however—his abrasive texture and his lurch-and-linger tempos—such imaginative sophistication seems unlikely in the extreme. While absolute evidence may never be available then, it is worth summarizing the testimony for Mark's connection to Peter—second-century tradition universally affirms it; what seem to be Petrine intimacies line the book itself; and finally, given the eminence of Peter and the growing threat to his life in Nero's Rome, such a literary genesis would be entirely consistent with known human practice through recorded history (a great teacher's pupils preserve his memory). But if we accept, even momentarily, the tradition that Mark was Peter's interpreter—that he was in fact the Mark mentioned by name in the closing of the canonical First Letter of Peter, which may or may not derive directly from Peter—and if that same Mark preserved Peter's recollections in a gospel, then close examination of the narrative and its claims may soon compel us to see that—for all Mark's rough-and-ready language and his haste—he has built those recollections and presumably other unknown sources into a minutely arranged story, one with far more psychic and literary complexity than his impatient surface suggests.

It may be useful at this point to recall my initial account of Mark's story, with its mention of numerous important pieces of knowledge which Mark silently assumes that the reader will bring to the story of Jesus. His imagined reader or listener will come to the story with at least a modest grounding in first-century Judaism, its partisan divisions with their powerful strands of eschatological hope, and the passionate expectation by some Jews of an anointed deliverer—Messiah. That ideal reader whom Mark is relying upon will also be grounded in the geography of the eastern Mediterranean rim and in the practical operations of Rome's imperial rule throughout the region—particularly in its most recalcitrant vassal, Palestine. With some such awareness then, we can try again to deduce and summarize the content of Mark—this time in the barest outline.

The reader will note that my outline implies a certain intellectual and emotional development in the mind of Jesus as his movements drift through Galilee and northward, then gradually focus on the fatal visit to Jerusalem. Many scholars claim now that, studying the gospels in relation to one another and noting their narrative and theological differences, we can no longer make legitimate deductions about Jesus' sense of himself or the actual shape of his career. Some have gone so far as to make the demonstrably untrue claim that ancient documents, as a rule, reveal little sense of cause and effect. Aware then of those objections, the following seems to me a justified, if hardly definitive, chart of the spine of Mark's story.

*

Near Jerusalem, John the Baptizer offers a ritual washing to signify repentance of wrong and God's forgiveness. Implic-

itly aware of his need for washing, Jesus from Nazareth comes to receive John's cleansing and, at that lustral moment, experiences the descent upon him of God's spirit and God's confirmation that Jesus is God's beloved son—in some sense unique in that relation.

After a solitary withdrawal to the wilderness and John's subsequent arrest, Jesus returns to his native district of Galilee and urges his listeners to turn and prepare for the imminent reign of God. He selects a group of intimate followers and simultaneously begins to discover extraordinary personal powers of healing, with their proof of his triumph over the demonic world.

At first those powers cause Jesus consternation—he warns the healed to suppress the source of their good fortune, and he flees the pressure of excited crowds—but compassion returns him to the world of suffering humanity. Soon his powers, his claim to forgive error, and his welcoming of outcasts begin to arouse the enmity of civil and religious authorities—authorities who will soon kill John the Baptizer but are more patient in halting Jesus. Yet Jesus continues his work in place, adding new wonders—personal power over physical nature and over death itself.

In time he elicits from his disciple Peter the conviction that Jesus is indeed the awaited Messiah, though for the present a concealed Messiah. Jesus confides to the disciples that the peculiar and never-explained nature of his anointment will require him to die at the hands of the authorities, then to rise from the dead. In confirmation of that confidence, he takes a core of three disciples on a private journey and permits them to witness an unprecedented moment in which he is changed in form to a supernatural radiance and meets for a never-disclosed purpose with the long-vanished Moses and Elijah.

Soon Jesus leads the baffled and fearful disciples to Jerusalem. He enters the city in a procession designed to make symbolic announcement of his messianic identity. He violently disrupts commercial activities in the Temple area and engages the authorities in a solemnly imperious ethical argument. After warning the disciples of an oncoming catastrophic intervention by God and his Son in history, Jesus joins the disciples at a Passover meal. There, in his only explanation of his fate, he tells the disciples he must die for the ransom of many. But alone in prayer, he begs God to spare him that death.

Quickly the authorities, inexplicably led by the disciple Judas, move to seize and question him. When Jesus acknowledges his divine anointment and threatens to return in divine judgment, they condemn him to death for blasphemy and receive the approval of the Roman governor Pilate. Roman soldiers torture and crucify Jesus as "King of the Jews." He dies on the eve of the Sabbath in agony and perhaps disillusionment, abandoned by all but a few women followers. At the moment of Jesus' death, the attending Roman officer concedes that Jesus was indeed Son of God. In haste, before the start of the Sabbath at sunset, Jesus is buried in a rock tomb with a heavy rock door.

Some thirty hours later, a small party of loyal women returns to Jesus' tomb to complete his hasty burial. There they find the tomb thrown open and a young man in white who tells them that Jesus has risen from the dead and has gone, as he promised, to Galilee. The women are instructed to tell the disciples that astonishing news, but in terror they maintain a frozen silence for an uncertain time.

*

What does Mark intend his audience to palpate in the spine of that story? If we assume, with the oldest tradition, that he wrote shortly before or after Peter's death—and that he wrote in Rome for the terrorized Roman church under Nero or Galba—then we may assume that Mark wrote primarily to remind his audience of bracing facts that they would have already known and valued. They would have experienced Mark's gospel as useful underpinning to a faith which they already held but which, like most faiths, could welcome support from a story that depended upon known eyewitness. And with their other sources of knowledge about Jesus and his meaning, Mark's earliest readers may well have heard something like this as the condensed residue of his story—*God recently exalted a single human creature to the heights of unique Sonship. He led that Son through a short earthly life to an agonized death, a death to which the Son assented as "a ransom for many." Am I one of that "many" in my own hour of trial? Will this Jesus the Son of Man, at his return with angels on clouds of glory, recognize and save me?*

There were of course millions of Romans, Jews, and assorted others throughout the known world who had heard nothing of Jesus and his story. But many of those who knew of Jesus rejected what they knew of his story as blasphemous or life-hating nonsense. The civil powers of Palestine and Rome, from the modest scholar through provincial governors to the emperor himself, had not only rejected the story (insofar as they knew it) but were thoroughly prepared to exterminate the followers of Jesus in ways that resembled their Lord's awful death. Tacitus, the first-century historian, describes Nero's actions in the attempt to find scapegoats for the fire which destroyed much of Rome in 64.

> He punished with the utmost refinements of cruelty a class of men despised for their vices, whom the crowd called Christians. . . . The confessed members of the sect were arrested. Then on their confessions, huge numbers were convicted, not so much on the charge of arson as for hatred of the human race. And mocking accompanied their end. They were covered with the skins of wild animals and torn to death by dogs; or they were hung on crosses and, when sun-

light failed, they were burned to serve as lamps at night.

Had Mark thought of his book as, in any sense, capable of reaching out to these sadistic enemies in the hope of convincing them of the truth of Jesus' claim (if Mark wrote in Rome in the sixties, the enemies were near at hand and threatened his own life), surely he could easily have provided narrative clarifications—writer-to-reader courtesies—for the numerous questions his elliptical voice leaves unanswered. Why should an unconvinced Roman not have heard, with the priests and Pilate, a threat of revolutionary danger to the Pax Romana? Could any reader, given the text of Mark but denied further information, come to believe in the Sonship of Jesus and to follow him toward painful death simply through blind faith in a literary hero?

If Mark's intended audience was an already-convinced assembly of Greek-speaking men and women, and his purpose was chiefly to provide them with a handbook for reference and reminder, then his book must have served them admirably. It reminded them not only of the voice of their revered Peter—with its vivid and rough-hewn but indubitable memories, its willingness to admit the most humiliating personal treacheries—its evocation of Peter likewise projected before their troubled inner eyes the inexorable movement of Jesus the Son of God himself toward a tortured death and the barely scrutable will of that Father who keeps all lives in his matchless and finally killing grasp. If Mark hardly encouraged his first audience toward, in Tacitus's words, "hatred of the human race," it may well have strengthened them to see the world around them as the fading cinder it plainly is while they faced the advent of their Lord on the clouds in glory with his angels, bringing the reign of God to Earth.

And despite the fact that, early in the life of the gospels,

Mark took last place among readers to Matthew, Luke, and John with their greater length and more abundant teaching, it has gone on serving in its homely astonishment ensuing centuries of baffled men and women. For any member of the Jesus sect, whether his or her trials were mortal or less, could watch on Mark's plain face the clearest moving action, more awful than most in its failure and grander than any in triumph but no less consoling in the voice of its hero who—deluded or well-informed—gave his life as an intended ransom from death and eternal night.

What does Mark offer a modern reader, from whatever background with whatever needs? If there was ever a "common reader" in the Western world, he or she has long since spun off from any stable center into a welter of eccentric private errands and wants. Even those millions who call themselves Christian have scattered into a contemporary range of religious response that runs from infinite mercy through loathing dismissal of all others to degrees of faith so intense that they declare themselves blind to any questions concerning the historical foundations of their sect and find themselves increasingly often involved in physical or psychic violence against presumed enemies.

There are, for instance, many members of modern Jesus sects who consider it a sacrilege even to wonder at the dozens of obvious narrative and theological contradictions among the four gospels—no two gospels are both more alike and, simultaneously, more resonantly different than Mark and John. Many such fundamentalists cannot permit themselves to question the extent to which the man Jesus saw himself as either a divine being or a special kinsman of God's. Conversely, there are likewise millions who turn aside in repugnance or worse at the very mention of Jesus or his cult name *Christ*; they are repelled by the odors of savage hypocrisy hung round his memory by millennia of normal human monsters.

Yet a random telephone poll of Americans, conducted in

1992 and published in *Time* magazine, found that among men and women between the ages of twenty-seven and forty-five, 65 percent agree that "religion is 'very important' to me"; and 73 percent agree that "the Bible is the 'totally accurate' word of God." Forty-three percent say that they "read the Bible in the past week." And the three percentages rise markedly as the respondents survive past age forty-five—to 79 percent, 80 percent, and 54 percent. So if we confine our view to Americans only and assume that some of these millions of Bible readers turn occasionally to the pell-mell pages of Mark, it is evident that the shortest of the gospels still exerts a strong appeal on a great many people, many of whom we must assume to be of average intelligence and decency. What is Mark giving them, here toward the end of an era unimaginably different from his own?

Those reared in observant Christian homes, or later converts to churchly Christianity, have likely received some preparation for their reading. Perhaps a majority of them possess a sketchy sense of the relations between Rome and first-century Palestine; they may have some sense of the Mosaic law which stands as a mountainous backing to Jesus' work and his eventual execution; they may well bring to Mark's very light indications of Jesus' personality and character their own useful, or entirely inappropriate, sense of Jesus which they have gathered from church attendance, religious art, and other reading—a man meek and mild or fiercely judging or both.

A raw reader though—one encountering Mark with slim preparation beyond the power to read—is potentially an even more interesting reflector of the nature of Mark's achievement. If that reader can be persuaded to persist past all obscurities of history and geography and custom, he may well arrive at one of three large possibilities.

1. This is the more-or-less-interesting fictional account of a sincere wonder-worker with megalomani-

acal political ambitions who comes to understandable grief.

2. This is the sparely related account of the career and death of a primitive lunatic with a talent for rhetoric and psychosomatic healing.

3. This is the maddeningly spotty—though credibly detailed, in its quirky haste, and ultimately convincing—account of a man whose life, death, and implied but undemonstrated resurrection from the grave suggest some possible validity for his claims of superhuman power.

At bottom—and as T. S. Eliot says "the bottom is a great way down"—that is all we know we have, all Mark the book and Mark the writer can or will give us. He almost surely halted, not ended, his story at Jesus' empty tomb precisely to force that hard truth upon us. If we make the unlikely assumption that Mark's original ending is lost and that he must have preserved at least one appearance by the risen Jesus, then since Matthew has copied more than 90 percent of Mark, the single resurrection scene at the end of Matthew may well reproduce Mark's lost conclusion.

Continuing, though, with the assumption that Mark really ends as the silent women flee the gaping tomb, then are we to assume that the "young man in white" has told the women the truth? Has Jesus actually risen from death, and will he await his disciples in Galilee? Or are the women the subjects of a hoax or the victims of a shared hallucination, a far from uncommon possibility? In short, has Jesus kept his promise; is he worth the disciples' trust—*anyone's* trust, from Mark's original audience to the modern reader's?

If Mark had continued past the women's silent fear and showed us one or more scenes in which the raised Jesus appears to his followers as convincingly as he does in the final scene of John for instance—and if readers succumbed to that spectacle with some degree of trust—then would the man Mark have claimed that a victory over death on the part of one other man has any meaning for other humans, in imperial Rome three decades after the first Easter morning or two millennia later? If the tradition is accurate and Mark was writing for a Greek-speaking Roman community under threat of tortured death, why did he fail to assure them more completely by providing details of the triumphant historical event which he and Peter believed to be a promise to all who follow Jesus?—*Jesus is risen from the grave; so will you be.*

Whoever constituted Mark's first audience, why omit that triumph? A possible answer, though the least rewarding, would be that Mark knew that Jesus had not risen—not in the flesh in any case, not in a manner that left his tomb empty (there have been past attempts to imagine a hoax—the disciples arranged to steal the corpse; the young man in white was a stranger or a secret follower persuaded to play a brief role). A second answer might be that—since an empty tomb is not mentioned in the earliest known record of the resurrection, which is contained in chapter 15 of Paul's First Letter to the Corinthians, written some twenty years after the alleged event—Mark invents the claim of an empty tomb but does not want to compound the fabrication by inventing his way beyond it to further lies, however benignly intended. Or perhaps he is uneasy with the empty tomb's place in his sources and cannot persuade himself to proceed past it to a claim of Jesus' risen appearance.

More likely, the empty tomb was present in Mark's sources and had been from the start. Though early rabbinical lore contains some denigrations of Jesus' mother's sexual virtue and her son's legitimacy, there is no surviving record that any of Jesus' adversaries denied that his corpse had disappeared from its tomb. And while Paul's recital of the resurrection appearances dates from about 56 and does not actually mention an empty tomb (though, again, Paul knew at least two of the disciples and one of Jesus' brothers), the first-century Jewish notion of resurrection would seem not to have acknowledged that a purely "mental" sighting—a vision or hallucination—could be considered proof of resurrection. Only a palpable resuscitated body would have been sufficient proof.

In fact, beyond the last scene of Mark, there are three other pieces of non-Marcan narrative evidence that Jesus' tomb was found empty thirty-some hours after his death. In Paul's list of those who witnessed resurrection appearances, Peter's name comes first; and the two travelers to Emmaus in chapter 24 of Luke tell the risen Jesus, whom they fail to recognize, of an initial angelic appearance near the empty tomb to "some women among us." In John, though Jesus' first appearance at the tomb is to Mary Magdalene, Peter is the first (once Mary has summoned him) to enter the empty tomb and confirm the presence of Jesus' abandoned burial wrappings. With the likelihood of a powerful and circumstantially convincing memory of Peter's behind him then, nonetheless Mark chose not to portray the risen Jesus. His first reason may well have lain beyond his own consciousness. Since he is plainly a Jew—a Semite in the broadest racial sense and therefore blood kin to the later visionary Mohammed— Mark's mind is deeply conditioned and hedged by the Semite's dread of *portraying* God or Allah. The risen Jesus, in his unity with the ineffable divinity, may not be painted in words. Even the writer of Exodus, in that imposing scene when God Yahweh hides Moses in a crevice of Mount Sinai and then passes near him, describes no more than the deity's back. In fact I know of only a single successful verbal theophany in the whole of literature before the final scene of John's gospel, and that is the long still moment in the *Bhagavad Gita* when the Lord Krishna accords the human Arjuna a vision of some of the forms of God's infinite nature. That display culminates in the desolating yet joyful revelation which Robert Oppenheimer recalled in 1945 as he watched the first atomic bomb's glare in the New Mexican desert—"I am come as Time, the waster of peoples."

More consciously though, Mark's final reason for the omission of a resurrection scene is surely part and parcel of his bedrock narrative strategy, his narrative faith throughout his book. Masterful as his writing hand has proved to be from the start of his tale, here at the end he faces the inexorable fact that words on a page, however attentive and carefully arranged, cannot of themselves produce belief and trust of the sort that a phenomenon like palpable resurrection from the dead demands of an audience. The supreme narrators—and Mark is one of them with the J writer of Hebrew scripture, Homer, the poet of the *Bhagavad Gita*, Shakespeare, Milton, Tolstoy, and a few film directors like Renoir and Kurosawa—can bring us to the very doorsill of the roofless chamber of total trust in the power of words to trigger belief. They transport us to that brink, not primarily by metaphorical brilliance or linguistic and visual freshness and precision but by a mysterious summoning before us of the fact-laden instant in which a visible undeniable human act approaches us with godly power—a power which, at the moment of reading or watching in any case, grips us and forces our full consent.

*

Early in his itinerant healing, Mark's Jesus—who is likely to be Peter's Jesus, and as near to the real man as we will ever come—reaches for the hand of a dead young girl, says two words in Aramaic, *"Talitha koum,"* and floods the child with life, a life so real that Jesus has nothing else to say to her parents but "Give her something to eat." And when the blind man at Bethsaida has the temerity to admit that Jesus' healing has partially failed—that he can only see "men that look like trees walking"—undeterred, Jesus spits again on his handful

80

of clay and thumbs it onto the hazy eyes. What reader can say that such moments—with their proffered sights of a credible powerful merciful hand moving through the lethal void of the world's indifference to confirm our absolute worth with the perfect reward of a second life or the gift of sight—are not among our greatest longings, our final hopes?

Mark and his small handful of peers in fiction, poetry, drama, and film can all but gratify that hope just outside the door to the room of heart's content. But the inherent limits on the power of words and the architecture of sentences or images force them to leave us there, on the edge of full sight—that room, just beyond us, in which all creation opens before us in its teeming variety and riotous individuality, as it really is, not "like trees walking." If we mean to take the single step onward, into full implication in the life of Abraham or Absalom or Anna Karenina or Jesus or the mind of the peregrine falcon diving on its hapless prey, then we must choose to take it ourselves—on our own volition, with our own severely limited energy—and make that final move through our own narrative and visual powers, that cell of our mind which is our best stage and screening room.

In the cases of Abraham, King David, Anna, Lady Macbeth, or the feeble Lear, we think that we know by instinct or by trained eye—as we move across actual or fabricated ground—that the life we enter is either a fictional or a real but vanished life. What is most original in Mark—most startling and potentially most offensive—is the writer's and perhaps Jesus' own insistence that the words of Jesus and Jesus' possible triumph over death not only press directly on the present life of the reader, in whatever time and place he or she exists, but may very well confront the reader with choices of belief and behavior that will decide the reader's fate throughout eternity.

Of all surviving ancient documents that continue to have an active force in the life of the world—from *Gilgamesh*, the

Vedas, and the *Gita* through the Hebrew scriptures with their refusal to predict an immortality for the individual soul and the Sanskrit memories and records of the Buddha — there are no documents earlier than Mark which confront the reader with what the document defines as a literal life-or-death choice. Whether we sit in the range of Mark's telling voice, or alone with his book before our eyes, it is not finally possible to ignore the enormous claim of his story — *Obey this man I have summoned before you; take your own cross and walk behind him.*

In the light of such unprecedented narrative audacity, consider a few more challenges set by Mark for his audience — whoever they may be, whenever they encounter him. One bold fact that is seldom remarked but nonetheless astonishing, especially if Mark works from the memories of Peter, is the fact that (unlike John and Luke) Mark never deigns to present his credentials for the story he offers, the demand his story makes. Nowhere in his length does he so much as hint at his own name and whereabouts, much less claim that he stands on the rock of Peter's knowledge or Paul's. It is worth noting here that, for centuries, readers have wondered if the otherwise inexplicable nude boy who flees Gethsemane when Jesus is arrested may not be Mark himself. Perhaps, the speculation runs, the youthful Mark was sent to warn Jesus of the imminent arrest and only managed to escape by a literal hair. In any case, the fleeing boy is unnamed and does not reappear — unless, and this is a desperate stretch, he is "the young man in white" at the empty tomb.

Whether or not Mark transmitted the eyewitness of Peter, it is equally extraordinary that he shows us throughout his length that all the disciples behave with an obtuseness which, in its own less immediately lethal way, is as real a betrayal as Judas's more public act (it is an obtuseness which also raises the question whether any of the disciples possessed an understanding sufficient to have written, or lain behind, any one of the four gospels; but if we answer No to the question, then how did a small handful of unknown men take up pens in the wake of Jesus and acquire the power to transcribe—or entirely invent—their gospels?). Even if Mark the writer had no direct tradition from Peter, it was inevitable that the memory of Jesus' words and acts could only have been preserved after his death by those very men and faithful women who dogged his steps, however blindly. By exhibiting frankly the male disciples' steady ignorance and failure of their Lord during his active career, Mark has risked impugning the very sources of his knowledge, his faith, and his story—who would believe these dismal dullards?

Far riskier, the God whom Mark's Jesus implies and all but proves throughout his early career to be a God of mercy, love, and forgiveness is the Father—Jesus' cherished familiar *Abba*, in one of the cruelest verbal ironies in the history of narrative. And *Abba* has planned, perhaps from the start of time as John will later suggest, to exalt this much-loved Son for the purpose of torturing him to death in the most excruciating manner available in the Roman world of the first century. The fact that the torture is previously understood by Jesus, even as late as his debates in Jerusalem a few days before his death, to be in the nature of a redeeming blood sacrifice to a supremely loving God—a ransom for the lives of erring humankind—only makes Jesus' early benign conception of the Father all the more cutting along its double edge.

Mark shows us unflinchingly that, until the nails first pierce Jesus or until his penultimate breath on the cross, the Son himself cannot have imagined the personal force of his abstract knowledge that the Father is not only loving but *just* in his final requirements of each human creature. And with this God—the God of Abraham and Isaac, Moses and David, Elijah and Jesus—justice always means blood, the appeasement of a just divine wrath. *Abba* Father craves seas of blood, and the blood of lambs and oxen was poured out to him in smoking torrents at the Temple which Jesus revered and haunted; but in the horrifying yet healing story at the core of Mark, the insufficient blood of dumb beasts is at last replaced by the one right offering—the blood of God's own unique Son, a man of enormous mercy and care: a sufficient feast for the hungriest Father.

No other gospel, even Matthew with its broad grounding in Hebraic lore, is quite brave enough to admit to that chasm yawning between the claims of Jesus and his agonized fate— a fate that may well yawn before each one of us, between here and death. Isn't that bravery—reckless, unnerving—the source of the pull that Mark the writer has exerted through all the life of his story: the radiant draw and the powerful thrust of Mark's forthright hand, a draw that works first on his near successors as they copy him faithfully and then on every subsequent human creature, whatever that creature's knowledge or ignorance of Mark the pamphlet? (The long triumph of the West over Africa and Asia spread Mark's meaning, however tortured, across the whole Earth.) And haven't that draw and its massive thrust continued through two thousand years to make for peace or frenzy, light or darkness, rescue or loss throughout the Earth? In the presence of what other book, from the length of history, could any sane reader even broach such a question?

THE GOOD NEWS
ACCORDING TO MARK

ACCORDING TO MARK

BEGINNING OF THE GOOD NEWS OF JESUS MESSIAH

As it was written in Isaiah the prophet
> *Look, I send my messenger before your face*
> *Who shall prepare your way.*
> *Voice of one crying in the desert*
> *"Prepare the Lord's way;*
> *Make his paths straight."*

John the Baptizer came into the desert declaring baptism of repentance for pardon of wrong.

All the country of Judea went out to him and those from Jerusalem and were baptized by him in the Jordan River admitting their wrongs.

John wore camel's hair and a leather belt round his hips, ate grasshoppers and wild honey and declared "He's coming who is stronger than I—after me—of whom I'm unfit stooping to loosen the strap of his sandals. I baptized you in water but he'll baptize you in Holy Spirit."

It happened in those days Jesus came from Nazareth in Galilee and was baptized in the Jordan by John. At once going up out of the water he saw the sky torn open and the Spirit like a dove descending to him.

There was a voice out of the sky "You are my Son the loved one. In you I have delighted."

At once the Spirit drove him into the desert. He was in the desert forty days tried by Satan and was with wild beasts.

The angels served him.

After John was handed over Jesus came into Galilee declaring God's good news and saying "The time has ripened and the reign of God has approached. Turn and trust the good news." Passing by the sea of Galilee he saw Simon and Andrew, Simon's brother, casting a net into the sea—they were fishermen—and Jesus said to them "Come after me and I'll make you fishers for men."

At once leaving the nets they followed him.

Going on a little he saw James—Zebedee's James—and John his brother right in the boat mending nets. At once he called them and leaving their father Zebedee in the boat with the hands they went after him.

They went into Capernaum and at once on the Sabbath entering the synagogue he taught.

They were amazed at his teaching for he was teaching them as if he had the right and not like the scholars.

At once there was in their synagogue a man with a foul spirit and he screamed "What are you to us, Jesus Nazarene? Did you come to destroy us? I know you for what you are—the Holy One of God!"

Jesus warned him saying "Silence! Come out of him."

Tearing him the foul spirit cried in a loud voice and came out of him.

All were stunned so they debated among themselves saying "What is this—a new teaching by right? He commands the foul spirits and they obey him."

Word of him went out at once everywhere all round the country of Galilee.

Going out of the synagogue at once they came to Simon and Andrew's house with James and John. Simon's mother-in-law was laid up with fever and at once they told him about her.

Approaching he raised her holding her hand.

The fever left her so she served them.

Then when dusk came and the sun set they brought him all the sick and the demoniac. The whole city was gathered at the door.

He cured many sick with various diseases and expelled many demons and did not let the demons speak because they knew him.

And very early—still night—he rose and went out and left for a lonely place and prayed there.

Simon and those with him tracked him down, found him and said to him "Everyone's looking for you."

He said to them "Let's go elsewhere to the nearest cities so I may spread the word there too. I came for this." And he spread the word in their synagogues in all Galilee and expelled demons.

A leper came to him begging him, kneeling and saying to him "If you will you can cleanse me."

Filled with pity stretching out his hand he touched him and said "I will. Be clean."

At once the leprosy left him and he was clean.

Then warning him sternly he ran him off and said to him "See you tell nothing to nobody but go show yourself to the priest and offer for your cleansing what Moses ordered as witness to them."

But he going off began to declare many things and spread the word.

So he could no longer enter a city openly but was out in desert places.

And they came to him from everywhere.

When he entered Capernaum again after days it was heard he was at home and many gathered so there was no room not even at the door and he spoke the word to them.

They came to him bringing a cripple borne by four men and unable to reach him because of the crowd they tore off the roof where he was and having broken in they lowered the pallet on which the cripple was lying.

Seeing their faith Jesus said to the cripple "Son, your wrongs are forgiven you."

But there were some scholars sitting there debating in their hearts "Why does this man speak thus? He blasphemes. Who can forgive wrongs but one—God?"

At once Jesus knowing in his soul that they were debating thus among themselves said to them "Why do you debate these things in your hearts? What is easier to say to the cripple 'Your wrongs are forgiven' or to say 'Stand. Take your pallet and walk'? But so you know the Son of Man has the right to forgive wrongs on Earth" he said to the cripple "To you I say stand, take your pallet and go home."

He stood and at once taking the pallet went out in sight of all so that all were astonished and praised God saying "We never saw the like."

He went out again by the sea and all the crowd came to him and he taught them. And walking along he saw Levi—Alpheus's Levi—sitting at the tax office and said to him "Follow me."

Rising he followed him.

Then it happened as he lay back in his house many tax collectors and wrongdoers lay back with Jesus and his disciples for there were many and they followed him.

The Pharisee scholars seeing him eating with wrongdoers and tax collectors said to his disciples "Does he eat with wrongdoers and tax collectors?"

Hearing Jesus said to them "The strong don't need a doctor but the sick do. I came not to call the just but wrongdoers."

Now John's disciples and the Pharisees were fasting and they came and said to him "Why do John's disciples and the Pharisees' disciples fast but your disciples don't fast?"

Jesus said to them "Can the sons of the bridal chamber fast while the bridegroom is with them? The time they have the bridegroom with them they can't fast. But days shall come when the bridegroom shall be taken from them and they'll fast on that day. No one sews a patch of unshrunk cloth on old clothes otherwise the new pulls on the old and a worse tear starts. And no one puts new wine into old skins or the new wine splits the skins and the wine is lost and the skins. No, new wine is put in fresh skins."

Then this happened as he was walking on the Sabbath through the grain fields and his disciples as they made a path began pulling stalks.

The Pharisees said to him "Look, why do they do on the Sabbath what's not right?"

He said to them "Didn't you ever read what David did when he was needy and hungry—he and those with him—how he entered God's house in the time of High Priest Abiathar and ate the presentation loaves which it's not right to eat except for priests and also gave to those with him?" And he said to them "The Sabbath was made because of man not man because of the Sabbath. So the Son of Man is also lord of the Sabbath."

He entered the synagogue again and there was a man who had a withered hand.

They were watching him closely whether on the Sabbath he would heal him so they might charge him.

He said to the man who had the withered hand "Stand in the middle here." And he said to them "Is it right on the Sabbath to do good or to do evil, to save life or kill?"

But they were silent.

Looking round at them with anger, grieved at the hardness of their heart he said to the man "Stretch out the hand."

He stretched it out and his hand was restored.

Leaving the Pharisees at once consulted with the Herodians against him so they might destroy him.

Jesus with his disciples withdrew to the sea.

And a great throng from Galilee followed and from Judea, from Jerusalem, from Idumea, from beyond the Jordan and round Tyre and Sidon a great throng hearing what he did came to him.

He told his disciples that a little boat should wait near him because of the crowd so they might not rush him for he healed many so that they fell on him to touch him as many as had torments. And the foul spirits when they saw him fell down before him and cried "You're the Son of God."

He warned them strictly that they not reveal him.

And he climbed the mountain and called to him the ones he wanted.

They went to him.

He appointed twelve to be with him to send out to spread the word and to have the right to expel demons. He appointed the Twelve and gave Simon the name Peter. And Zebedee's James and John, James's brother—he gave them the name *Boanerges* which is Sons of Thunder—and Andrew, Philip, Bartholomew, Matthew, Thomas, Alpheus's James, Thaddeus, Simon the zealot and Judas Iscariot who also handed him over.

He came into a house and again a crowd gathered so they could not even eat bread.

Hearing his family went out to seize him for they said "He's beside himself."

And the scholars who came down from Jerusalem said "He has Beelzebub and by the prince of demons he expels demons."

Calling them to him in parables he said "How can Satan expel Satan? If a kingdom is divided against itself that kingdom can't stand and if a house is divided against itself that house can't stand. And if Satan stood against himself and were divided he couldn't stand but would end. No man can—entering a strong man's house—plunder his goods unless he binds the strong man first. Then he shall plunder his house. Amen I say to you that all shall be forgiven people—wrongs and whatever blasphemies they may blaspheme—but whoever blasphemes against the Holy Spirit has no forgiveness to eternity but is subject to eternal wrong because they said 'He has a foul spirit.' "

His mother and his brothers came and standing outside sent to him calling him.

A crowd sat round him and said to him "Look, your mother and your brothers outside are hunting you."

Answering them he said "Who is my mother and my brothers?" and looking round at the ones sitting round him in a ring he said "Look, my mother and my brothers. Whoever does God's will that one is my brother, sister and mother."

Again he began to teach by the sea and a great crowd gathered to him so that climbing into a boat he sat on the sea and all the crowd was on land close to the sea. He taught them much in parables and said to them in his teaching "Listen. Look, the sower went out to sow and it happened as he sowed some fell by the road and birds came and ate it up. Another part fell on the rocky place where there wasn't much earth and at once it sprouted because it had no deep earth and when the sun rose it was burnt and because of not having root it withered. Another part fell into thorns and the thorns grew up and choked it and it bore no fruit. Another part fell into good ground and bore fruit growing up and increasing and bore in thirties, sixties and hundreds." Then he said to them "Who has ears to hear let him hear."

When he was alone those round him with the Twelve asked him about the parables.

He said to them "To you the mystery of the reign of God has been given but to those outside everything is in parables so
Seeing they may see and not find
And hearing they may hear and not understand—
Otherwise they'd turn and be forgiven."
And he said to them "Don't you know this parable? Then how will you know all the parables? The sower sows the word

and these are the ones by the road where the word is sown and when they hear at once Satan comes and takes the word sown in them. These are also the ones sown in rocky places who when they hear the word at once accept it with joy and have no root in themselves but are temporary. Then trouble or persecution coming because of the word at once they stumble. Others are the ones sown among thorns. These are the ones hearing the word and the cares of the time, the cheat of riches and the other passions entering choke the word and it becomes barren. And those are the ones sown in good earth who hear the word and welcome it and bear fruit in thirties, sixties and hundreds."

And he said to them "Does the lamp come so it can be put under the measuring bowl or under the couch, not so it can be put on the lampstand? For nothing is hidden that shall not be shown or veiled except it come into the open. If any has ears to hear let him hear."

And he said to them "Take care what you hear—with whatever measure you measure it shall be measured to you and added to you for whoever has to him shall be given and who has not even what he has shall be taken from him."

And he said "Such is the reign of God as if a man should throw seed on the earth and should sleep and rise night and day and the seed should sprout and lengthen he doesn't know how—on her own the Earth yields fruit, first a blade then an ear then full grain in the ear. And when the fruit offers itself at once he puts in the sickle for the harvest has come."

And he said "To what can we liken the reign of God? Or in what parable could we put it?—like a grain of mustard which when it's sown on the ground is smaller than all seeds on the Earth but when it's sown grows up and becomes greater than all plants and makes big branches so the birds of the air can live under its shadow." In many such parables he spoke the word to them as far as they could hear it but without a parable he never spoke to them though aside to his own disciples he explained everything.

He said to them on that day when evening had come "Let's cross over to the other side."

Dismissing the crowd they took him just as he was in the boat and other boats were with him. A violent windstorm came and waves poured into the boat so that it was now full.

He was in the stern on a pillow sleeping.

They woke him and said to him "Teacher, it's nothing to you that we're perishing?"

Awake he warned the wind and said to the sea "Silence. Be still."

The wind fell and there was great calm.

He said to them "Why be so cowardly? Where is your trust?"

They feared with great dread and said to each other "Who is this then that even the wind and sea obey him?"

They came to the far side of the sea to Gerasene country. When he got out of the boat at once a man from the tombs with a foul spirit met him—his home was in the tombs. Even with a chain no one could bind him since he had often been bound with shackles and chains and the chains had been broken by him, the shackles had been smashed and no one was able to tame him. Always night and day in the tombs and mountains he was screaming and slashing himself with rocks. Seeing Jesus from a distance he ran, fell to his knees and screaming in a loud voice he said "What am I to you, Jesus Son of the Highest God? I beg you by God don't torture me—"

For he had been saying to him "Out, foul spirit. Out of the man." He asked him "What is your name?"

He said to him "Legion is my name because we are many" and he pled hard with Jesus not to send them out of the country. Now there was there close to the mountain a big herd of pigs feeding and the demons pled "Send us to the pigs so we can enter them."

He let them.

Going out the foul spirits entered the pigs and the herd rushed down a cliff into the sea—about two thousand—and were choked in the sea.

The ones herding them fled and reported it to the city and the fields and they came to see what it was that had happened. They came to Jesus and saw the demoniac sitting dressed and in his right mind—him who had had the Legion—and they were afraid. Those who had seen how it happened to the demoniac told them and about the pigs so they began to plead with him to leave their district.

As he boarded the boat the demoniac pled to be with him.

He did not let him but said to him "Go to your home to your people and report to them how much the Lord has done for you and pitied you."

He left and began to spread word through Decapolis how much Jesus did for him.

Everyone wondered.

When Jesus had crossed into the boat again to the far side a great crowd swarmed to him—he was by the sea—and one of the synagogue leaders named Jairus came and seeing him fell at his feet and pled hard saying "My little daughter is at the point of death. Come and lay your hands on her so she may be cured and live."

He went with him.

And a great crowd followed him and pressed round him.

Then a woman who had had a flow of blood twelve years and had suffered many things from many doctors and spent all she owned and gained nothing but rather grown worse, hearing things about Jesus came up behind in the crowd and touched his coat saying "If I can touch just his clothes I'll be cured" and at once the fountain of her blood was dried and she knew in her body that she was healed from the scourge.

At once Jesus knowing in himself that his streaming

power had gone out of him turned to the crowd and said "Who touched my clothes?"

His disciples said to him "You see the crowd pressing you and you say 'Who touched me?' "

He looked round to see her who had done this.

So the woman—dreading and shaking, knowing what had happened to her—came and fell before him and told him all the truth.

He said to her "Daughter, your faith has cured you. Go in peace and be well of your scourge."

While he was still speaking they came from the synagogue leader's saying "Your daughter died. Why bother the teacher still?"

But Jesus ignoring the word just spoken said to the synagogue leader "Don't fear. Only trust" and he let no one go with him but Peter, James and John—James's brother.

They came to the house of the synagogue leader.

He saw a commotion, people weeping and wailing hard. Entering he said to them "Why make a commotion and weep? The child is not dead but sleeps."

They mocked him.

But expelling them all he took the child's father, mother and those with him and went in where the child was. Grasping the child's hand he said to her *"Talitha koum"* which is translated "Little girl, I tell you get up."

At once the little girl rose and walked round—she was twelve years old—and at once they were astonished with great wildness.

He ordered them strictly that no one should know this and told them to give her something to eat.

He went out of there and came to his own city and his disciples followed him. When a Sabbath came he began to teach in the synagogue.

Many hearing were amazed saying "From where did all these things come to this man and what is the wisdom given to him that such acts of power are done through his hands? Isn't this man the builder, the son of Mary and brother of James and Joses and Judas and Simon and aren't his sisters here with us?" They were offended by him.

Jesus said to them "A prophet is not dishonored except in his own city and among his kin and in his own house" and he could not do there any act of power except to a few sick—laying hands on them, he healed. He was amazed at their lack of trust.

And he toured the villages round there teaching. He called the Twelve to him and began to send them out two by two and gave them rights over foul spirits and ordered them to take nothing for the road except one stick—no bread, no wallet, no money in the belt—but be shod with sandals and not wear two shirts. He said to them "Wherever you enter a house stay there till you leave there and whatever place will not receive you or hear you, leaving there shake off the dust under your feet as a witness to them."

Going out they spread the word that people should change. They expelled many demons, anointed with oil many of the sick and healed them.

King Herod heard—his name became widespread and they were saying "John the Baptizer has been raised from the dead which is why acts of power work through him" but others said "It's Elijah" and still others said "A prophet like one of the prophets." But hearing Herod said "The one I beheaded—John: he was raised" for Herod himself had sent and arrested John and bound him in prison because of Herodias the wife of Philip his brother since he had married her. For John said to Herod "It's not right for you to have your brother's wife." So Herodias had a grudge against him and wanted to kill him but could not for Herod feared John knowing him a just and holy man and protected him and hearing him was shaken but gladly heard him. Then when a suitable day came Herod gave a supper on his birthday for his great men and the tribunes and leading men of Galilee. The daughter of Herodias herself entered and dancing pleased Herod and those lying back with him. So the king said to the girl "Ask me whatever you want and I'll give it to you" and he swore to her "Whatever you ask I'll give you up to half my kingdom." Going out she said to her mother "What must I ask?" She said "The head of John the Baptizer." At once entering eagerly to the king she asked "I want you to give me right now on a dish the head of John the Baptist." The king, anguished because of the oaths and those lying back with him, did not want to refuse her so at once sending an executioner the king commanded his head to be brought. Going he beheaded him in the prison, brought his head on a dish, gave it to the girl and the girl gave it to her mother. Hearing his disciples went, took his corpse and put it in a tomb.

And the ones sent out gathered back to Jesus and told him all they had done and taught.

He said to them "Come away by yourselves alone to a lonely place and rest a little" since those coming and going were many and they had no chance even to eat. They went off in the boat to a lonely place alone.

Many saw them going, knew and on foot from all the cities ran there together and preceded them.

Going out he saw a great crowd, pitied them since they were like sheep having no shepherd and began to teach them many things.

When it was late the disciples approached him and said "The place is lonely and it's late. Dismiss them so that going off to the neighboring farms and villages they can buy themselves something to eat."

But answering he said to them "You give them something to eat."

They said to him "Shall we go off and buy two hundred denars worth of loaves and give them to eat?"

He said to them "How many loaves do you have? Go see."

Knowing they said "Five and two fish."

He told them to lie back in parties on the green grass.

They lay back in groups by hundreds and fifties.

Then taking the five loaves and two fish looking up to Heaven he blessed and broke the loaves, gave them to the disciples to set before them and the two fish he spread among all.

All ate and were fed and they took up twelve full baskets of crumbs and fish. Those eating the loaves were five thousand people.

At once he made his disciples board the boat and go ahead to the far side of Bethsaida until he dismissed the crowd. And saying goodbye to them he went off to the mountain to pray.

When dusk came on the boat was in the middle of the sea and he alone on land and seeing them straining at the rowing for the wind was against them about three o'clock in the night he came toward them walking on the sea and wanted to pass them.

But seeing him walking on the sea they thought it was a ghost and cried out—all saw him and were frightened.

But at once he spoke with them and said "Courage. I am. No fear." And he went up to them into the boat and the wind dropped.

In themselves they were deeply astonished since they did not understand about the loaves as their heart was hardened.

Crossing over to land they came to Gennesaret and anchored.

When they came out of the ship at once knowing him they ran round all the countryside and began to haul the sick round on pallets where they heard he was and wherever he entered villages or cities or farms they put the sick in marketplaces and begged him to touch even the hem of his coat and as many as touched him were healed.

The Pharisees gathered to him and some of the scholars from Jerusalem and seeing some of his disciples eating bread with dirty hands—that is not washed (for the Pharisees and all the Jews do not eat unless they wash their hands with the fist keeping the way of the elders and coming from markets unless they rinse they do not eat and there are many other things which they have accepted to keep: washing cups, pitchers and kettles)—the Pharisees and scholars questioned him "Why don't your disciples walk after the way of the elders but eat bread with dirty hands?"

He said to them "Isaiah prophesied rightly about you hypocrites since it is written

This people honors me with lips
But their heart is far from me.
They worship me in vain
Teaching teachings which are men's commands.

Deserting God's command you keep man's way." And he said to them "Rightly you put aside God's command so you may keep your way for Moses said '*Honor your father and your mother*' and '*The one who reviles father or mother let him die.*' But you say if a man says to his father 'Whatever you might have got from me is *Korban*'" (that is *a gift*) "then you no longer let him do anything for his father or mother, canceling God's word in the way you've accepted. You do many such things."

Calling the crowd to him again he said "Hear me all of you and understand. There is nothing outside a man that entering him can defile him but the things coming out of a man are the ones that defile a man."

When he entered a house from the crowd his disciples questioned him about the parable.

He said to them "Then you too are stupid? Don't you understand that anything outside entering a man can't defile him because it doesn't enter his heart but his belly and goes into the privy purging all foods?" He said "The thing coming out of a man defiles a man. For from inside out of the heart of men bad thoughts come—fornications, thefts, murders, adulteries, greeds, malice, deceit, lust, evil eye, slander, pride, folly: all these evil things come from inside and defile a man."

Rising from there he went off to the district of Tyre. When he entered a house he wanted no one to know but he could not be hid.

At once a woman whose little daughter had a foul spirit heard of him and coming fell at his feet. The woman was a Greek, a Syro-Phoenician by race, and she asked him to expel the demon from her daughter.

He said to her "Let the children be fed first. It's not right to take the children's bread and throw it to pups."

She answered and said to him "Yes sir but pups under the table eat the children's crumbs."

He said to her "For that saying go. The demon has gone out of your daughter."

And going away to her house she found the child laid on the couch and the demon gone.

Going out again from the district of Tyre he came through Sidon to the sea of Galilee in the middle of the district of Decapolis. And they brought him a deaf man with a stammer and begged him to put his hand on him. Taking him apart from the crowd he put his fingers into his ears and spitting touched his tongue and looking up to Heaven groaned and said to him "Ephphatha" which is "Be opened."

His ears were opened, at once the block on his tongue was loosed and he spoke right.

He ordered them to tell nobody but the more he ordered the more wildly they declared it. They were wildly amazed saying "He has done everything right—he makes the deaf hear and the dumb speak."

In those days there was a big crowd again with nothing to eat and calling the disciples to him he said to them "I pity the crowd since they've been with me three days and have nothing to eat. If I send them off hungry to their homes they'll give out on the way—some of them are from far off."

His disciples answered him "Where could anyone get loaves to feed these people here in a desert?"

He asked them "How many loaves do you have?"

They said "Seven."

He ordered the crowd to lie back on the ground and taking the seven loaves and giving thanks he broke and gave to his disciples to serve.

They served the crowd.

They had a few little fish and blessing them he said for those to be served too.

They ate and were fed and took up seven trays of excess scraps—now they were about four thousand—and he sent them off.

At once embarking in the boat with his disciples he came to the region of Dalmanutha.

The Pharisees came out and began to debate with him, demanding from him a sign from Heaven, tempting him.

Groaning in his soul he said "Why does this generation demand a sign? Amen I tell you no sign will be given this generation." And leaving them again embarking he went off to the far side. They forgot to take bread—except for one loaf they had nothing with them in the boat—and he ordered them saying "Look, watch out for the Pharisees' leaven and Herod's leaven."

They argued with one another that they had no bread.

Knowing he said to them "Why argue that you have no bread? Don't you see yet or understand? Has your heart been hardened? *'Having eyes don't you see? Having ears don't you hear?'* Don't you remember? When I broke the five loaves for the five thousand how many basketsful of scraps did you take?"

They said to him "Twelve."

"When the seven for the four thousand how many trays filled with scraps did you take?"

They said "Seven."

He said to them "You still don't understand?"

They came to Bethsaida.

And they brought a blind man to him and begged him to touch him.

Taking the blind man's hand he led him out of the village and spitting in his eyes and laying hands on him he questioned him "Do you see anything?"

Looking up he said "I see men that look like trees walking."

So again he put his hands on his eyes.

Then he looked hard, was restored and saw everything clearly.

He sent him home saying "You may not go to the village."

And Jesus and his disciples went out to the villages of Caesarea Philippi. On the way he questioned his disciples saying to them "Who do people say I am?"

They told him " 'John the Baptist' " and others " 'Elijah' " but others " 'One of the prophets.' "

He questioned them "But you—who do you say that I am?"

Answering Peter said to him "You are Messiah."

He warned them not to tell anyone about him and began to teach them that the Son of Man must endure many things and be refused by the elders and chief priests and scholars and be killed and after three days rise again—he said the thing plainly.

Peter taking him aside began to warn him.

But he turning round and seeing his disciples warned Peter and said "Get behind me, Satan, since you think not of God's things but men's things."

And calling the crowd to him with his disciples he said to

them "If anyone wants to come after me let him disown himself and lift his cross and follow me for whoever wants to save his life shall lose it but whoever shall lose his life because of me and the good news shall save it. For how does it help a man to get the whole world and forfeit his soul? For what can a man give to redeem his soul? Whoever is ashamed of me and my words in this adulterous and wrongful generation the Son of Man shall also be ashamed of him when he comes in the glory of his Father with the holy angels." And he said to them "Amen I tell you that there are some of those standing here who shall never taste death till they see the reign of God come in power."

After six days Jesus took Peter, James and John and led them up into a high mountain by themselves alone. He was changed in shape before them and his clothes became a very shining white such as no bleacher on Earth can whiten. And Elijah appeared to them with Moses and they were talking with Jesus.

Speaking up Peter said to Jesus "Rabbi, it's good for us to be here. Let's make three tents—one for you, one for Moses and one for Elijah." He didn't know what he said—they were terrified.

There came a cloud covering them and there came a voice out of the cloud "This is my Son the loved one. Hear him."

Suddenly looking round they no longer saw anyone but only Jesus alone with themselves.

Coming down from the mountain he ordered them to tell no one the things they saw except when the Son of Man should rise from the dead.

They kept that word to themselves discussing what is "To rise from the dead." And they questioned him "Why do the scholars say that Elijah must come first?"

He said to them "Elijah in fact coming first shall restore everything. How has it been written of the Son of Man—that he should endure much, suffer and be scorned? But I tell you that Elijah has come already and they did with him what they wanted as it was written of him."

And coming to the disciples they saw a big crowd round them and scholars arguing with them.

At once seeing him all the crowd were much stunned and running up greeted him.

He questioned them "What are you arguing with them?"

One of the crowd answered him "Teacher, I brought you my son who has a dumb spirit. Wherever it seizes him it flings him down and he foams and gnashes his teeth and goes stiff. I told your disciples to expel him but they couldn't."

Answering them he said "O unbelieving generation, how long shall I be with you? How long must I bear you? Bring him to me."

They brought him to him.

And seeing him at once the spirit convulsed him fiercely and falling to the ground he wallowed foaming.

He questioned his father "How long is it since this happened to him?"

He said "Since childhood. Often it throws him into fire and water to destroy him but if you can do anything take pity on us. Help us."

Jesus said to him " 'If you can'?—everything can be for a believer."

Crying out at once the boy's father said "I believe. Help my unbelief."

Seeing a crowd running together Jesus warned the foul spirit saying to it "Dumb and deaf spirit, I order you to come out of him and enter him no more!"

Screaming and convulsing him greatly it came out and he was lifeless so that many said he was dead.

But Jesus taking hold of his hand pulled him and he stood.

When he entered a house his disciples asked him privately "Why couldn't we expel it?"

He told them "This kind comes out for nothing but prayer."

Leaving there they passed through Galilee. He wanted no one to know since he was teaching his disciples. He told them "The Son of Man is handed into men's hands. They shall kill him and being killed after three days he shall rise."

They were ignorant of the prophecy and afraid to ask him.

And they came to Capernaum and once in the house he questioned them "What were you discussing on the way?"

They were silent for on the way they had argued with one another who was greater.

Sitting he called the Twelve and said to them "If anyone wants to be first he shall be last of all and slave of all." Then taking a child he set him in their midst and folding him in his arms he said to them "Whoever welcomes one child like this in my name welcomes me and whoever welcomes me welcomes not me but the one who sent me."

John said to him "Teacher, we saw someone expelling demons in your name. We stopped him since he doesn't follow us."

But Jesus said "Don't stop him. No one will do a powerful thing in my name and soon speak evil of me. Whoever is not against us is for us and whoever gives you a cup of water to drink because you are Messiah's—amen I tell you that he shall no way lose his reward. And whoever causes one of these little ones who trust to stumble it would be better for him if a great millstone were set around his neck and he were thrown in the sea. If your hand makes you stumble cut it off. It's better you enter life maimed than having two hands go off into Gehenna into unquenchable fire. If your foot makes you stumble cut it off. It's better you enter life lame than having two feet be thrown into Gehenna. And if your eye makes you stumble gouge it out. It's better you enter the reign of God one-eyed than having two eyes be thrown into Gehenna *where their worm never dies and the fire is not quenched.*' For everyone shall be salted with fire. Salt is good but if salt goes bland how will you season it? Have salt in yourselves and keep peace with one another."

Rising from there he came to the region of Judea and the far side of Jordan. Crowds followed him again and as usual he taught them.

Coming up Pharisees questioned him if it was right for a man to dismiss his wife—testing him.

Answering he said to them "What did Moses command you?"

They said "Moses allowed us *'to write a notice of divorce and to dismiss her.'*"

Jesus said to them "For your hardheartedness he wrote you this command. But from the start of creation *'He made them male and female and because of that a man shall leave his father and mother and the two shall be one flesh'* so that they're no longer two but one. Thus what God yoked man must not divide."

Back in the house the disciples questioned him about this.

He said to them "Whoever dismisses his wife and marries another commits adultery on her. And if she dismissing her husband marries another she commits adultery."

They brought him children to touch but the disciples warned them.

Seeing Jesus was indignant and said to them "Let the children come to me—don't stop them—for the reign of God belongs to such. Amen I tell you whoever doesn't welcome the reign of God like a child shall never enter it." And folding them in his arms he blessed them by putting his hands on them.

As he went out onto the road a man ran up and kneeling to him asked him "Kind teacher, what must I do to inherit eternal life?"

Jesus said to him "Why do you call me kind? No one is

kind but one—God. You know the commandments '*Do not kill, do not commit adultery, do not steal, do not give perjured witness,*' do not cheat, '*honor your father and mother.*'"

He said to him "Teacher, all these things I've kept since my youth."

Then Jesus gazing at him loved him and said to him "One thing is lacking you. Go sell what you have and give to the poor—you'll have treasure in Heaven. Then come follow me."

But he was shocked by the word and went away grieving since he had great belongings.

Looking round Jesus said to his disciples "How strenuously the rich shall enter the reign of God!"

The disciples were stunned at his words.

But Jesus speaking again said to them "Children, how strenuous it is to enter the reign of God! It's easier for a camel to go through a needle's eye than for a rich man to enter the reign of God."

They were much amazed saying to themselves "Who can be saved?"

Gazing at them Jesus said "With people it's impossible but not with God for everything is possible with God."

Peter started saying "Look, we left everything and followed you—"

But Jesus said "Amen I tell you there is no one who left home or brothers or sisters or mother or father or children or farms for my sake and the sake of the good news but shall get a hundredfold now in this time—houses and brothers and sisters and mothers and children and farms with persecutions—and in the age to come eternal life. Many first shall be last and last first."

They were on the road now going up to Jerusalem and Jesus was preceding them. They were stunned and the followers were afraid.

Taking the Twelve again he began to tell them the things about to happen to him. "Look, we're going up to Jerusalem and the Son of Man shall be handed to the chief priests and scholars. They'll condemn him to death and hand him to the Gentiles. They'll mock him, spit on him, flog him and kill him. Then after three days he'll rise again."

James and John—Zebedee's two sons—came up to him saying to him "Teacher, we want you to do whatever we ask for us."

He said to them "What do you want me to do for you?"

They said to him "Grant that one on your right and one on your left we may sit in your glory."

Jesus said to them "You don't know what you're asking. Can you drink the cup I'm drinking or be baptized with the baptism I'm to be baptized with?"

They said to him "We can."

And Jesus said to them "The cup I drink you'll drink and the baptism I'm baptized in you'll be baptized in. But to sit on my right or left is not mine to give, rather for the ones for whom it was prepared."

Hearing the ten began to be indignant at James and John.

So calling them to him Jesus said to them "You know that the self-styled rulers of the Gentiles lord it over them and their great ones exercise power over them. But it's not so among you. Whoever wishes to be great among you shall be servant of all and whoever wishes to be first among you shall be slave of all for even the Son of Man didn't come to be served but to serve and give his life a ransom for many."

They got to Jericho and as he was leaving Jericho with his disciples and a sizable crowd Timeus's son—Bartimeus a blind beggar—sat by the road. Hearing that it was Jesus the Nazarene he began to cry out "Son of David, Jesus, pity me."

Many warned him to be quiet.

But he cried out even more "Son of David, pity me."

Stopping Jesus said "Call him."

So they called the blind man saying to him "Cheer up.

Stand. He's calling you." Throwing off his coat and jumping up he came to Jesus.

Answering him Jesus said "What do you want me to do for you?"

The blind man said to him "Rabboni, to see."

Jesus said "Go. Your faith has cured you."

At once he saw and followed him in the road.

And as they neared Jerusalem at Bethphage and Bethany toward the Mount of Olives he sent two of his disciples and told them "Go to the village opposite you and at once entering it you'll find a tethered colt on which no one has yet sat. Untie it and bring it. If anyone says to you 'Why are you doing this?' say 'The Lord needs it and at once he'll send it back.' "

They went and found a colt tied at a door outside in the street and they untied it.

Some of those standing there said to them "What are you doing untying the colt?"

They said to them what Jesus said.

So they let them go.

They brought the colt to Jesus and threw their coats on it. He sat on it.

Many spread their coats in the road and others branches of leaves cut from the fields. The ones leading and the ones following cried out " 'Hosanna! Blessed he who comes in the Lord's name!' Blessed the coming reign of David our father! Hosanna in the heights!"

So he entered Jerusalem and the Temple and looking round at everything—the hour now being late—he went out to Bethany with the Twelve.

On the next day as they went out from Bethany he hungered and seeing a fig tree in the distance in leaf he went to see if maybe he could find something on it. Coming to it he found nothing but leaves since it was not the time for figs. Speaking out he said to it "Let no one never again eat fruit from you."

The disciples heard him.

Then they came to Jerusalem and entering the Temple he began to expel those selling and buying in the Temple. He upset the money changers' tables, the dove sellers' chairs and did not let anyone carry anything through the Temple. Then he taught them "Hasn't it been written that '*My house shall be called a house of prayer for all nations*'? But you have made it '*a bandits' cave.*'"

The chief priests and scholars heard and looked for how they might destroy him since they feared him and all the crowd was amazed by his teaching.

When it was late they went out of the city.

And passing along early they saw the fig tree withered from the roots.

Remembering Peter said to him "Rabbi, look. The fig tree which you cursed has withered."

Answering Jesus said to them "Have faith in God. Amen I tell you that whoever says to this mountain 'Be raised and thrown into the sea' and has no doubts in his heart but believes that what he says is happening, it shall be his. So I tell you all what you pray and ask for, trust that you get it and it shall be yours. And when you stand praying forgive if you have anything against anyone so your Father in Heaven may also forgive you your wrongs."

They came again to Jerusalem and as he walked in the Temple the chief priests, scholars and elders came to him and said to him "By what right do you do these things? Or who gave you this right that you do these things?"

Jesus said to them "I'll ask you one thing. Answer me and I'll tell you by what right I do these things. John's baptism — was it Heaven's or men's? Answer me."

They argued among themselves "If we say 'Heaven's' he'll say 'Then why didn't you trust him?' but if we say 'Men's'" they feared the crowd for everybody held that John was certainly a prophet. So answering Jesus they said "We don't know."

Jesus said to them "Neither will I tell you by what right I do these things" and he started speaking to them in parables. "A man planted a vineyard and put a fence round it, dug a wine vat and built a watchtower. Then he leased it to tenants and went far away. At the right season he sent a slave to the tenants to get some fruit from the vineyard. Taking him they beat him and sent him away empty. Again he sent them another slave. They struck him on the head and insulted him. So he sent another and they killed that one and many more, beating some, killing others. He had one left, a much-loved son. He sent him to them last saying 'They will honor my son.' But those tenants said to themselves 'This is the heir. Come let's kill him. The inheritance will be ours.' Taking him they killed him and flung him outside the vineyard. What will the lord of the vineyard do? He'll come, kill the tenants and give the vineyard to others. Haven't you read this text?

> *A stone which the builders rejected —*
> *This became the cornerstone.*
> *This was from the Lord*
> *And is wonderful in our eyes."*

They longed to arrest him but feared the crowd since they knew he had told the parable on them. So leaving him they went away and sent to him some Pharisees and Herodians to snare him in a word.

Coming they said to him "Teacher, we know you're honest and that no one counts heavily with you since you don't regard people's faces but truly teach God's way. Is it right to pay tribute to Caesar or not? Should we pay or not pay?"

But knowing their hypocrisy he said to them "Why tempt me? Bring me a denar so I may see."

They brought one.

And he said to them "Whose picture is this and whose inscription?"

They told him "Caesar's."

So Jesus said to them "Caesar's things give back to Caesar and God's things to God."

They were dumbfounded by him.

Then Sadducees came to him who say there is no resurrection and asked him "Teacher, Moses wrote for us that if *'anyone's brother die and leave a wife and leave no child then his brother may take the wife and rear seed for his brother.'* There were seven brothers and the first took a wife and dying left no seed. The second took her and died not leaving seed and the third likewise. The seven left no seed. Last of all the wife died too. At the resurrection when they rise again which of them will she be wife to for the seven had her as wife?"

Jesus said to them "Aren't you wrong in not knowing the scriptures or God's power?—for when they rise again from the dead they neither marry nor are given in marriage but are like angels in the heavens. But about the dead that they are raised—didn't you read in the scroll of Moses how at the bush God spoke to him saying *'I am the God of Abraham, the God of Isaac, the God of Jacob'*? He's not God of the dead but the living. You're deeply wrong."

One of the scholars approaching, hearing their discussion and knowing he answered them well asked him "What commandment is first of all?"

Jesus answered "First is *'Hear, Israel, the Lord our God is one Lord and you shall love the Lord your God with all your heart, with all your soul and with all your strength.'* Second, this—*'You shall love your neighbor like yourself.'* There is no other commandment greater than these."

The scholar said to him "True, Teacher. You say rightly that there is one and no other beside him and to love him with all the heart, with all the understanding and with all the strength and to love one's neighbor as oneself is more than all the burnt offerings and sacrifices."

Jesus seeing that he answered wisely said to him "You're not far from the reign of God."

Nobody dared question him further.

And going on as he taught in the Temple Jesus said "How can the scholars say that Messiah is David's son? David himself said through the Holy Spirit

The Lord said to my Lord
'Sit at my right
Till I put your enemies under your feet.'

David himself calls him Lord so how is he his son?"

The great crowd heard him gladly.

In his teaching he said "Beware of the scholars—the ones liking to parade in flowing robes, to be greeted in the markets, to have the best seats in synagogues and the best places at banquets, the ones consuming widows' houses under cover of long prayer: these shall get greater damnation."

And sitting opposite the Treasury he saw how the crowd put coppers into the Treasury. Many rich people put in much but one poor widow coming put in two lepta which make one penny. So calling his disciples to him he said to them "Amen I tell you that this poor widow put in more than all those contributing to the Treasury for they put in out of their surplus but this woman out of her need put in everything she had, all her living."

When he went out of the Temple one of his disciples said to him "Teacher, look what great stones, what great buildings!"

Jesus said to him "See these huge buildings? There shall no way be left stone on stone which shall not surely be thrown down."

And when he sat on the Mount of Olives opposite the Temple, Peter, James, John and Andrew asked him privately "Tell us when these things will be and what will be the sign when all these things are about to be done?"

So Jesus began to say to them "Watch so nobody leads you wrong. Many shall come in my name saying 'I am' and shall lead many wrong. But when you hear of wars and tales of wars don't be frightened. It must happen but the end won't be yet for nation shall be set against nation and kingdom against kingdom. There'll be earthquakes in places; there'll be famines—these are the onset of birth and pain. But see to yourselves.

"They'll hand you over to courts, you'll be beaten in synagogues, you'll stand before governors and kings for my sake to witness to them since to all nations the good news must first be announced. When they lead you out and hand you over don't worry yourself with what you'll say but what's given you in that hour say that for you're not the ones speaking but the Holy Spirit. Brother shall hand brother over to death and a father his child, children shall rise against parents and kill them and you'll be hated by everyone because of my name but the one surviving to the end—that one shall be saved.

"Still when you see the desolating horror stand where it shouldn't"—let the reader understand—"then those in Judea let them flee to the mountains. Him on the roof let him not climb down or go in to take anything from his house. And him in the field let him not go back to the rear to take his coat. But woe to pregnant women and them suckling in those days. Pray for it not to happen in winter for those days shall be a trial such as has not come since the start of creation which God created till now and shall no way ever come again. Unless the Lord shortened the days no flesh would be spared but because of the chosen whom he chose he shortened the days.

"So if anyone tells you 'Look here, Messiah! Look there!' don't trust it. False Messiahs and false prophets shall appear and do signs and wonders to lead the chosen wrong if possible. But you, see!—I've warned you of everything. In those days after that trial

> The sun shall turn dark,
>> The moon give none of her light,
>> The stars shall be falling from Heaven
>>> And the powers in the Heavens shall quake.

Then they'll see 'the Son of Man coming on clouds' with great power and glory and then he'll send the angels and they'll gather his chosen from the four winds from pole of Earth to pole of Heaven.

"Now learn a parable from the fig tree—when its branch is tender again and puts out leaves you know that summer is near. So too when you see these things happen know that he is at the doors. Amen I tell you that no way shall this generation pass till these things all happen. Heaven and Earth shall pass but my words shall not pass.

"But about that day or hour nobody knows—neither the angels in Heaven nor the Son, only the Father. Watch. Stay awake for you don't know when the time is. It's like a traveler leaving his house and putting his slaves in charge each with his own work and he ordered the doorman to watch. You watch then since you don't know when the lord of the house is coming either late or at midnight or at cock-crow or early or coming suddenly he may find you sleeping. What I say to you I say to all—watch."

Now it was the Passover, the feast of unleavened bread, after two days and the chief priests and the scholars searched for how seizing him by deceit they might kill him for they said "Not at the feast or there'll be an outcry from the people."

When he was in Bethany in the house of Simon the leper as he lay back a woman came with an alabaster flask of costly pure nard ointment. Breaking the alabaster flask she poured it over his head. Some were indignant among themselves "Why has this waste of ointment occurred? This ointment could be sold for more than three hundred denars and given to the wretched." They scolded her.

But Jesus said "Let her be. Why make trouble for her? She did a good deed on me. The wretched you always have with you and whenever you want you can do good to them but me you don't always have. What she could she did. She was early to anoint my body for burial. Amen I tell you wherever the good news is declared in all the world what this woman did shall also be told as a memory of her."

Then Judas Iscariot one of the Twelve went to the chief priests so he might hand him over to them.

Hearing they were glad and promised to give him silver.

And he looked for how he might conveniently hand him over.

On the first day of unleavened bread when they slaughtered the Passover lamb the disciples said to him "Where do you want us to go and arrange for you to eat the Passover?"

He sent two of his disciples and told them "Go into the city. You'll be met by a man carrying a jug of water. Follow him. Wherever he goes in tell the owner 'The teacher says "Where is my guest room where I can eat the Passover with my disciples?" ' He'll show you a big room upstairs all spread and ready. Prepare for us there."

The disciples went out, entered the city and found it as he told them. Then they prepared the Passover.

As evening fell he came with the Twelve and as they lay back and ate Jesus said "Amen I tell you that one of you shall hand me over, the one eating with me."

They started grieving and saying to him one by one "Surely not I?"

He said to them "One of the Twelve, him dipping with me in the common bowl. For the Son of Man is really going his way as was written of him but woe to the man through whom the Son of Man is handed over. Better for him if that man were not born."

As they were eating he took a loaf and blessing it he broke and gave it to them and said "Take. This is my body." And taking a cup and giving thanks he gave it to them.

All drank of it.

He said to them "This is my blood of the promise poured out for many. Amen I tell you never in no way will I drink of the fruit of the vine till that day when I drink it new in the reign of God."

After singing the hymn they went out to the Mount of Olives.

And Jesus said to them "All of you shall stumble since it was written

I will strike down the shepherd
And the sheep shall be scattered.

But after I'm raised I'll go ahead of you to Galilee."

Peter said to him "Even if everybody stumbles not I."

Jesus said to him "Amen I tell you, you today, tonight before the cock crows twice you'll deny me three times."

But he just kept saying "If I must die with you no way would I deny you."

All said likewise too.

They came to a piece of land whose name was Gethsemane and he said to his disciples "Sit here while I pray." He took Peter, James and John with him and began to be deeply appalled and harrowed so he said to them "My soul is anguished to death. Stay here and watch." Going on a little he fell on the ground and prayed that if it were possible the hour might turn away and he said "*Abba*, Father, everything is possible to you. Take this cup from me—still not what I want but you."

He came and found them sleeping and said to Peter "Simon are you sleeping? Couldn't you watch one hour? Watch and pray so you don't come to testing—oh the spirit is ready but the flesh weak."

Going off again he prayed saying the same words.

Coming back he found them sleeping since their eyes were growing heavy and they didn't know how to answer him.

He came the third time and said to them "Sleep now and rest. It's paid. The hour came. Look, the Son of Man is handed into wrongdoers' hands. Get up. Let's go. Look, the one who's handing me over is nearing."

At once while he was still speaking Judas appeared—one of the Twelve—and with him a crowd with swords and sticks from the chief priests, scholars and elders. The one handing him over had given them a sign saying "Whomever I kiss is he. Seize him and take him off securely." At once coming up to him he said "Rabbi!" and kissed him lovingly.

They got their hands on him and seized him.

But one of the bystanders drawing a sword struck the High Priest's slave and cut off his ear.

Speaking out Jesus said to them "Did you come out as if against a rebel with swords and sticks to arrest me? Daily I was with you in the Temple teaching and you didn't seize me. But the scriptures must be done."

Deserting him they all ran.

One young man followed him dressed in a linen shirt over his naked body. They seized him but leaving the shirt behind he fled naked.

Then they took Jesus off to the High Priest and all the chief priests, elders and scholars followed.

Peter followed him far off right into the High Priest's courtyard, sat with the servants and warmed himself by the blaze.

Now the chief priests and all the Sanhedrin looked for testimony against Jesus to execute him but they found none since many witnessed falsely against him and the testimonies were not the same. Some standing witnessed falsely against him saying "We heard him saying 'I'll tear down this Temple made by hand and after three days I'll build another not handmade.' " Even so their witness was not consistent.

Standing in the center the High Priest questioned Jesus "Won't you answer anything these men testify against you?"

But he was silent and answered nothing.

Again the High Priest questioned him "You are Messiah the son of the Blessed?"

Jesus said "I am and

> *You shall see the Son of Man*
> *Sitting at the right of Power*
> *And coming with clouds of Heaven."*

The High Priest tearing his robes said "What further need do you have for witnesses? You heard the blasphemy. How does it look to you?"

They all condemned him worthy of death. Some began to spit at him, cover his face, hit him and say to him "Prophesy!" and the servants treated him to blows.

When Peter was down in the courtyard one of the High Priest's maids came and seeing Peter warming himself she looked at him and said "You were with the Nazarene Jesus."

But he denied it saying "I don't know or understand what you're saying." Then he went out into the porch and the cock crowed.

Seeing him the maid began again to say to those standing round "This man is one of them."

But again he denied it.

After a little again those standing round said to Peter "Surely you're one of them. It's plain you're a Galilean."

He began to curse himself and swear "I don't know this man you mention." At once a second time a cock crowed and Peter remembered the word Jesus said to him "Before the cock crows twice you'll deny me three times" and dwelling on that he wept.

At once in the morning the chief priests held council with the elders, scholars and all the Sanhedrin and binding Jesus they led him off and handed him to Pilate.

Pilate asked him "You're the king of the Jews?"

Answering him he said "You say."

The chief priests charged him with many things.

But Pilate asked him again "Will you answer nothing? See how much they charge you with."

But Jesus still answered nothing.

Pilate wondered.

At each feast he freed for them one prisoner whom they requested. There was one named Barabbas held with the rebels who had committed murder in the rebellion. So the crowd came up and began to ask for his usual act.

But Pilate answered them "Do you want me to free you the king of the Jews?"—he knew the chief priests had handed him over out of envy.

But the chief priests incited the crowd to free them Barabbas instead.

So Pilate spoke out again to them "What must I do then with the one you call king of the Jews?"

They again shouted back "Crucify him!"

But Pilate said to them "Why? What evil has he done?"

They shouted louder "Crucify him!"

Then Pilate wanting to pacify the crowd freed them Barabbas and handed over Jesus having flogged him so he could be crucified.

The soldiers led him off into the courtyard called Pretorium and summoned the whole cohort. They put on him a purple robe and plaiting a thorn crown they put it round him. Then they started saluting him "Hail, king of the Jews!" They hit his head with a reed, spat on him and kneeling down worshiped him. When they had mocked him they took the purple off him and put on his own clothes. Then they led him out to crucify him. They forced one Simon a Cyrenean from the country, the father of Alexander and Rufus, to carry his cross. So they brought him to the place Golgotha which means "Skull Place." They gave him wine drugged with myrrh but he would not take it. Then they crucified him and divided his clothes casting lots for them what each might take. It was nine in the morning when they crucified him. The notice of the charge against him was written above "The King of the Jews." With him they crucified two thieves one on his right and one his left.

Those passing by insulted him wagging their heads and saying "So! The one who would destroy the Temple and build it in three days! Save yourself. Get down off the cross."

In the same way the chief priests joking with each other and with the scholars said "He saved others. He can't save himself. Messiah king of Israel!—let him get down off the cross so we can see and believe."

And those crucified with him reviled him.

At noon darkness came over the whole land till three and at three Jesus shouted in a loud voice " *'Eloi Eloi lema sabachthani?'* " which means " 'My God, my God, why did you forsake me?' "

Some of the bystanders hearing said "Look, he's calling Elijah" and running one filled a sponge with vinegar and putting it round a reed gave him to drink saying "Let him be. Let's see if Elijah comes to take him down."

But Jesus giving a loud cry breathed his last.

The Temple curtain was torn in two from top to bottom.

The centurion standing opposite seeing that he breathed his last that way said "Surely this man was Son of God."

There were women too at a distance watching among whom were both Mary the Magdalene, Mary the mother of the younger James and mother of Joses and Salome who followed him when he was in Galilee and served him and many other women who had come up with him to Jerusalem.

Now when evening came since it was Preparation which is the day before the Sabbath Joseph from Arimathea, an important councilor who was himself also expecting the reign of God, came and boldly went in to Pilate and asked for Jesus' body.

Pilate wondered if he was already dead and summoning the centurion questioned him how long ago he died. Then learning from the centurion he presented the corpse to Joseph.

Having bought new linen and taken him down he wrapped him with the linen, put him in a tomb hewn from rock and rolled a stone across the entrance of the tomb.

Mary the Magdalene and Mary the mother of Joses watched where he was put.

When the Sabbath passed Mary the Magdalene, Mary the mother of James and Salome bought spices so they could come and anoint him. Very early on the first day of the week they came to the tomb as the sun was rising. They said to each other "Who'll roll the stone off the tomb door for us?" and looking up they saw that the stone had been rolled back for it was huge. Entering the tomb they saw a young man sitting on the right dressed in a white robe and they were much stunned.

But he said to them "Don't be stunned. Are you looking for Jesus the crucified Nazarene? He was raised. He isn't here. Look, the place where they laid him. But go tell his disciples and Peter 'He's going ahead of you to Galilee. There you'll see him as he told you.' "

Going out they fled the tomb—they were shuddering and wild—and they told no one nothing for they were afraid.

THE STRANGEST STORY

A PREFACE TO

THE GOOD NEWS ACCORDING TO JOHN

THE Good News According to John is the most mysterious document that survives from the early years of the Jesus sect. It is stranger even, in its history and contents, than its infinitely explicated companion in the New Testament—The Revelation to John—and the New Testament is as filled with mysteries of date, authorship, and intent as any important book in human history. But say for a moment that the oldest surviving tradition about The Good News According to John is correct. Then it was written by John bar Zebedee (John son of Zebedee), the Beloved Disciple of Jesus; and it appeared in the city of Ephesus around AD 90, spreading rapidly throughout the Roman empire and—within a century—establishing its unique understanding of Jesus as the central view of all succeeding orthodox Christianity.

Though it makes no detectable pretense to the formal order and beauty of a work of art, consider John's predecessors in Western narrative. They include early Middle Eastern epics, from the Babylonian creation poem *Enuma Elish* (which is at least as old as the twenty-second century BC) through the tales and lives of Hebrew scripture. They continue through all of Greek narrative poetry, drama, and prose with their cult of the great man and his burdened family, their tragic gaze and worship of Eros, their bracing obscenity; and then they end in the prime Latin classics—shocks like the scurrilous narrative lyrics of Catullus, the urbane sideline comment of Horace, the mockery of Juvenal, and Petronius's salacious *Satyricon*. That much at least lies behind John's brief story, and some of it may have been known to his first audience. We may well ask further if—deeply Hebraic though his mind clearly is—John himself had encountered Greek tragedy, history, and Platonic metaphysics.

Given the traditional author and date for the book, and despite such flamboyant narrative predecessors, a powerful case can still be made that this last gospel—little more than a pamphlet and written in a curiously shackled Greek prose— is the most outrageously demanding work, in any type of prose or verse, that had yet appeared in the West or Near East. Even its companion gospel Mark, some twenty-five years older and a reckless pioneer, is tamed a little in the dazzling light of John. And if two thousand years of pious handling had not dimmed both John's story and its demand, his gospel would still be seen as the burning outrage it continues to be, a work of madness or blinding revelation. Its plain but supremely daring verbal strategies, the human acts it portrays, and the claim it advances—from the first paragraph— demand that we make a hard choice. If we give John the serious witness it wants, we must finally ask the question it thrusts so flagrantly toward us. Does it bring us a life-transforming truth; or is it one gifted lunatic's tale of another lunatic, wilder than he?

*

Again, who wrote it—when, where, and why? Any brief discussion of such matters must simplify ruthlessly; but a number of serious students continue to agree with the early tradition which claims that The Good News According to John originated and was shaped to its present form in the vicinity of the city of Ephesus, then in Asia Minor, now western Turkey. The current wide-ranging tendencies are to date its composition and eventual publication to the years between the death of Jesus, near AD 30, and the end of the first century, sixty-odd years later—no long wait, in narrative cul-

tures where stories pass from mouth to ear, often down startling reaches of time. Any veteran of a society devoted to the
spoken transfer of urgent memory—a culture like that of the
American South till the 1970s or immigrant American Judaism or most Native Americans—will know how easily vivid
tales and speeches can pass intact through generations, even
centuries.

My nieces, for instance, never knew their grandfather
Will Price. He was born in 1900 and died in 1954, well before
their births. Yet since infancy, they have heard my brother
and me tell stories of our father's acts, traits, and memories.
The oldest oral memory of his which we preserve is my father's repeated recollection that his own father Edward Price,
born in 1861, died in eastern North Carolina in the late 1920s
while hallucinating a violent uprising of African Americans.
That fear was almost surely planted in Edward Price in childhood by his own parents' recollections of the notorious Nat
Turner slave rebellion of 1831 which had occurred only some
sixty miles north of their home. My nieces can now repeat
many such stories more or less precisely in the form conveyed to them. And they have retained the stories apparently
because the actual words in order give them an obvious but
complex pleasure—a pleasure *in the words* which they are
likely to pass to their children, who may well be born a century after my father. Admittedly, my nieces have heard no
claims that Grandfather (or Great-grandfather) Price was the
only Son of God; so the stories they know are devoid of worship, though not of a strong family hope to win their collu-
sion in acts of individual human perpetuity.

In his two-volume commentary, Raymond Brown, the
most judicious recent exhaustive student of The Good News
According to John, concludes that the gospel appeared between AD 90 and 100; and papyrus evidence found in Egypt
tends to confirm a late first-century date. Whenever and by
whomever John was written, edited, and published—and

there are serious objections confronting any of the major candidacies for authorship—our first external evidence that its author was the disciple John, "the disciple whom Jesus loved," comes in brief mentions by Ptolemy the Gnostic in about 150 and by Theophilus of Antioch in about 180, some sixty to ninety years after the gospel's publication.

More extensive confirmation comes from Bishop Irenaeus, writing as a missionary from Lyon in Roman Gaul in about 185, some eight or nine decades after the gospel first appeared. Irenaeus tells us that, as a boy in Asia Minor, he had listened avidly to the memories of old Polycarp, a pupil of Jesus' own pupil, John (apparently the son of Zebedee, though Irenaeus does not specify). Irenaeus adds that—apparently after Mark, Matthew, and Luke had published their gospels—The Good News According to John was published in Asia by John, that same disciple who had leaned on Jesus' chest at the supper before his arrest. Irenaeus adds also that John lived in Ephesus down into the reign of the emperor Trajan, who came to power in 98 and died in 117. We know further that Irenaeus's predecessor as bishop at Lyon was Pothinus, who died in 177, having passed the age of ninety. Since the churches in Lyon and the nearby Vienne included other natives of Asia Minor, it may be that Pothinus's own memories included contact in the East with firsthand witnesses of Jesus. Well before Irenaeus, Justin Martyr speaks of John as having resided in Ephesus (Justin had been in Ephesus in about 135); and the apocryphal *Acts of John* from about 150 likewise places John in Ephesus. It hardly seems credible that a false tradition could have developed so rapidly, given the strong likelihood of a continuing oral tradition through the late first and early second centuries in a city as important as Ephesus and its populous environs.

With a clear awareness of the dangers attending the transmission of facts in a time and place so different from our own—and in full awareness that some sixty years lay between

John's supposed death and the earliest surviving testimony—still such an assertion as Irenaeus's might seem unexceptionably credible to a student of human memory and its modes of conversion to story. Yet New Testament scholars are often comically nervous at the prospect of simple or eminently logical solutions. And by the mid-twentieth century, a majority of scholars had come to doubt Irenaeus and his claimed informants—sometimes to the point of alleging conscious falsehood (it has, for instance, more than once been suggested that Irenaeus lied about hearing Polycarp or was mistaken about which of several men named John might have been known to Polycarp). Many scholars dismissed scornfully the possibility that "a simple Galilean fisherman" could have written such a strange and elevated work. But in recent decades, with rapid advances in our knowledge of a multitude of widespread and unorthodox theologies in first-century Palestine, more and more students are returning to at least a saner view—one that sees no overwhelming human or literary obstruction to the acceptance of some version of the testimony of men who claim to have met and heard pupils of John bar Zebedee, the Beloved of Jesus.

Again I hack a path through hundreds of theories and a few serious objections; but my own study convinces me that no skeptic has shown sufficient cause to doubt the core of our oldest surviving tradition as relayed by Irenaeus, a witness of no demonstrable confusion or guile (though one who is not, elsewhere, immune from occasional good-faith errors of fact). In the face of the gospel's own unrelenting display of accurate geographical and cultural knowledge of first-century Palestine and despite its pervasive atmosphere of eyewitness to the public and private career of Jesus—a store of detailed memory that seems quite independent of other gospels—then the suggestion that a young fisherman who studied with Jesus might not, in latter years, have been as competent a theologian as his modern doubters is amusingly small-minded (John advances, after all, no idea which is not at least implicit in the early Mark).

Whatever the answers to the mysteries of John, they are all concealed in the space of a single lifetime, one that might credibly have spanned the six or seven decades after Jesus' death and resurrection. And if we assume that John bar Zebedee was a man in his early twenties when he followed Jesus in about AD 28, then we may reasonably guess that at least the first edition of the gospel was the product of a man in his eighties or a little older—hardly an anomalous situation in the history of literature. In all the mountain ranges of commentary on John—the all but endless attempts to explain John's alleged dislocations, his stops and jolting starts, his glaring clarities and sudden fogs—I have met with no sustained attempt to see the heart of John's final draft as, specifically, an old man's book. Yet an arresting case can be made for its being the product of a single large but aging mind, a mind at hurried final work on the scenes and words of its distant youth—now precise and lucid, now vague and elliptical in its movement, all its memories screened through the thought of intervening years. Whoever wrote the core of its tale, the hand of a clear-minded thoughtful eyewitness to the acts and mind of Jesus laid the massive foundations for our surviving John. Surely no one who was not known to have accompanied Jesus yet remained alive till the end of the first century could have issued, or stood behind, so uniquely audacious yet plainly authoritative a document.

The first indisputable fact is that, not long after the end of the first century, the document which we know as The Good News According to John was widely (if not yet universally) acknowledged throughout the scattered and threatened world of the Jesus sect as one of four unparalleled stories of the acts and the meaning of Jesus. With the possible exception of the apocryphal *Gospel of Thomas*, which confines itself strictly to sayings of Jesus, none of the other first-century gospels alluded to by Luke in the preface to his own gospel has yet come to light in its entirety. So John with all its bafflements—and above all with its unique claim of firsthand authority—has, from near the first, been seen as the unmatched pearl of the four. And it stands unchallenged as the crown of firsthand witness to a life as shocking, and as crucial to the history of the world, as any life known.

Yet again, the heart of that shock is seldom noticed. And a poll of modern readers would likely show that John stands with Luke as the most beloved of gospels, primarily because of its many consolations. A further poll might show that, among possible readers, Christian readers prize John for two reasons—his steady picture of a Jesus who boldly announces his godhead yet knows our human weakness so well that he promises the love and hope which most hearts crave. Few readers versed in Anglo-Saxon culture fail to know some of the words by heart, and in the King James Version—

> For God so loved the world, that he gave his only begotten Son: that whosoever believeth in him, should not perish, but have everlasting life. . . . Let not your heart be troubled: ye believe in God, believe also in me. In my Father's house are many mansions; if it were not so, I would have told you: I go to prepare a place for you . . . that where I am, there ye may be also.

But centuries of familiarity with such assurance—and with John's near omission of that awful Judge who spreads his terror through the other gospels—has muffled the rank outrage of John. Seen head-on, John demands that his readers choose—is he a truthful reporter, as he vows, or a fantast? Is he fraudulent or raving? And if we feel that John's report rings true, then all the questions must be judged once more in the matter of his hero. Is this man Jesus a whole-cloth fictional creation, a village lunatic, a deluded visionary, a skill-ful charlatan, the "only begotten Son of God"; or as John's Jesus announces, is he somehow the power of God himself? If veteran readers of John can make the effort to approach his gospel freshly, in a new and relatively literal translation, they may begin to see what atheists and agnostics will sight at once—the hair-raising newness of one slender tract. Anyone coming to the book afresh will spot that newness at once.

*

Forget that you ever read a gospel; forget you ever heard of Jesus. Read John watchfully and what do you see? For me, first and last, he offers two things. The things are a few human acts, some of which John calls "signs," and a number of speeches. The story concerns the final years of one man's life. The important speeches come from that man. Alone among gospel writers, John claims that he himself witnessed the signs and heard the speeches (the second such claim, at the end of the gospel, appears to be made by John's surviving disciples). He claims to report a few of those significant mo-ments—and to report them truly—and he adds in clarifica-tion at the very end, "There were many other things Jesus did which if each were written I think the world couldn't hold the books written." Also near the end, and again in his own voice (or that of his stenographer or editor), John says that he makes his record for an urgent reason—to convince each reader "that Jesus is Messiah, the Son of God and that trust-ing you may have life in his name." Compared with the world's other urgent stories, however—the early books of He-brew scripture, the Koran, and the founding texts of most Eastern religions for instance—John delivers his strike in a few thousand words and ends. He can be read through in little more than an hour; and he stands, after Mark, as the second-shortest of the gospels.

What is the story John can tell so quickly? Does he mean us to read it as "realistic," even by his time's different standards of veracity? If he writes symbolically, allegorically, anagogically, does he give us sufficient signals when he goes into a nonrepresentational gear, into rigged descriptions of acts that never happened or improvisations on the gestures and voice of a distantly remembered Jesus? (Ancient writers and readers of John's time make it amply clear that they were capable of differentiating between a visible historical event and the transmutation of that event into metaphor.) Again, is John's evident passion to change at least the lives of his initial readers a folly, a delusion, or a sanely built plan?

*

With unprecedented daring, he packs the whole story—veiled but intact—into his first three paragraphs. A further surprise in traversing the length of John's pamphlet comes in our eventual discovery that we knew his whole story from the first page but were unaware of our knowledge. "At the start was the Word. The Word was with God and God was the Word—he was at the start with God." The Word, then, or the Idea, is one of God's presumably infinite natures—a nature that was present before the creation of things and that caused all things. After a glance at another John, who will forerun Messiah, John the gospel writer races with a speed and aim as sure as the start of Genesis toward his first shock. Though he would be refused by the world, "the Word became flesh and tented among us. We watched his glory, glory like that of a father's one son full of grace and truth." In the early years of our era then, God's active power embodied itself in a visible man called Jesus.

Having calmly hung the assertion before us, John begins his human story. The Word has now been among us through the concealed years of Jesus' childhood and has grown to manhood in ways likewise undescribed. Now at a moment of historical time that ends in the known Palestinian governor-ship of Pontius Pilate, the Word in its tent of flesh—Jesus from the village of Nazareth in Galilee—comes south to the teacher called John (the writer never calls him *the Baptizer* or *the Baptist*). This John is performing a ritual washing of sinners near Jerusalem. Though the writer omits the scene itself, Jesus apparently accepts this rite that he (as a sinless God-man) cannot need. At once John both recognizes Jesus as Messiah and predicts his unsuspected nature, the shock and scandal he will bring to his people.

Jesus Messiah will not be the longed-for chieftain to lead his people in victory over Rome. He will be more nearly the Suffering Servant whom Isaiah foresaw—"He was despised and rejected by men . . . by his wounds we are healed." In another flare of insight, this Baptizer finds yet another name for the man Jesus who walks before him—"Look, the Lamb of God who cancels the wrongs of the world." Lambs are common objects of affection. They are also slaughtered by the thousand, in sacrifice to God's just wrath, in his Temple a few miles west of the baptism site. But while the Baptizer sees so far at the start, even he fails to glimpse the horror to come in the life of this lamb and the glory to follow.

Among those around the Baptizer are five particular men. At least three of them are from Galilee—Andrew, his brother Simon (whom Jesus soon calls *Peter* or *Rock*), and Nathanael (a man not mentioned in the other gospels). The fourth is Philip. Is the unnamed fifth that man whom John later calls "the disciple [or pupil] whom Jesus loved"? Since John bar Zebedee is named in each of the other gospels as one of the first four disciples called by Jesus, the guess is likely. In any case, all five men seem young, impressionable, and game to roam; and they are so impressed by the Baptizer's witness, by the undescribed magnetism and wit of Jesus, by Jesus' assent to Nathanael's belief that here indeed is Messiah, that they promptly leave the Baptizer and follow Jesus north.

Back in Galilee, Jesus soon impresses the new disciples, his mother, and numerous others with a first display of power, the first unearthly sign. In a forthright kitchen wonder—the response to nothing more urgent than a friend's social embarrassment—Jesus changes water to delicious wine at a wedding in Cana, a town near Nazareth. Despite the symbolic meanings deduced by two millennia of commentators, it seems unlikely that John would describe such a homely feat unless he had been present and convinced of its actual and inexplicable occurrence. If not, why invent—for the inaugural sign of Jesus' great career—a miraculous solution to a mere social oversight?

Then with his disciples, his mother, and now his brothers, Jesus visits the fishing town of Capernaum on the Lake of Galilee. The other gospels tell us that, hereabouts, Jesus found and enlisted more disciples, to a final number of twelve. John will later mention others—Judas, Thomas Didymus, and "the disciple whom Jesus loved"—but he passes over their calling in silence. And he omits the numerous early Galilean signs and wonders described by Mark and repeated in Matthew and Luke.

Next Jesus and the disciples go to Jerusalem for Passover, the solemn spring feast in memory of the night when God's angel of death spared those Hebrew sons with lamb's blood on their doors. It is the first of three such visits to the capital described by John; the other gospels describe only one. And here at Jesus' first appearance on the main stage of his country, he at once scores his fame on the public air by committing a serious breach of the civil and religious peace. In the other gospels such a breach comes only a few days before Jesus' death and is clearly a weighty matter in his condemnation; with John's own unapologetic authority, he sets it as the headpiece of Jesus' dealings with the interlopers who defile his Father's house. With an impromptu whip, Jesus drives the licensed livestock dealers and money changers from the Temple (though John does not specify, it seems implicit that his Jesus actually strikes some of the dealers; in Mark he merely over-turns their tables). Unaccountably, such an alarming out-burst goes unpunished—in fact, it is never again alluded to by Jesus' enemies—and on the same visit Jesus is free to perform other signs, unspecified.

Then he moves in bold contrast to the Jesus of Mark, who demands that his disciples keep silent about his nature. John's Jesus moves from his violent breach to a meeting with a member of the same hierarchy he has challenged. Poised on the edge of national fame, Jesus tells Nicodemus (who is a member of the Jewish ruling council and visits Jesus by night) that he Jesus is the only Son of God. He has been sent, here and now, from the depths of God's love to save whoever believes in him. Here and constantly hereafter, Jesus affirms that eternal life is available to those who believe in him, and to them alone. In the teeth of such a blasphemous claim, strangely Nicodemus makes no reply; but when Jesus is dead, it is John alone who tells us that Nicodemus shares the burial costs with Joseph of Arimathea.

In the remaining three-fourths of the gospel, Jesus will give more signs; he will suffer death and rise from the dead. By the end of Jesus' first visit to Jerusalem, however, John's story has set its pattern and made its sole demand—*Trust in this man or die forever.* But who is the man and what do we mean if we say we "trust or believe in him"? How would that belief change our daily lives, our thoughts and acts? What would be the long-range outcome of such a vague faith? The balance of the story, and the speeches, work at telling us, with no trace of doubt (though not always clearly) in the voice of the teller.

At this point in my own reading, I begin to notice John's strangest departure from the memories of Jesus recorded in other gospels. John takes almost no notice of the man's ethi-cal teaching, even less than Mark's sparse attention to ethics.

The parables of Mark, Matthew, and Luke, with their implicit lessons on daily life and their guideposts to eternity; the eloquent moral teaching which Matthew and Luke record in such quantity, with such awful threats for failure, and their sometimes tedious suspension of narrative thrust—John has no room for a syllable of these. He surely remembers or knows of the teaching. In so many cases, he knows of place names, times, customs, acts, and speeches that ring entirely true but are absent from the other gospels. Yet the fact is that John omits Jesus' teaching with the same ease as that with which he bypasses many other things we may eventually want from him—some account of Jesus' early life and education, a physical description of the man, and much more.

The fact that we read John in the context of its three companion gospels obscures the astonishing realization that, if John's were our only report, not even Christians could claim that Jesus was a moral teacher, a probing witness of human life who declared God's will that we love our neighbors as we love ourselves (and the converse, so often ignored by Christians—that we love ourselves as we do our neighbors). Admittedly John reports that, as Jesus bids farewell to his disciples at the Last Supper, he says "This is my command that you love each other as I loved you. Greater love than this no one has, that one should lay down his life for his friends." But though the command is taken by later members of the Jesus sect to apply to all human beings, Jesus gives it to his disciples only, alone in a dark room fouled with the threat of his death. Did he mean it for the world? And what can be the reason for this absence of moral precept, the most enormous of John's many omissions? The silent fact, with which we are left, is that John did not think the preservation of Jesus' ethical teaching important to his urgent purpose in the gospel he was writing for his own community and the far wider community and history which he might well have suspected to lie beyond his lifetime.

From that flagrant first visit to Jerusalem, Jesus leads the disciples into the Judean countryside where, with the authority of their master, they proceed to baptize. And we hear that John the Baptizer again acknowledges that Jesus is Messiah—"He must increase but I must decrease." Word also reaches Jesus of the beginning of hostility from the liberal political-religious party, the Pharisees; and he and the disciples return to Galilee. Hereafter John's story is revealingly strung on the twin poles of Western realistic narrative—country and city: Galilee and the capital, a three- or four-day walk apart. Among numerous differences, the country Jesus is far more human and humane than the coruscating mage he becomes in Jerusalem.

On the return trip north, for instance, when the disciples leave him briefly alone, Jesus meets a woman by a well near Shechem in Samaria. That a male Jew should associate freely with a hated Samaritan, much less a woman, is scandal enough. But in the midst of an initially lighthearted conversation, in which Jesus tells the woman that he knows she has had five husbands and is now living with yet another man, he launches an image that—if we credit John—comes from the core of Jesus' sense of mission and that states his literal offer to humankind. He tells this restless, plainly famished pariah that, in his person, he is somehow sustenance—food—for humanity. He is all forms of nourishment for hungry humanity, *Partake of me and live forever*. The implicit response, beyond taunting laughter or flat dismissal, would seem to be *But how do I partake of you?* Strangely though, no one in all John's gospel asks him.

Through the remainder of the story, Jesus will ramify the terms of his offer in increasingly daring ways. But here, still near the start, he offers this likably feisty reprobate "a spring of water welling up to eternal life." At first she scarcely hears him. What wins her sudden unwarranted belief that he is Messiah is his uncanny knowledge of her past. But when she calls her townsmen, and they prevail upon Jesus to stay for two days and explain himself further (an explanation we do not hear), they also accept his words. And with no further sign, these Samaritans, so long shunned by orthodox Jews, come to believe his one demand—"We trust since we've heard for ourselves that this man is truly the savior of the world."

The entwined lightness and gravity of Jesus' dialogue with the woman at the well is ample occasion for noting what seems to be a strain of wit, even humor, in John that goes unmatched in any other gospel. Despite the writer John's unflagging commitment throughout to the visible earthly divinity of the man Jesus, John paradoxically of all the gospel writers seems to have heard and recalled a resourceful capacity for wit in his God. And while nothing is more difficult to identify with certainty in ancient documents than subtle wit and low-pitched laughter, surely we are deftly invited to hear the wit in Jesus' byplay with the Samaritan, in his teasing of Nathanael at their first encounter—"Because I told you I saw you under the fig tree you trust? You'll see greater things." There is a fiercer but paradoxical wit in his light-handed treatment of the old Nicodemus who has been too timid to visit by daylight but whom Jesus confronts with the unimaginable errand of being "born again" or "born from above," in the later razor-edged dialogues with his enemies in the Temple, and finally in his lethal arraignment before Pilate. A few other characters share in John's proclivity for wit—the man born blind meets his doubters with a pleasantly flat-footed humor; even Pilate shows a cold-edged grin. These hints, among others, are strong implications that the man Jesus and his friends and foes may well have been recalled by John— the same John who likewise saw Jesus as God—as at least occasional smilers; and Jesus can be glimpsed, at odd moments, ambushing his listeners in sudden amusement.

Back in Galilee on another visit to Cana, Jesus gives his

second sign on home ground. He heals the son of an official in the employ of the king, one of the lesser Herods. The man has come from Capernaum to beg his help—"Sir, come down before my boy dies." For the first time this sovereign Jesus sounds a complaint often heard in other gospels—"Unless you see signs and magic you won't trust me." But then in words alone, at some twenty miles' distance and with no mention of pity or compassion, he heals the boy by telling the father, "Go. Your son's alive." The man believes, heads downhill to Capernaum, and is met by servants who tell him that the boy was cured at one o'clock the previous afternoon, at the moment Jesus spoke.

The other gospels begin Jesus' adult career with pictures of his first long rush of compassionate healing. John has waited this late, a fourth of the way through his story, to introduce the single strand of Jesus' public acts that appears to have gained him his widest contemporary attention. And John has all but concealed the common thread of such reports by the other gospel writers—their insistence that trust in the power of Jesus is somehow a condition of his love, his unearthly power to free the victims of demonic possession. In John we almost never hear the other gospels' awesome pre-echo of King Lear's threat to an apparently ungrateful daughter—"Nothing will come of nothing." This John's Jesus *can* act and *will*, whether we trust him or not. And in John, he is far more sparing of his power than in any other gospel.

As if to prove his mastery of fate, Jesus returns to Jerusalem for an unspecified feast; and there on the Sabbath, he goes to the curative pool called Bethzatha or Bethesda (a site whose detailed description by John has only lately been confirmed by archaeologists). Here he cures a man lame for thirty-eight years. Because Jesus heals in the Sabbath rest, and because the sign is followed by his defense of such work, many readers see the sign chiefly as a demonstration that Jesus is Lord of the Sabbath and free to dispense with the rules for its observance. Those readers are partly right but surely at the expense of sufficient notice that, in this his first face-to-face cure, Jesus heals instantly and without requesting trust or thanks. Nor does John say, like the other gospel writers, that Jesus heals from a loving heart. This man can and *does*, when and where he wills, for his own inscrutable reasons. His power exists for himself, as *evidence* of his divinity. If he heals us, the motive may only be reflexive—the light of our amazement reveals his grand face, though it may not warm our hearts.

When those authorities in the city, whom John calls simply "the Jews" (*Iudaioi* in Greek), learn of this breach of the Sabbath, they challenge his right. Jesus tells them "My Father is even now working and I'm working." The flat assertion is his first public announcement in Jerusalem of quasi-divine authority, but it is barely a warning of the full claim yet to come. Understandably, we hear of a mounting hatred—"Because of this then all the more the Jews were trying to kill him." Heedless, Jesus expands on the powers of his Sonship—

> . . . an hour is coming when all those in the tombs will hear his voice and come out, the ones that did good to a resurrection of life; those that did evil to a resurrection of judgment.

So in words that more than compound his deeds, Jesus casts his fatal die in the game that will kill him and work his triumph. John never says why the enemies fail to kill him on the spot. They have more than ample provocation, though they cannot know how much more they have yet to bear.

Next we learn only that Jesus is back in Galilee by the lake, healing the sick and drawing crowds. For the first time we are told that, though Jesus and the disciples withdraw to a mountain for Passover, a crowd of five thousand gathers. Again at this point John avoids the chance to let his Jesus teach (so, oddly, do the other gospels—perhaps a memory of the real occasion: with so many round him, perhaps teaching was impractical). Jesus' one expressed concern is for their nourishment, "Where can we buy bread so they may eat?" This far into our knowledge of Jesus, the question strikes an odd note—how can this tense and exalted man lower his gaze and plan a mass picnic? Yet he does. On the crowd's hunger, Jesus builds a new sign, another practical kitchen wonder that works his deeper purpose. For only when he transforms a boy's lunch of bread and fish into an overabundance for the crowd are they convinced that Jesus is "really the prophet that's coming into the world," an understandably false identification by people more impressed with multiplied crumbs than the streaming power of Jesus' presence.

Knowing that these men are about to seize him and make him king, Jesus slips off alone. This is the one moment in any of the four gospels when we are plainly told that numbers of men have begun to see Jesus as not only a spiritual but a political leader (and thus a far graver threat to the Jerusalem authorities and the Roman overlords than a mere rural thaumaturge with blasphemous delusions).

Evening comes and the disciples leave also, by boat for Capernaum. When they have gone three or four miles—the lake there is seven miles wide—night overtakes them; and a storm blows up. Suddenly they see Jesus walking toward them on the water and are rightly afraid. But as he nears the disciples, Jesus says—for the first time in their hearing—a phrase that means literally "I am. No fear." And they welcome him aboard, with no sign of having just heard a wonder.

In Mark's account of the same incident, Jesus says nearly the same, employing the identical Greek pronoun and verb—*Egō eimi*. Most English versions translate the Greek clause as "It is I." So far as it goes, that translation is correct. But *Egō eimi* or *I am* is also the name that God reveals to Moses in Exodus 3:14: "Tell the Israelites 'I Am has sent me to you.' " John has used the clause one previous time when, alone with the Samaritan woman at the well, he responds to her knowledge that Messiah is coming. Jesus says "I am [he], speaking to you." Here also translations blur the possibility that, even so early, John's Jesus confides to an outcast not merely his exclusive Sonship but his very identity with God the Father. If the storm-tossed disciples hear even a trace of the claim, it seems a wonder that they stay in the boat and do not leap out to swim for dry ground.

Next day, missing Jesus, the crowd finds him at Capernaum. And at last he speaks to them in the first of the startling "I am [something]" metaphors. He has told the Samaritan woman that he possesses living water to give, but he has not claimed that he himself is the water. Now though he is ready for a bolder leap, "I'm the bread of life. . . . Who comes to me will never hunger." This man speaks not in the short-story parables of other gospels but in self-made metaphors that show John's Jesus as a lyric visionary poet, not a prose story-teller. We cannot know how such self-regarding claims sounded to John's first readers, much less to Jesus' own audiences (assuming that the speech begins in a memory of John's and is not a whole-cloth creation). But we can share their amazement, if not revulsion, when in a matter of moments Jesus thrusts his metaphor of nourishment a further horrific step—"Amen amen I tell you unless you eat the flesh of the Son of God and drink his blood you have no life in you."

To say that one can give "living water" may be no more than the poetic claim of a spiritual teacher. To call oneself the "bread of life" approaches the ludicrous, even the megalomaniac. But for one man to thrust through the Hebrew dread of eating blood and of human sacrifice and apparently to demand the actual consumption of his physical body is a deed that cries for drastic response—exile, confinement for lunacy, immediate stoning. Or obedience.

For by now, a third of the way through his pamphlet,

John has boldly shown us (we who know Mark, which John may not) that even the rawboned first gospel writer evades telling us how entirely Jesus *means* what he says. The man is no fraud, no country magician with God on the brain. He has shown his power over inhuman nature—water to wine, the storm on the lake. He has healed the sick whom no doctor could heal. Crowds of the desperate follow his tracks. He wields language as though he were making it, word by word, from the empty air (by implication of course, he has made it—as the Word of God, he made the air and he willed human language as well as the tongues of angels and the stars who sang while all things rose from nothingness). And though again the Jews balk at immediate stoning, John admits that "From then on many of his disciples went back and no longer walked with him." By the end of this taut passage, a third of the way through his tale, John's revelation of his man's meaning is all but complete. The greater part of Jesus' remaining acts and words will only cut old impressions deeper and compound the outrage.

Next we learn that because Jesus is not yet ready to die in Jerusalem, he continues to "walk" in Galilee, presumably giving more signs. John specifies no one action from the time; but if we are to take his chronology literally, Jesus "walks" about at home from the early spring Passover to the autumn feast of Tabernacles. Some of the signs done in those months are almost surely described in other gospels; but John has only three more deeds to describe in his shapely story—Jesus' penultimate affront to "the Jews" (raising a putrid corpse from the tomb), then his own acceptance of judicial death, and his resurrection.

Though his disbelieving brothers, blood kin apparently, urge him to visit Jerusalem for the feast (are they eager for his death?—in any case, they taunt him with the fact that, since he means to be famous, he should show himself in the big world), and though Tabernacles had by now become the feast most associated with the messianic hope of the Jewish people, Jesus refuses to go. But once the brothers depart for the south, Jesus slips into the city secretly. Knowing of the deadly hostility against him, and having told his brothers "My time isn't yet come," why does he take the risk? John makes no guess but we may suspect that his all-knowing Jesus fore-knows that his doom is some way off.

Only midway through the observance of Tabernacles does Jesus suddenly show himself and begin to teach in the Temple. (The famous story of Jesus and the woman caught in adultery is often inserted at this point in John. In fact, though the story has the ring of authentic tradition, it is lacking from the oldest and best manuscripts of all four gospels; and I have omitted it from my translation.) As always, at Tabernacles John withholds any precepts which Jesus may have given. In-stead John launches an extended report of one more wrestle between this man and his enemies. And another of John's boldest strokes is visible in all the stages of this match as it spreads through the center of his story. John permits us to see—and in raking light, as no other gospel writer sees or dares—that the enemies of Jesus are, by their standard of rea-son, more than justified in their fierce revulsion from the man, if not their brute vengeance on him.

If nothing else exculpates them for a modern reader—even the injunction *Eat me, flesh and blood*—then let the reader suspend any bias for or against John and his Jesus and look again at the end of the scene that occurs near the Tem-ple as the climax of this Tabernacles visit. I am aware of no more audacious scene in literature nor of one more carefully built toward its climax—a blinding, unforeseeable bloom of vast megatonnage.

> The Jews answered him "Aren't we right to say that you're a Samaritan and have a demon?"
>
> Jesus answered "I don't have a demon but I

honor my Father and you dishonor me. I don't seek my own glory—there is one who seeks it and judges. Amen amen I tell you if anyone keeps my word he'll no way see death through eternity."

The Jews said to him "Now we know you have a demon. Abraham died and the prophets and you're saying 'If anyone keeps my word he'll no way taste death through eternity'? Are you greater than our father Abraham who died—and the prophets died? Who are you making yourself?"

Jesus answered "If I glorify myself my glory is nothing. My Father is the one glorifying me, the one you say is your God though you haven't known him. I know him. If I say that I don't know him I'll be a liar like you but I do know him and I keep his word. Abraham your father was glad to see my day. He saw it and delighted."

So the Jews said "You're not yet fifty and you've seen Abraham?"

Jesus said to them "Amen amen I tell you before Abraham was I am."

They took up stones then to throw at him but Jesus was hid and went out of the Temple.

We heard Jesus in private, in the storm, say "I am" to the disciples, with the chance of a simpler meaning. Unmistakably though, his assertions of "I am [something]" have continued metaphorically—*I am bread, drink, the light of the world.* But here in the Temple, God's literal home—and in the hearing of mortal foes—at last Jesus stamps out any remaining doubt of his meaning with an outright definition. He does not say "I am food" or "I am light for your path," not even "I am the only Son of God" but "I am God himself, here and now; I have always been, will always be." In Leviticus 24:16, Moses commanded that "anyone who blasphemes the name of Yahweh must be put to death. The whole assembly must stone him." And only by hiding himself at this moment does Jesus—a man who has now claimed to be God Yahweh—escape a lynch mob, one with an ample stock of stones at their feet: shards from the Temple construction around them, the Temple that only forty years hence will be again a hill of rubble, destroyed by Rome.

Any reader who has begun to feel that John is the master artificer among gospel writers—that, working with similar but highly individual memories, he cuts and splices with a freer and more imaginative hand—must face, at the end of the great "Abraham/I am" confrontation, the odd fact that John does not sustain this vast surge of force and climb to the next and tallest of his towering waves of theophany. Maybe, however, his art has not failed him. May he not be hewing to his irresistible memory of the visit? In any case, from that first climax, he swoops to Earth and describes a further Sabbath cure in Jerusalem.

Through the medium of clay which Jesus makes from his own spit, he heals a man born blind. Though the sign precipitates a touching response from the man and comic confusion among the Pharisees, it does little more in the ongoing story than deflate the pressure generated by Jesus' near stoning in a new but familiar round with the Pharisees, who by now are predictable straight men.

Then with no description of Jesus' actions and whereabouts from early October till mid-December, John hurries to the next Jerusalem visit, at the feast of Hanukkah. The Jews approach him with a question that at first seems to predate his recent claim to divinity—"How long will you hold our souls suspended? If you're Messiah tell us plainly." But then we recall that nothing in our present understanding of the messianic hope suggests that the Jews expected a *divine* Messiah, only a strong wise man. This time Jesus, as he so often does in other gospels, sidesteps. He says that his acts declare his identity and mission. "The deeds I do in my Father's name witness to me. But you don't trust. . . . I and the Father are one."

Here an alert reader may begin to reflect that the Jews have an advantage denied to us. They can watch Jesus' acts in progress; yet they are still doubtful, having already revealed that they believe in demons and black magic. What of us, these two millennia later, who see the acts only through ancient words? Do we accuse John of lying, delusion, or insufficient evidence? Considering that the techniques of full-blooded narrative realism will not be developed till the nineteenth century, what more could John give us than this film of words? Whatever we, as vicarious witnesses, may wish to believe or do at this crux of the story, Jesus' live audience seizes its familiar stones to kill him. But again he escapes and withdraws a few miles across the Jordan to the Baptizer's old baptismal site. There Jesus is visited by many, and many believe.

We are now in the exact midst of John's campaign to win or hold us. Only two more signs remain to unfold. After the vertiginous heights of the Tabernacles confrontation, where else can John take us? In the relative calm of Jesus' Transjordanian retreat, he learns of the sickness of his friend Lazarus, the brother of Martha and Mary of Bethany, a village near Jerusalem. Till now John has told us nothing of this family, but here he specifies that Jesus loved them (the only ones beyond the circle of disciples for whom John claims such an honor). Despite his love, Jesus refuses to hurry. He lingers a further two days. And then against the fearful advice of his disciples, he goes up to Bethany to find that Lazarus is already dead and has been in the tomb four days.

Meeting Jesus in the road, Martha rebukes his delay; but with words as prized as any in the New Testament, Jesus makes her the promise that anyone bereaved of a loved one wants—"Your brother will rise again. . . . I'm the resurrection and the life. Who trusts in me even if he should die will live." Still, at a second rebuke from Mary, at the sight of Mary's tears and those of "the Jews" around her, Jesus groans "in spirit" and also weeps—the nearest approach to a human passion shown by this man who is also God. In John's only other entirely human moment, in the scene at the Samaritan well, he told us that Jesus was tired from a journey; but what is the trigger now of his tears—the thought of the suffering that preceded his loved friend's death or the disbelief of Mary and the bystanders, despite their hearing his affirmation of Lazarus's rising? Composed again, Jesus asks that the door stone be taken off the tomb. Martha, the forthright sister, says "Lord, by now he stinks." But the stone is removed. Jesus looks up and—for the stated purpose of informing his audience—he thanks God for hearing his prayer, a peculiarly unlikable moment (as if our *liking* had any weight). Then he shouts "Lazarus, come out."

Any reader with a willing imagination can watch the great moment; anyone who saw the filmed *Last Temptation of Christ*, with its hauntingly portrayed raising of Lazarus, knows the visual and emotional force, the terror and joy, that lurk in those words. In the two other raisings—of virtual children, Jairus's daughter in Mark and the widow's son in Luke—we see no detail of the corpses' reaction to the rousing word and touch. But in John we have the hard facts—this stinking body was once a live man with two quite different sisters, a man of sufficient wealth to own a tomb cut into live rock. And without an actual touch by Jesus, in prompt response to words alone, the Greek says literally

> Came out the one having died, having been bound
> his feet and hands with bandages and his face bound
> round with a napkin. Jesus says to them "Free him
> and let him go."

However much more we want from the story—Lazarus's first words, the response of his sisters and the mourners (what do you do with a friend and brother who was four days dead?)—John ruthlessly turns our eyes elsewhere. The great deed is done; we are left in the hope of more information, but John is aware that his story plunges on. There is no time now for wondering reflection or an outcry of "Fraud!" We rush ahead to the ominous reaction of those men who gather in the Sanhedrin, the ruling council presided over by Caiaphas the High Priest.

In a scene that stands—with Mark's account of the death of John the Baptist—as one of only two scenes in the pair of gospels in which Jesus is neither present nor stands as the central figure, these powers that be explicitly grant the fact of the miracle. Again it is odd to note how none of the gospels takes the chance to point out that the mortal enemies of Jesus never question his inhuman power or attempt to expose its fraudulence, though some of them claim that his power is demonic. But for the first time here, the enemies privately sound a calculating note, far grimmer than the old impulsive anger—"If we leave him like this everyone will trust in him and the Romans will come and take our place and our nation." Caiaphas deepens the tone by sounding a blindly ironic note, "It's better for us that one man die for the people and all the nation not be lost." Serious plans begin for a human sacrifice.

Somehow Jesus learns of the plan (is his source the nameless disciple who is later said to know the High Priest, and is that disciple also "the Beloved"?). Again Jesus retreats with the disciples, this time to Ephraim in the desert. Apparently he stays there till, six days before the spring Passover, he comes back to Bethany—less than a mile from Jerusalem—for a supper at the home of Lazarus and his sisters. John says nothing of Jesus' purpose in the dangerous visit. But when sister Mary un-expectedly bathes Jesus' feet with an exorbitant amount of ex-pensive perfume, and Judas protests the waste, Jesus then foreshadows his purpose—"Leave her be so she may keep it for the day of my burial." He knows that his fateful hour is near and that Mary's open heart has unknowingly prophesied his end. Six nights from now, he will lie torn, dead, and cold.

The remainder of the book, nearly half its length, will unroll John's version of that last week—the man who is God agrees to die, as the High Priest has dimly foreseen, and to "be glorified," whatever that may mean. The external lines of the story are scored as deeply in Western minds as any other narrative lines, in high and low art; and I will not follow that line as closely as before. What seems more useful is a chart of John's differences from other gospels in his description of the last full days—differences of act, focus, and meaning, many of which strongly signal the guiding hand or voice of an authoritative eyewitness.

First and basic to the entire account is John's claim that Jesus both enacted and confirmed his divinity in Galilee a few years ago. Here in Jerusalem in sight of the Temple for the past two years, in acts and metaphors, Jesus has bruited his claim at center stage. And within the Temple courts and in a suburb only yards away, in the months from the winter solstice till now, Jesus has thrown down his wildest "I am" gauntlet and publicly raised the rotting corpse of a man of evident wealth and standing. So when Jesus next courts messianic identity in making his ass-back reentry to the city, John (in contrast to the welcoming crowd) sees him, not as the teacher-Messiah-king of the other gospels but as something utterly new on Earth—a chance once given and not to be repeated.

In other gospels the four days that lie between this hollow triumph and Jesus' final supper with the disciples are packed with incident and speeches. But John vaults through them. Jesus makes repetitive and oddly unremarkable statements of his mission. The thermonuclear flare of the clash at Tabernacles is never revived, not before his death; and he works no further wonder in the city. Likewise "the Jews" seek no more debate. Their course—and Jesus' intent—are firmly set for lethal collision, as we have known since Lazarus rose (and since the very prologue to John's story). In the light of John's earlier authentic-feeling textures, it hardly seems possible that he lacks a richly detailed memory or a good deal of hearsay concerning the time. The remarkable leanness of his passion-story line then is likely explained by two things—the fact that he has already established "the Jews'" grounds for violence, and John's own understandable if lamentable rush toward Jesus' farewell and "glory."

John's third large innovation in the passion story appears in his memory of Jesus' last supper with the disciples on Thursday evening. Knowingly or not, John contradicts the chronology of the other gospels. Mark, Matthew, and Luke state that the supper is the Passover feast. John calmly states that the supper is "[the night] before the feast of Passover" and leaves us a quandary—is his memory accurate, and the other gospels wrong; or has he jogged the calendar by a day to provide a synchrony he will soon reveal?

Then John alone gives us the moment during supper when Jesus strips, girds himself with a towel, pours water into a basin and washes the feet of each disciple, including presumably Judas. Each time the act begins before my reading eyes, I pull back and think "The withering or frozen I Am of John would not do this." And in fact it is I Am's most human act since his early chat with the Samaritan woman, since spitting on dirt to heal the blind man, or weeping at the thought of Lazarus dead.

Scholars have proposed dozens of implicit theological meanings for the foot washing. I have read many of them in the hope of understanding a significance beyond the obvious, but at last the theological claims seem foolish excess baggage for a moment so charged with the credible shock of human meeting and bitter farewell. For as the moment of the washing moves to its end—when Jesus reaches Peter and Peter objects—John may win us to a trust in the historical likelihood of the scene with a last exchange, the unforesee-able depth of which even Mark, with his notes of Peter's memories, cannot match:

> Peter said to him "No way will you wash my feet not till eternity."
> Jesus answered him "Unless I wash you you have no part in me."
> Simon Peter said to him "Lord, not just my feet but also my hands and head."

Then while the other gospels report a few of Jesus' words at the supper—the establishment of a bread and wine memorial to himself, the news of his coming betrayal—John is alone in reporting long final speeches from Jesus. In fact, a glance at one of those useful New Testaments with the words of Jesus printed in red will indicate that where Matthew is reddest near the start, and Mark and Luke red fairly evenly throughout, John's long red stretch is withheld till now, very near the end.

It is this long arc of speech, packed into so short a space of narrative time (perhaps twenty minutes), that gives John an air of weight and ponderosity equal to Matthew's and Luke's, where speech so often impedes story. In John the disciples ask a few questions and occasionally whisper among themselves, but the valedictory voice of Jesus fills the air of a long slow evening. A substantial portion of the favorite texts of Christians come from these very speeches; yet few believers notice or mind that (in context) they are puzzlingly repetitious, though readers of John's Greek will notice that only in these passages does Jesus seem to lack the words and syntax to clarify his meaning. At least some of the more static repetitions of the farewell discourse may result from a later editor's anxiety to tack on to John's first edition yet another surviving report on Jesus' words or a meditation about them. But for

•

me, and for many non-Christian readers, the lengthy wait does not simply leave us impatient for the coming doom—or at least some resolving action to end the circling speech. It leaves us wondering what, if anything, is new and indispensable—to either John's purpose or to our own stake while we read—in the slow and uncharacteristic farewell.

If we trust that John is reporting Jesus' actual leave-taking, then we face a document at least as fascinating as, say, the last words of Cleopatra or Francis of Assisi. If we cannot make that trusting leap but do assume that John is attempting a faithful memory—a scrupulous *impression* of what Jesus said and meant at the actual meal—we may conclude that first-century Middle Eastern eloquence was as coiling and numbing as it can be today. Then we may search for any new matter.

First, we see that the words are spoken to the disciples in a private gathering, to a small group that has been with Jesus almost from the start. To what extent are we to assume that whatever Jesus says is valid also for other and later believers? The question is seldom noticed—modern readers often sweep past it—and since it goes unanswered by John, I will not risk a public guess, however strongly the words have braced the lives of millions of readers. For the remainder of the speech, the following points seem new both to the disciples and to us readers.

Jesus is going away to the Father. And he goes specifically to prepare a place where the disciples may follow him. Only then will he return for them. In his absence meanwhile he will ask the Father to send a substitute, a spirit whom Jesus calls the Advocate or the Counselor (the Greek word is *paraklētos*). Late in the supper speeches, when Jesus makes his first clear reference to a punishment of human sin, he adds that the Advocate will convict the world of failing to believe in him. He goes on twice more to urge the disciples that, with the help of that Spirit, they obey his second command—"Love each other as I loved you" (the first command is "Trust that I Am").

And then, for the first time in the gospel, Jesus makes an ethical observation which he seems to claim as valid for all humankind (it is not a precept, notice)—"No one has greater love than this, that he lays down his life for his friends." Newly tender now, Jesus grants a new status to the disciples by calling them *servants* no longer but *friends*. He promises that the disciples will suffer for his sake but that, on his return, their joy will abound. Then they will know the answers to all questions—"I've said these things to you in metaphors; an hour's coming when I'll no longer speak to you in metaphors but plainly I'll declare the Father to you."

At last the disciples, who have hardly understood more than the tragicomic bunglers who are their counterparts in Mark and to some extent Matthew and Luke, show a redeeming insight—"Now we know that you know everything and don't need anyone to question you. So we trust that you came out from God." Here I always recall that, of the four gospel writers, John is much the least harsh on the disciples; he is in fact the only recorder who grants them more than a modicum of dignity. Can that fact be weighed with the many other pieces of evidence, or manufactured hints, which suggest or insist that the author or source of John was one of the Twelve—and one who, in being the Beloved Disciple, was spared the self-loathing of Peter which so vividly colors Mark's gospel? (It is perhaps worth noting at this point that none of the four gospels presents us with the portrait of a single disciple who seems capable of a sustained narrative, which is not to say that a disciple's testimony does not in fact lie behind Mark or John, Matthew or Luke.)

Next, as if the disciples' final expression of warmth has completed some long-delayed circuit of power, Jesus prays. Now that "those you gave me" have trusted, "glorify me, Father, along with yourself with the glory I had with you before the world was." With a further prayer for those who will come to believe through the disciples' teaching—but strangely with no request for a bread and wine memorial—Jesus rises and leads his friends downhill, out of the city and across a small stream to a garden, a familiar haunt. Except for the final sign he will give, his communication with the disciples is ended. From first till last, from the time with John the Baptist till now, John tells us no more of Jesus' will for his pupils than can be contained in one sentence—*Believe that I Am and love one another.* And at no point has Jesus explained his reason for the death he has all but begged from "the Jews" and now strides to embrace.

It is generally assumed that John's sense of Jesus as all knowing and divinely serene compels him to omit the next scene reported by the other gospels—that appalling hour when the disciples sleep oblivious while Jesus prays that the crisis pass somehow and he not die. In the oldest account of this nadir, Mark's scene in Gethsemane, the muffled horror of Jesus' dread is conveyed with a power matched only by John's account of the towering crest of Jesus' claim for himself—"Before Abraham was I am." And it may well be that John chose to suppress the awful moment as a private human lapse by Jesus, undeserving of public scrutiny.

But given the gritty eyewitness nature of so many narrative details in John, another possibility suggests itself. If, as Mark reports, John bar Zebedee was one of the sleeping disciples, then the same man—the aged John, writing his gospel—may have had no direct memory of the moment and declined to accept another's witness, even Peter's. (Though Mark's details have the ring of hard fact, and though the eloquence of his Jesus' words far surpasses any other speech recorded elsewhere by Mark, Mark never tells us who witnessed Jesus' solitude and conveyed its memory to later times. Any modern traveler who knows the topography of those few square yards in the narrow valley between Temple

Mount and the Mount of Olives may easily assume that one or more of the sleepers roused briefly and overheard Jesus' agonized prayer. Or did the mysterious boy, who flees the arrest naked—and who has often been thought to be Mark himself—overhear the dark ordeal and recall it?) Certainly John's unique details of the ensuing arrest in the garden suggest either eyewitness or a canny novelistic fabrication—the torches and lanterns of the posse, their stumbling panic when Jesus again says "I Am," the name of the man whose ear Peter lops off in the fracas. And if John is largely a canny novelist, how odd that he exerted those powers so seldom in his gospel.

Each of the gospels has a varied account of the remaining events of that Thursday night and Friday morning. The ensuing action includes further details unique to John. First comes the news that one of the pupils (John himself?) is known to the former High Priest Annas and so gains admission for himself and Peter to the courtyard near where Jesus is first questioned. John gives us Jesus' unremarkable reply to Annas—he has always spoken the truth publicly, never in secret. Though John is the only gospel writer to include an interrogation at the home of Annas, a power behind the current High Priest's throne, there is nothing in the disappointingly undramatic scene to suggest imaginative heightening where it might well be expected. Is the explanation as simple as the fact that John did not gain entrance to the interrogation itself and lacked a firsthand witness of that event?

And though John says that Annas sent Jesus on to the High Priest Caiaphas for further questioning, John tells us nothing of that meeting, though the other gospels call it a meeting of the priests and elders or the Sanhedrin. Thus John misses the chance to reiterate the only explanation he offers for Jesus' death—the early ironic foresight by Caiaphas that "it's better for us that one man die for the people and all the nation not be lost." Again was John simply absent from the meeting and lacking in direct memory? (Compare Mark's charged account. When Caiaphas asks Jesus if he is Messiah, Jesus replies *Egō eimi*—"I am," a reply whose admission goes well beyond the scope of the question. Caiaphas hears the full meaning; he tears his robe, the ritual response to high blasphemy.) By now it is early morning; and "the Jews" lead Jesus on to the residence of Pilate, the Roman governor.

All the gospels insist on the blood hatred felt by the priests and the Pharisees and by the Passover crowds who, five days earlier, had greeted Jesus as king. Each of the four writers implies that a fearful rejection by certain factions from Jesus' own people is finally the trigger of his execution. Some readers find a hotter anti-Jewish hostility in John than elsewhere in the gospels, but I see no greater bias on his part. In fact, John is the one gospel that fairly states the degree to which the Jewish authorities had strong grounds for fear that Jesus would trigger a nationally devastating Roman violence. Only Mark's trial scene, with Jesus' frank assumption of divine prerogative, matches the effrontery of many scenes in John where Jesus towers in truth or lunacy above his own blood kin; and even Mark has no match for John's claim that (after the feeding of the multitude) five thousand people wanted "to come and seize [Jesus] to make him king."

And right or wrong, John is the one gospel writer who says why "the Jews," having made their decision to execute Jesus for blasphemy, bring him to the Roman governor for confirmation—they do not have the judicial right of capital punishment (as opposed to their early near-lynching attempts). Though John joins the other gospels in mitigating the responsibility of Pilate, he does not give us Matthew's scene in which Pilate washes his hands of guilt. And nowhere does John echo the historically disastrous moment in Matthew where "all the people" are reported as crying "Let his blood be on us and our children."

From whatever distance of foresight and awareness of his own divinity, John's Jesus endures his mental and physical trials; at no point does he yield an inch to his accusers. His final words to Pilate are, from Pilate's point of view, so absurd as to guarantee harmless lunacy.

> "You'd have no right over me unless it was given you from above. . . ."
> From there on Pilate tried to free him but the Jews shouted "If you free this man you're no friend of Caesar! . . ."
> Pilate hearing these words brought Jesus out and sat on the bench [and condemned him].

As John warned us in the prologue, "his own failed to take him." And though their refusal gets slim sympathy from John, he is again the one gospel writer who grants how understandable and, from their point of view, entirely rational is the rage of Jesus' enemies for his elimination.

John's account of the crucifixion and burial is also strikingly idiosyncratic. One of the most important differences is John's implication, never directly stated but in firm contradiction of the chronology of the other gospels, that Jesus is crucified at the hour when, a few hundred yards away in the Temple courts, priests are slaughtering thousands of Passover lambs—ritual substitutes to bear God's wrath and thus spare the people. John proceeds to omit some of the credible details of the other gospels (Mark's note that Simon of Cyrene helps carry the cross, for instance, or the fact that the men with whom Jesus is crucified are thieves); but John adds minor details that are known to be historically plausible (that four Roman soldiers are in the execution party; that the soldiers come to break Jesus' legs and hasten death but, finding him apparently dead, pierce his chest with a lance for good measure). And there are two striking innovations.

The first is to be expected. None of the four gospels pays special attention to the brutal agonies of mind and body implicit in crucifixion; they can assume that each of their contemporary readers has witnessed the common ghastly sight, one that appalled even so hardened a lawyer as Cicero. In fact, the condemned was fastened to an upright wooden cross or other scaffolding with spike-sized nails and rope (the Greek word for *cross* means *stake*); sometimes the body was supported by a rudimentary footrest, sometimes by a thick peg in the fork of the body; then the condemned simply hung suspended, stripped, in all weathers till he died or was dispatched, sometimes by a breaking of the long leg bones (if the condemned could not press up on his legs to draw deep breaths, he would soon suffocate).

Despite their avoidance of such basic information, Mark, Matthew, and Luke do provide ample incidents to dramatize the private pain of Jesus and the sympathy of nature itself—the mockery of witnesses, Jesus' words with the thieves who hang beside him, lowering skies, an earthquake that opens tombs and raises "many bodies of the sleeping saints." Though John's Jesus gives almost no signs of suffering, he does uniquely say that he is thirsty and then sucks a drink of sour wine from a sponge held toward him. But he spares us Jesus' desolate cry from Mark and Matthew, "My God, my God, why have you abandoned me?" And in John his last words are a richly ironic claim of relief, acceptance, and triumph—"It's done" (or "finished"): Jesus' death is one of the least finished acts in human history.

From the point of view of narrative texture, the second important innovation is John's report of something not mentioned in other gospels—Jesus' mother is present at the cross. Though John has not referred to Jesus' mother since the wedding in Cana, he tells us that Jesus on the cross provides for her care, bequeathing her to the disciple "whom he loved." In contrast to other gospels, which imply that no disciple was brave enough to stand by the cross, John affirms that the Beloved Disciple was not only present but "from that hour the disciple took her to his home." Her actual name, given elsewhere as Mary, and the name of the Beloved are never recorded in John. Of the other disciples mentioned till now, none other's name has been suppressed except that of James, the brother of John bar Zebedee.

Despite a century of busy debate on the identity of the Beloved and on the symbolic significance of Jesus' addressing his mother only as *woman*, it seems inescapable for any student of Western narrative strategy that, whatever *beloved* connotes for John, the disciple in question is intended by the writer to be identified as John bar Zebedee. And the strange interjection at this late point of the Beloved's credentials is nothing less than an underlining of the fact that "the one who saw this has witnessed. His witness is true and he knows he speaks truly so you too may trust for these things happened so the scripture be fulfilled. . . ."

That intense air of personal recall, the one relief in such a long stretch of painful matter, is suspended for a quick account of the surprisingly lavish embalming and burial of the corpse in a new garden tomb near Golgotha. John reports that the burial is handled by two secret adherents of Jesus, the till-now-unmentioned Joseph of Arimathea and Nicodemus, whom we encountered on the first Passover trip to Jerusalem. Like other gospels, John tells us nothing of the thirty-odd hours of Friday night and Saturday when Jesus lies dead. Where are the disciples and what are they doing? After all, it is Jesus' story, not theirs. And with Sunday morning, and throughout the resurrection appearances, John comes to life most startlingly as a grainy and credible eyewitness. Again his version is independent and has the feel of authority. All the gospels admit a fact detrimental to their case in first-century Palestine—the empty tomb was discovered by women, women being thought unreliable witnesses. But where the other gospels mention small groups of women, John tells us only that Mary the Magdalene comes to the tomb early, while it is still dark; and finding the stone removed from the door, she runs to tell Peter and the Beloved (it is worth noting that, in her telling, the Magdalene may imply other companions in her visit—"We don't know where they have put him").

Peter and the Beloved of course run toward the tomb, the Beloved outstripping Peter, stopping at the open door, and bending to look inside. He sees the grave clothes lying there empty; but for unexplained reasons, the Beloved does not enter. Some readers think that John praises the Beloved (perhaps himself) tacitly—the Beloved does not need to make a thorough inspection; he understands at once. When Peter arrives, with characteristic boldness, he steps in and sees not only the grave clothes but the head cloth, folded separately. If those details are provided for us by the Beloved, it is significant that he scrupulously preserves what might easily be interpreted as Peter's greater courage.

A similar conclusion may well be drawn from the four remaining scenes that John reports. The Beloved is absent for the tomb-side meeting between Jesus and Mary the Magdalene (another example of John's emotional generosity and the only detailed gospel record of a risen appearance to a woman). The Beloved also plays no special part in Jesus' first appearance to the disciples—the Twelve minus Judas and Thomas—or in the next appearance, when doubting Thomas is the center of attention. Even in the final muted but deeply resonant appearance by the Lake of Galilee, though the Beloved is the first of the disciples to recognize Jesus when he calls to them from shore, the Beloved receives no special notice in the scene that follows—not till Peter calls him to Jesus' attention.

The resurrected Jesus who returns in visible form to his disciples and friends in Matthew, Luke, and John has been studied more obsessively than any other figure in Western narrative. By comparison, Hamlet and Don Quixote are barely noted. Paul's flat-footed account of the resurrection appearances in The First Letter to the Corinthians 15:3–8 is our earliest surviving record, written about twenty years after the events and specifically insisting on its accuracy as a tradition previously "received" by Paul (as might be expected of Paul, he omits the initial appearance to the Magdalene). Mark as well has no scenes that show the risen Jesus. The appearances mentioned at the end of Mark, as that end is found in most modern editions, are a later non-Marcan addition to the original which stops with the flight of the terrified women. In Matthew the risen Jesus meets his assembled disciples only once, on a nameless mountain in Galilee—there is no report of physical contact nor any physical detail, only a visible presence and words. Luke gives detailed accounts of two meetings, one between the risen Jesus and two of his prior followers on the road from Jerusalem to Emmaus and a second scene in which Jesus surprises the disciples at a meal, asks them for food, eats "part of a broiled fish," then leads them out to Bethany and departs to Heaven.

Of the four resurrection appearances in John, only one seems to parallel another gospel's—John's first Jerusalem appearance may harmonize with Luke's appearance to the disciples behind locked doors. John's early morning appearance to the Magdalene is unique, like the second Jerusalem appearance to the disciples—the occasion on which Thomas is invited to probe the actual hand and side wounds of the risen Jesus, to acknowledge this palpable being as his "Lord" and "God" and then, like the others, to receive the unthinkable power to forgive sin (a power unmentioned elsewhere).

What is most extraordinary—and for me most compelling and convincing as story—is the complex event recorded at the end of John. Students now widely acknowledge that the earliest edition of John must have ended with the statement that follows Jesus' final Jerusalem appearance.

The statement defines, in retrospect, the scope and purpose of John's whole book.

> Jesus did many other signs before his disciples which are not written in this book but these have been written so you may trust that Jesus is Messiah the Son of God and that trusting you may have life in his name.

The whole of the ensuing scene feels very much like an appendix then but one with such intimate connection of manner and tone to the original text as to seem unquestionably a piece of the same firsthand tradition, saved here perhaps by a later editor, if not by the original writer himself in a subsequent draft. I will look at the scene closely later.

It is a natural inference that this final appearance reports Jesus' last meeting with the disciples. We can at least know that John has told all he wanted to tell—*The man returned from the tomb and forgave us; feeding us one last time, near home.* So with two brisk but emphatic repetitions, the appendix ends; and the book ends again—the Beloved is the source of this story too, and Jesus did so much more among us that the world itself could not hold the books if all his acts were described.

*

That seems a fair outline of John's story. Yet the outline can be pressed further down, to a sentence—*The force that conceived and bore all things came here among us, proved his identity in visible human acts, was killed by men no worse than we, rose from death, and walked again with his early believers, vowing eternal life beside him to those who also come to believe that he is God and loves us as much as his story shows.* None of the other active world religions says anything remotely similar or comparable. John's story, which—more than the story of the other gospels—became the orthodox Christian faith, is in fact repugnant to Judaism, Islam, Buddhism, and to all the indigenous beliefs of India and Japan. There is likewise no parallel in the theologies of John's contemporaries—the dead myths of Greece or Rome, with their demigods and deified bureaucrats. Again, John hands us a brand-new thing.

Then what do we think? Were we meant to read it at all? As he wrote, did the Beloved or whoever wrote on his behalf imagine an audience of almost utterly alien people, Christian or otherwise, two thousand years later? If John could have glimpsed our existence, in a century of profound doubt, would he repeat for us his hope to win our trust in the uniquely divine nature of Jesus? Would he think his gospel still a useful, if not sufficient, brief in the case? Or was he chiefly thinking, there in his old age and near the end of his century, of the small community of his own already convinced pupils in Asia? They were anyhow friends whom he would soon leave; and he may well have written at their urging in the prospect of their no longer having his speaking memories and meditations, the unsurpassed power of his comprehending voice.

If John meant to write for such a private audience, then he was essentially providing them with a prompt book—this careful, though occasionally clumsy, set of a few sketchily rendered acts and a few more important speeches (from a hoard of both) to coach the memories of pupils already learned in the lore and meaning of the Beloved Disciple's Jesus. But what if we could have asked John a further question—did he so much as guess that his brief document, as it left his hands, could be expected to win and hold the belief of generations who would lack a direct eyewitness teacher and perhaps have no other account than his own pamphlet with its stupendous claim and promise?

Whatever John's hopes, surely no other ancient firsthand document continues to press its force on so many lives (I assume that Mark is secondhand). The only recoverable, incontestable fact is that we have it. With all its mysteries of authorship, editing, and the nature of its editors (again perhaps no more than two or three people are involved), it has stood in the midst—sometimes near the head—of our culture for this long. How can an interested reader use it, here and now?

This late in the life of the Jesus sect and its heirs in Christianity, it seems more than unlikely that a sane non-Christian first-time reader can spring to the belief that the Jew Jesus of Nazareth, crucified by Roman authority in about AD 30, was an earthly condensation of the God who made everything, known and unknown, in our universe at least. Without a powerful goad from that same invisible God—whose nature is further obscured by the disasters of our own history—how can a rational mind yield its modern self to an old and preposterous tract which asks no less than an absolute change of mind and heart? (The ignorant and mad yield daily to less.)

What would yielding mean? The question brings us once more to the one broad command of John and his Jesus—*Believe that Jesus is Messiah, the Son of God, and God incarnate.* Suppose that I assent, *I do believe.* What next? Despite the fact that, late in his life, Jesus urges the disciples to keep his commands, it is important to recall that only one other command is reported by John, the last-minute injunction that the disciples "love each other" (his earlier observation to Nicodemus that "unless a person is born from above he can't see the reign of God" is not an injunction, only a statement of fact). Nowhere in John does Jesus commend the Mosaic law, as he does in other gospels. His miraculous signs are benign in effect—healings but no exorcisms, feedings, two resurrections—yet are far past all human hope of emulation.

And the least attempt to copy Jesus' acts, his gestures and words, will promptly land us in blasphemy, if not jail or the mental ward. So far as we can learn from John then, individual assent to the divinity of Jesus is the one vital act of response that a reader must make—eternal life will follow, whatever that is (and in Jesus' long farewell during the last supper, it appears to be a continuing existence with Jesus in some extraterrestrial good place, though again Jesus himself makes the promise solely to the disciples, not to a subsequent world of believers).

*

Say that John is the one surviving gospel. Given the disappearance of a great many once-known early documents from the Jesus sect, John might easily be the chief survivor. Say that we have no other believing *narrative* testimony to the man and his meaning. Then would the Jesus sect have survived the death of the last disciples and apostles? Would the memory of Jesus have lingered any more powerfully in the world's imagination than the memory of Socrates, Alexander, Joan of Arc, or an eloquent (though made-up) figure like Shakespeare's Hamlet?

Unless the Holy Spirit had inspired abstract belief in many more hearts, the answer is surely No. Original and powerful as he is, John would not be enough. Neither would Matthew nor Luke, though their reports of the teaching would lodge Jesus firmly in the history of ethics. Paul and all the other writers of the New Testament would have gathered dust as eccentric exhibits in the history of Judaism and the Hellenistic mystery religions. Only Mark—with his blunt air of no-nonsense reportage, his bat-out-of-hell commitment to vivid action over slowed-down speech, and his readers' terminal brick-wall collision as the terrified women flee the empty tomb—might have gone the long way toward keeping Jesus strong among us: a young man coming to John the Baptizer for cleansing, learning in that instant of God's will for him, choosing disciples, working compassionate miracles, incurring the wrath of officialdom, revealing his mystic status as Son in a nighttime mountaintop transfiguration, then choosing death as a substitute for the human race and apparently—*apparently*—rising from the tomb. It's at least a story worth hearing and weighing.

What of John though, with his patent design on human lives (lives in his own time, if not ours) and his huge demand? It turns out, to his good, that three more gospels also survive and that each provides a good deal that we miss in John—three more distinct angles on the presence, acts, and words of an extraordinary life. I have noted numerous ways in which John, with a tranquil mastery worthy of his teacher, stakes down the tent of his own story with the hard pegs of contemporary Palestinian detail, then floats it on the literal air of a voice unlike any other on human record. But a glance back at the central great Tabernacles confrontation will strengthen the point—Jesus' rising voice, insane if not true, and the all but murderous countervoices, mounting as unstoppably as the peroration of an organ fugue. The delicate comedy of the well-side meeting in Samaria is another scene in which acts and words seem to mock the likelihood of invention (though no one is present but Jesus and the woman; will Jesus tell the disciples later?). And nothing reported from Jesus' earthly life is more convincing as *story* than the homely but ghoulish prelude to the raising of Lazarus. Our worst fear has happened; our best hope may follow—and suddenly does. Yet the scene that mostly defeats my doubts, that bears the homeliest signs of straight reportage, is the most uncanny of all.

For nothing in John is more impressive, because unexpected, than the nature of the three resurrection appearances he chooses to give. As the single gospel writer who has shown us an intensely self-aware Jesus from the start—the conscious Man-God striding through his world with dauntless eyes and unstillable voice—John should almost certainly have shown us (if he felt any freedom to invent or seriously alter his memory of the risen Jesus or the stories he had heard) an even more uncannily transformed and glorified figure: a gleaming and all but unwatchable God on Earth for however briefly before he departs to await his followers at the glorious right hand of the Father. Far from it though. The risen Jesus is as still as light itself, in its progress through night toward our dim eyes.

*

Look back at the whole of the final scene, the dawn appearance of Jesus by the lake to his fisher friends. Even a sanely conservative student like Raymond Brown suspects that the scene is an amalgam of two memories of the resurrection, one involving Peter and a miraculous haul of fish and another involving a meal and the commissioning of Peter as shepherd of the flock. To indicate the tortures that even the most sensible Biblical commentators inflict upon themselves, I should add that Brown's suspicion rises mainly from the lack of any mention of a meal in other early references to a resurrection appearance to Peter. I might point out that there is likewise no early mention of swimming or nudity; but that does not perturb Brown—nude swimming being, it would seem, more natural to nocturnal fishermen than breakfast. As a reader who has known the story for more than fifty years, who has read it dozens of times and translated it, I continue to respond to what I see as a patently seamless web of story—the large amount that is said so quickly, the larger amount that goes unsaid. An experiment in extrapolation, however risky, will sketch my point.

After the appearances of a risen Jesus in Jerusalem, seven

of the disciples—for whatever reasons—have returned to their home and their old work (though we know their old work from other gospels, not John's). Peter is already their leader. He decides to fish at night, a propitious time on the Lake of Galilee; and six others agree to come with him. They work all night and catch nothing. Dawn commences and they see a strange man standing on shore. In their village world, a stranger is rare. He calls to them "Boys, anything to eat?" (The Greek noun is the plural of *paidion*, a diminutive of *pais* or *boy*—thus an easy greeting.) When they shout back their failure, the man suggests that they cast to the right. Impressed perhaps by his strangeness, they gamble on a throw; and at once they haul an enormous catch.

"So," John says, "the disciple whom Jesus loved said to Peter 'It's the Lord.' " Does the Beloved know Jesus first because of their special intimacy (as he may, for that reason, have trusted in the resurrection without close scrutiny); or does he know him because of the bountiful gift of fish?—never in the gospels do the disciples catch a single fish without help from Jesus. Yet so certain is the Beloved that he stays aboard to draw the heavy net to shore.

The headstrong Peter, elated, tucks up his shirt for speed—under it, he is naked—and throws himself in, to swim toward Jesus. (Was Peter insufficiently convinced by the prior appearances? Is he afraid that this uncanny risen Lord will disappear before the boat can reach shore? Is he hell-bent on asking forgiveness?) The five others stay aboard with the catch. Even a further appearance of the Lord does not force them to sacrifice their welfare, only a hundred yards from shore. John's focus continues on those laboring disciples through the next moments—their landing, their seeing a charcoal fire with fish and bread.

Despite his apparent readiness for breakfast, Jesus invites them to bring their own fish. And only now does the focus return to Peter. "Simon Peter got up and dragged the net to land full of a great many fish—a hundred fifty-three and with so many still the net wasn't torn." So Peter *gets up*—from *where*? I may be crossing legitimate bounds, but here again I suspect the skipping movement of an old man's memory. Peter has dropped from John's gaze for the time of the rash independent swim; what John most remembers is what the Beloved was doing, conserving a haul. But now Peter returns to mind; he gets up from where he is panting on shore, or kneeling near Jesus, and resumes his earthly duty. He helps his friends draw in the fish that will feed their dependents (we know from Mark that Peter at least has a family).

Jesus calls them to eat. Still awed, they hang back, knowing but speechless—even the Beloved is silent (in any case, he speaks only twice in the gospel: at the last supper he asks the traitor's name, "Lord, who is it?"; and now at dawn he has said "It's the Lord"—a total of six words in the Greek). So Jesus "came over, took the bread and gave it to them, also the fish." John tells us nothing about the meal itself. Did Jesus partake; were there any relaxed exchanges, the domestic meal-talk of old road companions? As with Peter's swim, John again jerks forward in the action—"So when they'd eaten. . . ." And the threefold questioning of Peter begins, rising in Jesus' laconic intensity, Peter's shamed answers, and Jesus' repeated "Feed my lambs." *I was the shepherd. Now I am leaving. Serve awhile in my stead.*

From here to the end, John's eye is fixed on Peter with only a glance toward the Beloved; we hear nothing more of the other five pupils. And no words to them or to the Beloved are reported. If the Beloved is identical with John the writer of the gospel, then whatever his part in this last meeting, he effaces its memory with silence. The Beloved is mysteriously noted only one last time. After Jesus' prediction of Peter's death by crucifixion, Peter turns, sees the Beloved, and says to Jesus "Lord, and what about this one?" Jesus speaks his haunting peremptory last words, "If I want him to stay till I come, what's it to you? You follow me." And again with the confirmation that the same Beloved "is the disciple witnessing to these things and writing these things and we know that his witness is true," John (or his own later pupil) rests his case.

Again the risen Jesus has made no ethical demands and, after the meal, no practical request to anyone but Peter—no exhortation, as in Matthew, to spread the word of his glory worldwide. I have suggested that, given the godly Jesus of John, we might have expected signs heightened with an extra degree of wonder after his rising, acts of the glorified Son of God. But his risen acts are all of a piece with his former life—if anything, more modest. He speaks with a woman, breathes the Holy Spirit onto the Eleven, satisfies a doubter, and assists a failed boatload of fishermen. As ever, again he enacts his name—*I Am. Grasp only that.*

Nothing in all this unprecedented book, nothing in any other gospel, consistently comes so near to convincing me of reliable human witness as this last scene of John. By its *reliability* I mean its tenor of honest report—*I saw this happen; now I tell it to you plainly.* There are hundreds of invented scenes in Western fiction and drama that win our momentary belief. To mention only two, look at Mistress Quickly's description of Falstaff's death in the second act of Shakespeare's *Henry V* or Anna Karenina's final moment before she flings herself under the train in Tolstoy's mammoth novel. But nothing that I have encountered elsewhere, in a lifetime's reading, surpasses the simple conviction, the pure-water flow of the last scene in John.

As literate a scholar as C. S. Lewis has said much the same of John's whole story.

> I have been reading poems, romances, vision literature, legends, myths all my life. I know what they are like. I know that none of them is like this. Of this

text there are only two possible views. Either this is reportage—though it may no doubt contain errors—pretty close to the facts, nearly as close as Boswell. Or else, some unknown writer in the second century, without known predecessors or successors, suddenly anticipated the whole technique of modern, novelistic, realistic narrative. If it is untrue, it must be narrative of that kind. The reader who doesn't see this has simply not learned how to read.

And to Lewis's salutary desk thumping, I can add one unquestionable fact. The whole of the end of John can be converted into first-person narrative by a simple change of pronouns. Note the effect in a few examples:

> Simon Peter said to us "I'm going fishing." We said "We're coming with you." So we went out, and got into the boat and all that night caught nothing. . . . We others came on in the little boat dragging the net of fish since we were only about a hundred yards from land. When we got out on land we saw a charcoal fire laid, a fish lying on it and bread. . . . Jesus came, took the bread and gave it to us, also the fish. This was the third time Jesus was shown to us raised from the dead.

Admittedly, such a recasting is not sufficient proof that a firsthand narrative memory lies behind the end of John; but all fiction writers and most careful readers know that third-person narratives—with their detachment, their stance well back from the action—can seldom be satisfactorily converted by a mere switch of pronouns. The phenomenon applies, though less directly, to all John's narratives of miracles—the water to wine, the healings, the raising of Lazarus—the trial and crucifixion, the race to the empty tomb, and the other two resurrection accounts that involve the disciples. Hovering just at the edge of each event, or caught in its center, is the powerful sense of a pair of human eyes, so fixed in a lover's rapt attention as to vanish nearly from our reading minds and leave us face-to-face with the act itself and the moving bodies.

Is it all "true" then—a prosaic report, screened no doubt through long decades of thought and teaching but an earnest try at the visible, audible facts of a life lived in an actual place and time? Was John the Beloved a young man possessed of photographic memory with an added genius for verbal recall? Even in a few hurried years of following Jesus on his restless swings through Palestine, was the young John making the kinds of careful notes that recent findings of scrolls and papyri have proved were possible, not only in settled communities but among endangered fugitives? On the face of the book before us, neither chance is unlikely. If John's raw notes—his travel diary, say—were to be discovered tomorrow in a desert cave and we knew thereby that he appeared to document his life at the heels of Jesus, then what would be changed?

To look at only one change of many—at once the inadequacies of other gospels would glare in a new light. None of the other three make specific claims to be an eyewitness account. But if our John is really the Beloved Disciple, then we would not only need to adjust the narrative itinerary and chronology of Mark, Matthew, and Luke (Papias, after all, recorded in about AD 130 that Mark set down Peter's memories, "though not in order"). To the other gospel writers' accounts of Jesus' ethical teaching, we would have to add John's theophanic shockers—the man's equations of himself to God, the elaborate metaphors of himself as food. And John's account of the resurrection would, more than ever, complicate our response to an unimaginable action that John insists we take as *event*, not symbol—hard, palpable, edible event that aims at every human heart, "whoever trusts."

Beyond such practical adjustments in our view of the remainder of the New Testament, each reader would then
make whatever private changes seemed apt, urgent, or neither. At the least, those responses would range from an unquestioning conversion to trust in Jesus' claims all the way to
a repelled dismissal of the mad outrage or massive fraud of
his pretension. As I have noted, a number of sober students
have lately moved in an older direction, hearing and seeing
the steady presence of John bar Zebedee, the Beloved, behind the full length of the charged few pages—a voice at
least that means "to stay," as Jesus granted, till he comes
again. Once you have moved that far, of course, your questions and choices have only begun.

Still, with every large-scale manuscript discovery of the
past century, we come closer to understanding that, once we
concede the nearly intolerable premise of John's theology,
nothing in his book is past the scope of a watchful sensible
man of his time and place—certainly nothing past the mental or narrative reach of a man who stood, to the end of his
long life, as the single pupil who could be called Beloved in a
group of twelve. With the availability of uncluttered new
translations, attentive to the rapt storytelling of the Greek, we
can meet John's knowledge face to face. Bizarre as it is in so
many parts, his gospel speaks—in the clearest voice we
have—that sentence all humankind craves from stories: *The
Maker of all things loves and wants me.* In no other book our
culture possesses can we see a clearer graph of that need, that
tall enormous radiant arc—fragile creatures made by the Father's hand, hurled into space, then caught at last by a man
in some ways like ourselves, though the ark of God.

THE GOOD NEWS
ACCORDING TO JOHN

ACCORDING TO JOHN

At the start was the Word. The Word was with God and God was the Word—he was at the start with God. Everything came to be through him and apart from him nothing that has come came to be. In him was life. The life was the light of humankind. The light shines in the dark and the dark didn't quench it.

Came a man sent from God, John by name. He came as a witness so he might witness about the light so all might trust through him—he wasn't that light but so he might witness to that light. The true light that lights everyone was coming into the world.

He was in the world—the world came to be through him—but the world didn't know him. He came to his own and his own didn't take him. Still as many as took him he gave them the right to be children of God—those trusting in his name, those born not of blood nor will of the flesh nor man's will but born of God. So the Word became flesh and tented among us. We watched his glory, glory like that of a father's one son full of grace and truth.

John witnessed to him and cried out "This is he of whom I said 'The one coming after me has come before me since he preceded me.' "

(From his fullness we all took grace on grace. The law was given through Moses; grace and truth came through Jesus Messiah. No one has ever seen God yet an only Son God—the one in the Father's bosom—he explained him.)

This was John's witness when the Jews sent priests and Levites from Jerusalem to ask him "Who are you?"

He confessed and didn't deny it but confessed "I'm not Messiah."

They asked him "What then—are you Elijah?"

He said "I'm not."

"Are you the prophet?"

He answered "No."

They said to him "Who are you?—so we may give an answer to those who sent us. What do you say about yourself?"

He said "I am

> A *voice crying in the wilderness*
> *'Straighten the Lord's way!'*

as Isaiah the prophet said."

Those sent were from the Pharisees. They asked him "Why baptize then if you're not Messiah nor Elijah nor the prophet?"

John answered them "I baptize in water. Among you stands one whom you don't recognize, the one coming after me whose sandal strap I'm unworthy to loosen." These things happened in Bethany across the Jordan where John was baptizing.

The next day he saw Jesus coming toward him and said "Look, the lamb of God who cancels the wrongs of the world. This is he of whom I said 'After me comes a man who comes before me since he preceded me and I didn't recognize him.' But so he might be shown to Israel I came baptizing in water." And John witnessed "I saw the Spirit descending like a dove out of Heaven and it stayed on him. I didn't recognize him but the one who sent me to baptize in water said to me 'On whomever you see the Spirit descending and staying he's the one who baptizes in Holy Spirit.' I've seen and witnessed that this is the Son of God."

The next day again John was standing there and two of his disciples. Seeing Jesus walking he said "Look, the lamb of God."

The two disciples heard him speaking and they followed Jesus.

Turning and seeing them following Jesus said to them "What are you after?"

They said *"Rabbi"* which translated means *Teacher* "where are you staying?"

He said to them "Come and see."

So they went and saw where he was staying and stayed with him that day. It was about four in the afternoon.

It was Andrew the brother of Simon Peter one of the two hearing John and following him. First he found his own brother Simon and said to him "We've found Messiah" which means *Anointed*. He led him to Jesus.

Looking at him Jesus said "You're Simon son of John. You'll be called Cephas" which is translated *Peter* or *Rock*.

The next day he wanted to go to Galilee so he found Philip and Jesus said to him "Follow me."

Now Philip was from Bethsaida, Andrew and Peter's town. Philip found Nathanael and said to him "The one Moses wrote about in the law—and also the prophets—we've found him, Jesus son of Joseph from Nazareth."

Nathanael said to him "Can anything good be from Nazareth?"

Philip said to him "Come and see."

Jesus saw Nathanael coming toward him and said of him "Look, a true Israelite in whom there's no guile."

Nathanael said to him "From where do you know me?"

Jesus answered "Before Philip called you I saw you under the fig tree."

Nathanael answered "Rabbi, you're the Son of God. You're king of Israel."

Jesus said to him "Since I told you I saw you under the fig tree you trust? You'll see greater things." And he said to him "Amen amen I tell you you'll see Heaven opened and the angels of God rising and falling on the Son of Man."

On the third day there was a wedding in Cana in Galilee and Jesus' mother was there. Jesus and his disciples had been invited to the wedding too and when wine ran short Jesus' mother said to him "They're out of wine."

Jesus said to her "What's that to me and you, woman? My hour hasn't come."

His mother said to the servants "Just do what he tells you."

Now six stone jars for the Jews' washing custom were standing there. Each could hold twenty or thirty gallons.

Jesus said to them "Fill the jars with water."

They filled them to the top.

He said to them "Now draw some and take it to the head servant."

They took it.

When the head servant tasted the water turned to wine, not knowing where it came from—though the servants knew, the ones who'd drawn the water—the head servant called the bridegroom and said to him "Everybody brings out the good wine first and once the guests are drunk brings out the poor stuff. You've kept the good wine till now."

Jesus did this the start of his signs in Cana in Galilee and showed his glory.

His disciples trusted in him.

After this he, his mother, his brothers and his disciples went down to Capernaum and stayed not many days.

The Passover of the Jews was near and Jesus went up to Jerusalem. In the Temple he found people selling oxen, sheep and doves and the money changers sitting there. Making a whip from cords he drove them all out of the Temple all the sheep and oxen. He scattered the money changers' coins and upset their tables and to the dove sellers he said "Get all this out of here. Stop making my Father's house a market."

His disciples recalled that it was written of him *'Zeal for your house will consume me.'*

The Jews said to him "What sign can you show us for doing such things?"

Jesus answered "Destroy this temple and in three days I'll raise it."

The Jews said then "This Temple was built over forty-six years and in three days you'll raise it?"

But he was speaking of the temple of his body.

So when he was raised from the dead his disciples recalled him saying this and they trusted the scripture and the word which Jesus said.

When he was in Jerusalem during Passover at the feast many seeing the signs he did trusted in his name.

But Jesus wouldn't trust himself to them since he understood people and needed no one to witness to people since he understood what was in people.

Now there was a man from the Pharisees named Nicodemus a leader of the Jews. He came to him at night and said to him "Rabbi, we know that you've come from God a teacher since no one could do these signs you do unless God is with you."

Jesus answered "Amen amen I tell you unless a person is born from above he can't see the reign of God."

Nicodemus said "How can a man be born being old? He can't enter his mother's womb a second time to be born."

Jesus answered "Amen amen I tell you unless a person is born from water and Spirit he can't enter the reign of God. What's born from flesh is flesh. What's born of the Spirit is spirit. Don't wonder that I told you it's necessary to be born again. The wind blows where it wants and you hear its sound but don't know where it comes from and where it goes—the same with everyone born from the Spirit."

Nicodemus answered "How can such things happen?"

Jesus answered "You're the teacher of Israel and you don't know these things? Amen amen I tell you what we know we tell and what we've seen we witness to. You don't accept our witness. If I tell you earthly things and you don't trust, how will you trust if I tell you heavenly things? No one has risen to Heaven except the one who came down the Son of Man. And as Moses raised the snake in the desert so must the Son of Man be raised so all who trust in him may have eternal life. For God loved the world so much that he gave his only Son so all who trusted in him might not be lost but have eternal life.

"God didn't send the Son into the world to judge the world but so the world might be saved through him. A person who trusts in him isn't judged but the one not trusting is judged already since he didn't trust in the name of the only Son of God. And this is the judgment that the light has come to the world and people loved the dark instead of the light since their deeds were evil. For everyone doing wrong hates the light and won't come to the light so his deeds won't be exposed. But the one doing the truth comes toward the light so his deeds are shown as done through God."

After this Jesus and his disciples went into the Judean countryside. He stayed there with them and baptized.

John was also baptizing in Aenon near Salim since there was plentiful water there and people kept coming and were baptized—John hadn't yet been thrown into prison.

Now there was a dispute between John's disciples and a Jew about purification. They came to John and said to him "Rabbi, the one who was with you across Jordan to whom you witnessed—look, he's baptizing and everyone's coming to him."

John said "No one can get anything if it hasn't been given him from Heaven. You yourselves witness that I said 'I'm not Messiah but have been sent ahead of him.' The one with the bride is the bridegroom but the friend of the bridegroom the one standing there hearing him rejoices joyfully in the bridegroom's voice. So this joy of mine has been fulfilled. He must increase but I must decrease."

(The one coming from above is over all. The one from the Earth is of the Earth and speaks of the Earth. The one coming from Heaven is over all. What he has seen and heard he witnesses to and no one takes his witness. Who takes his witness attests that God is true since he whom God sent speaks God's words for he gives the Spirit without measure. The Father loves the Son and has given all into his hand. Who trusts in the Son has eternal life but the one who disobeys the Son won't see life—the wrath of God stays on him.)

So when the Lord knew that the Pharisees had heard how Jesus made and baptized more disciples than John—though Jesus himself didn't baptize but his disciples did—he left Judea and went off again into Galilee. But he had to pass through Samaria so he came to a Samaritan town called Sychar near the plot of land that Jacob gave Joseph his son. Now Jacob's well was there so Jesus tired from the trip just sat down by the well—it was near noon.

A Samaritan woman came to draw water.

Jesus said to her "Give me a drink"—his disciples had gone off to the town to buy food.

So the Samaritan woman said "How can you a Jew ask a Samaritan woman for a drink?" (Jews won't use the same dishes as Samaritans.)

Jesus answered "If you knew of God's gift and who's saying to you 'Give me a drink' you'd have asked him and he'd have given you living water."

She said "Sir, you've got no bucket and the well's deep—where do you get living water? You can't be greater than our father Jacob who gave us the well and drank from it himself with his sons and his flocks."

Jesus answered "Everyone drinking this water will be thirsty again but whoever drinks the water I give them will never be thirsty again. The water I give him will be a spring gushing into eternal life."

The woman said "Sir, give me this water so I won't be thirsty nor come here to draw water."

He said to her "Go call your husband and come back here."

The woman answered "I've got no husband."

Jesus said to her "Well said 'I've got no husband' since you've had five husbands and the one you've got now isn't your husband. You spoke truly."

The woman said "Sir, I see that you're a prophet. Our fathers worshiped God on this mountain but you say that Jerusalem's the place where we must worship."

Jesus said "Trust me, woman, that an hour's coming when neither on this mountain nor in Jerusalem will you worship the Father. You worship what you don't know; we worship what we know since salvation is from the Jews. But an hour's coming—and now is—when true worshipers will worship the Father in spirit and truth for the Father really seeks such people to worship him. God is spirit and those worshiping him must worship in spirit and truth."

The woman said to him "I know that Messiah is coming, the one called Anointed. When he comes he'll lay out everything to us."

Jesus said to her "I'm he, the one speaking to you."

At this his disciples came and were amazed that he was talking with a woman but no one said "What are you hunting or why are you talking with her?"

So the woman left her water jar and went back into the town and said to the people "Come see a man who told me everything I ever did. Can he be Messiah?"

They went out of the town and came toward him.

Meanwhile the disciples were saying "Rabbi, eat."

But he said to them "I have food to eat that you don't know of."

So the disciples were saying to each other "Surely no one brought him anything to eat."

Jesus said to them "My food is to do the will of who sent me and to finish his work. Don't you say 'Four more months and the harvest comes'? Look, I tell you raise your eyes and see the fields since they're white for harvest. Already the reaper's taking his pay and gathering fruit for eternal life so the sower and reaper may be glad together for here the saying is true 'One sows, another reaps.' I sent you to reap what you never worked on. Others worked and you've entered their work."

From that town many Samaritans trusted in him because of the word of the woman witnessing "He told me everything I've done." So when they approached him the Samaritans asked him to stay with them.

He stayed there two days.

Many more trusted because of his word and they said to the woman "It's no longer because of your talk that we trust since we've heard for ourselves and know that this is truly the savior of the world."

After two days he went from there on to Galilee for Jesus himself had witnessed that a prophet gets no honor in his own country. But when he got to Galilee the Galileans welcomed him having seen all he did in Jerusalem at the feast— they'd gone to the feast too.

So he came again to Cana in Galilee where he'd made the water wine and there was this royal officer whose son was sick in Capernaum. The man hearing that Jesus had come from Judea to Galilee went to him and asked that he come down and heal his son for he was about to die.

Jesus said to him "Unless you see signs and magic you won't trust me."

The royal officer said "Sir, come down before my boy dies."

Jesus said "Go. Your son's alive."

The man trusted the word Jesus told him and left.

And on the way down his slaves met him saying that his son was alive.

So he asked them the time when he'd improved.

They told him "Yesterday at one in the afternoon the fever left him."

So the father knew that it was the same time when Jesus told him "Your son's alive" and he himself trusted and all his household.

Here again Jesus worked a second sign after coming from Judea to Galilee.

After this there was a feast of the Jews and Jesus went up to Jerusalem. Now in Jerusalem by the Sheep Gate there's a pool the one called in Hebrew *Bethzatha* with five porches. On these were lying a crowd of the sick—blind, lame, withered—and there was one man there who'd been sick thirty-eight years.

When Jesus saw him lying, knowing how long he'd been there he said to him "Do you want to get well?"

The sick man answered "Sir, I don't have a man when the water's troubled to put me into the pool. While I'm going in somebody goes down ahead of me."

Jesus said to him "Stand. Take your pallet and walk."

At once the man got well. He took his pallet and was walking around.

It was a Sabbath that day so the Jews were saying to the healed man "It's the Sabbath and it's not lawful for you to carry your pallet."

But he answered them "The one that made me well told me 'Take your pallet and walk.' "

They asked him "Who is the man who told you 'Take it and walk'?"

But the healed man didn't know who it was for Jesus had vanished—there was a mob in the place.

After this Jesus found him in the Temple and said to him "Look, you're well. Stop going wrong or something worse may happen to you."

The man went off and told the Jews that Jesus was the one who'd made him well.

So the Jews started bearing down on Jesus since he was doing such things on the Sabbath.

But he answered them "My Father is even now working and I'm working."

Because of this then all the more the Jews were trying to kill him since he was not just breaking the Sabbath but also calling God his own Father and making himself equal to God.

Jesus said to them "Amen amen I tell you the Son can't do anything himself except what he sees the Father doing since what he does the Son does likewise. For the Father loves the Son and shows him all he does and will show him deeds greater than these so you may marvel. Just as the Father raises the dead and revives them so too the Son revives whom he wants. The Father judges no one but has given all judgment to the Son so all may honor the Son as they honor the Father. The one not honoring the Son doesn't honor the Father who sent him. Amen amen I tell you that the one hearing my word and trusting the one who sent me has eternal life and does not come to judgment but is passed from death into life.

"Amen amen I tell you the hour is coming—it's now—when the dead shall hear the voice of the Son of God and those hearing shall live. For as the Father has life in himself so he gave life also to the Son to have life in himself. He gave him the right to render judgment since he is the Son of Man. Don't wonder at this—an hour is coming when all those in the tombs will hear his voice and come out, the ones that did good to a resurrection of life, those that did evil to a resurrection of judgment. I do nothing from myself. As I hear I judge and my judgment is just since I don't seek my will but the will of the one who sent me.

"If I witness about myself my witness is not true. There's another who witnesses about me and I know that the witness he witnesses about me is true. You sent to John and he witnessed to the truth but I get no witness from humankind though I say these things so you may be saved. That man was a lamp burning and shining and you were willing for an hour to joy in his light. But I have a witness greater than John's for the deeds the Father has given me to finish. The deeds I do witness about me that the Father has sent me and the Father that sent me has witnessed about me. You've neither heard his voice nor seen his form and his word doesn't stay with you since you don't trust the one he sent. You search the scriptures because you think to have eternal life in them—they witness to me—but you won't come to me so you might have life.

"I get no glory from humankind but I know you that you lack the love of God in yourselves. I've come in the name of my Father and you don't take me. If another comes in his own name you'll take that one. How can you trust, taking glory from one another and not seeking the glory that comes from the only God? Don't think I'll accuse you to the Father. There is one accusing you—Moses in whom you hope. If you trusted Moses you'd have trusted me for he wrote about me. But if you don't trust his writings how will you trust my words?"

After this Jesus went off across the sea of Galilee or of Tiberias.

And a big crowd followed him because they saw the signs that he did on the sick.

Jesus went up to the mountain and sat there with his disciples. Passover was near, the feast of the Jews. So Jesus raising his eyes and seeing a big crowd coming toward him said to Philip "Where can we buy bread so they may eat?" He said this testing him since he knew what he was set to do.

Philip answered him "Two hundred denars worth of loaves aren't enough for them for each to take a little."

One of the disciples said to him—Andrew, Simon Peter's brother—"There's a boy here who has five barley loaves and two fish but what are those among so many?"

Jesus said "Make the people lie back"—now there was a lot of grass in the place.

So the people lay back some five thousand in number.

Jesus took the loaves then and giving thanks passed them out to those lying back, also the fish as much as they wanted. Then when they were full he told his disciples "Pick up the leftover pieces so nothing is lost."

They picked them up and filled twelve baskets with pieces of the five barley loaves which were left over by those who'd eaten.

So when the people had seen the sign he did they said "This is really the prophet who's coming into the world."

Jesus knowing that they were about to come and seize him to make him king went off again to the mountain by himself alone.

When evening came the disciples went down to the sea and pushing off in a boat went across the sea to Capernaum. Dark had now fallen and still Jesus hadn't come to them and since a strong wind was blowing the sea was rising. Rowing on about three or four miles they saw Jesus walking on the sea and nearing the boat and they were scared.

But he said to them "I am. Don't be scared."

So they wanted to take him into the boat and at once the boat was at the place where they were going.

Next day the crowd that stood on the far side of the sea saw there was no other boat there but the one the disciples had left in and that Jesus hadn't gone with the disciples in the boat but the disciples had left alone (though there came other boats from Tiberias close to the place where they'd eaten bread after the Lord gave thanks)—when the crowd saw that Jesus wasn't there or his disciples they pushed off and came to Capernaum hunting Jesus. Finding him on the other side of the sea they said to him "Rabbi, when did you get here?"

Jesus told them "Amen amen I tell you you don't hunt

me because you saw signs but because you ate the bread and were full. Don't work for the food that spoils but the food that lasts to eternal life which the Son of Man will give you since God the Father has sealed him."

They said to him "What can we do to do God's deeds?"

Jesus answered them "This is God's work to trust in the one he sent."

So they said to him "What sign can you do then so we can see and trust you? What can you perform? Our fathers ate manna in the desert. It's written *'He gave them bread from Heaven to eat.'*"

Jesus said to them "Amen amen I tell you it wasn't Moses who gave you bread from Heaven. My Father gives you the real bread from Heaven for God's bread comes down from Heaven and gives life to the world."

Then they said "Sir, always give us this bread."

Jesus said to them "I'm the bread of life. Who comes to me will never hunger and who trusts in me will no way thirst again ever. Yet I told you that you've seen me and still don't trust. All that the Father gives me will come to me and the one who comes to me I no way throw out since I've come down from Heaven not to do my will but the will of the one sending me. This is the will of the one sending me that all he's given me I shall not lose any of it but raise it again on the last day. For this is my Father's will that everyone seeing the Son and trusting in him may have eternal life and I will raise him on the last day."

The Jews muttered about him then because he said "I'm the bread come down from Heaven" and they said "Isn't this man Jesus, Joseph's son, whose father and mother we know? How's he now saying 'I've come down from Heaven'?"

Jesus answered them "Don't mutter among yourselves. No one can come to me unless the Father who sent me draws him; then I'll raise him on the last day. It's written in the prophets *'They'll all be taught by God.'*

"Everyone who hears from the Father and learns comes to me—not that anyone has seen the Father but the one who's from God he's seen the Father. Amen amen I tell you the one who trusts me has eternal life—I'm the bread of life. Your fathers ate manna in the desert and died. This is the bread coming down from Heaven so anyone may eat it and not die. I'm the living bread, the bread coming down from Heaven. If anyone eats this bread he'll live to eternity. And the bread I give is my flesh for the life of the world."

So the Jews quarreled among themselves "How can this man give us his flesh to eat?"

Jesus said to them "Amen amen I tell you unless you eat the flesh of the Son of Man and drink his blood you have no life in you. The one who eats my flesh and drinks my blood has eternal life and I will raise him on the last day for my flesh is real food and my blood is real drink. The one eating my flesh and drinking my blood lives in me and I in him. As the living Father sent me and I live because of the Father so the one eating me, that same one will live because of me. This is the bread which came down from Heaven not what your fathers ate and died. The one eating this bread will live to eternity." He said these things in the synagogue teaching in Capernaum.

Many of his disciples then hearing said "This is a hard saying. Who can hear it?"

But knowing in himself that the disciples were muttering about this Jesus said to them "This makes you stumble? What if you see the Son of Man rising to where he was before? The Spirit is the thing that quickens; the flesh gains nothing. The words I've said to you are spirit and life but there are some of you who still don't trust"—from the start Jesus knew the ones not trusting and the one who'd hand him over. And he said "So I told you that no one can come to me unless it was given to him by the Father."

From here on many of his disciples went back and no longer walked with him.

So Jesus said to the Twelve "Don't you too want to leave?"

Simon Peter answered "Lord, to whom shall we go? You have the words of eternal life. We've trusted and known that you're the holy one of God."

Jesus answered them "Haven't I chosen you Twelve and one of you is a devil?" He spoke of Judas son of Simon Iscariot for he was about to hand him over, one of the Twelve. After these things Jesus walked in Galilee for he didn't want to walk in Judea since the Jews were hunting to kill him.

Now the Jews' feast of Tabernacles was near and his brothers said to him "Leave here and go to Judea so your disciples will see the deeds that you do. No one does anything in secret and wants to be public. If you're doing these things show yourself to the world." His brothers didn't trust him.

So Jesus said to them "My time isn't yet come but your time is always ready. The world can't hate you but it hates me because I witness about it that its deeds are evil. You go up to the feast. I'm not going up to this feast because my time isn't yet ripe." Saying these things to them he stayed in Galilee. But when his brothers went up to the feast then he went up too not openly but as if concealed.

So the Jews hunted him at the feast and said "Where is that man?" and there was much muttering about him in the crowds. Some said "He's a good man" but others said "No he deceives the crowd." Nobody though spoke openly about him for fear of the Jews.

But in the middle of the feast Jesus went up to the Temple and taught.

The Jews wondered saying "How does this man know his letters never having studied?"

Jesus answered them "My teaching isn't mine but from the one that sent me. If anybody wants to do his will he will know about the teaching whether it's from God or I speak from myself. Anyone speaking from himself seeks his own glory but the one hunting the glory of whomever sent him, this man is true and there's no injustice in him. Didn't Moses give you the law yet none of you keeps the law? Why do you try to kill me?"

The crowd answered "You've got a demon. Who's trying to kill you?"

Jesus answered them "I did one deed and you're all astonished at it. Moses gave you circumcision—not that it's from Moses but the fathers—and on a Sabbath you circumcise a man. If a man gets circumcised on a Sabbath and the law of Moses isn't broken why are you angry with me because I made a whole man well on the Sabbath? Don't judge by appearances but judge right judgment."

Some from Jerusalem said "Isn't this the man they're hunting to kill? Look, he's talking openly and they say nothing to him. Maybe the leaders know that this is Messiah. But we know where this man is from. When Messiah comes no one will know where he's from."

So Jesus cried out in the Temple teaching "You know me and also know where I'm from. I haven't come from myself but the one who sent me is true. You don't know him. I know him because I'm from him and he sent me."

They tried to seize him and no one laid a hand on him because his hour hadn't yet come.

But many of the crowd trusted in him and said "When Messiah comes will he do more signs than this man did?"

The Pharisees heard the crowd muttering these things about him and the chief priests and the Pharisees sent guards to arrest him.

Jesus said "Just a short time I'm with you and I go to the one who sent me. You'll hunt me and find nothing and where I am you can't come."

So the Jews said to themselves "Where's this man about to go that we won't find him? He's not about to go to the Greek dispersion and teach the Greeks. What's this word he said 'You'll hunt me and find nothing and where I am you can't come'?"

Now on the last day the great day of the feast Jesus stood and cried out "If anyone thirsts let him come to me and drink. The one trusting in me as the scripture says *'Rivers of living water will flow from his belly.'* " He said this about the Spirit whom the ones trusting in him were about to receive for there was no Spirit yet since Jesus was not yet glorified.

Some of the crowd hearing these words said "This man's really the prophet." Others said "This man's Messiah" but others said "Surely Messiah's not coming from Galilee? Doesn't the scripture say that Messiah's coming from the seed of David and from Bethlehem, David's town?" So a split grew in the crowd because of him and some of them wanted to arrest him but no one laid hands on him.

Then the guards came back to the chief priests and Pharisees.

And they said "Why didn't you bring him?"

The guards answered "No man ever spoke as this man speaks."

So the Pharisees answered them "Haven't you too been deceived? Did anyone from the leaders or the Pharisees trust in him? This crowd who don't know the law are cursed."

Nicodemus said to them—the one who came to him first being one of them—"Does our law judge the man unless it hears from him first and knows what he's doing?"

They answered him "Are you from Galilee too? Search and see—no prophet is raised from Galilee."

Jesus said to them again "I'm the light of the world. The one following me will no way walk in darkness but will have the light of life."

The Pharisees said to him then "You witness to yourself. Your witness isn't true."

Jesus answered them "Even if I witness to myself my witness is true because I know where I came from and where I'm going but you don't know where I come from or where I'm going. You judge by the flesh; I judge no one. Even if I do judge my judgment is true because I'm not alone but am with the one who sent me. It's written even in your law that the witness of two men is true. I'm the one witnessing to myself and the Father that sent me witnesses."

They said to him "Where's your father?"

Jesus answered "You don't know me or my Father. If you knew me you'd also know my Father." He said these words in the Treasury teaching in the Temple and no one seized him since his hour hadn't yet come.

So he said to them again "I'll go off and you'll hunt me and die in your wrong—where I go you can't come."

The Jews said "Surely he won't kill himself yet he's saying 'Where I go you can't come'?"

He said "You're from below. I'm from above. You're from this world. I'm not from this world. So I said to you that you'll die in your wrongs. If you don't trust that I am you'll die in your wrongs."

Then they said "Who are you?"

Jesus said to them "Why should I even speak to you? I've got much to say about you and to judge but the one who sent me is true and what I heard from him I speak in the world."

They didn't know that he spoke to them of the Father.

So Jesus said "When you lift up the Son of Man then you'll know that I am and from myself I do nothing but speak only the things the Father taught me. The one who sent me is with me. He hasn't left me alone since I always do what's pleasing to him."

When he said these things many trusted in him.

So Jesus said to the Jews that trusted him "If you keep on in my word you're really my disciples. You'll know the truth and the truth will free you."

They answered him "We're the seed of Abraham and

have never been slaves to anyone. How can you say 'You'll be set free'?"

Jesus answered "Amen amen I tell you that everyone doing wrong is the slave of wrong. But the slave can't stay in the house forever; the Son stays forever. So if the Son frees you then you'll really be free. I know you're the seed of Abraham but you're trying to kill me because my word finds no place in you. What I've seen with the Father I tell; now do what you've heard from the Father."

They answered him "Our father is Abraham."

Jesus said to them "If you're children of Abraham you'd do his deeds. But now you're trying to kill me, a man who's told you the truth which I heard from God. Abraham never did this. You're doing the deeds of your father."

They said to him "We weren't born of fornication. We have one father—God."

Jesus said to them "If God was your father you'd have loved me since I came out from God and am here. I haven't come from myself; he sent me. Why don't you recognize my voice? It's because you can't hear my word. You're from your father the Devil and long to do your father's wishes. He was a killer from the start and he never stood in the truth since the truth isn't in him. When he tells a lie he speaks from himself because he's a liar and the father of lies. But I, since I tell the truth you don't trust me. Who among you blames me for wrong? If I'm telling the truth why don't you trust me? The one from God hears God's word but you're not hearing since you're not from God."

The Jews answered him "Aren't we right to say that you're a Samaritan and have a demon?"

Jesus answered "I don't have a demon but I honor my Father and you dishonor me. I don't seek my own glory—there is one who seeks and judges. Amen amen I tell you if anyone keeps my word he'll no way see death through eternity."

The Jews said to him "Now we know you have a demon.

Abraham died and the prophets and you're saying 'If anyone keeps my word he'll no way taste death through eternity'? Are you greater than our father Abraham who died—and the prophets died? Who are you making yourself?"

Jesus answered "If I glorify myself my glory is nothing. My Father is the one glorifying me, the one you say is your God though you haven't known him. I know him. If I say that I don't know him I'll be a liar like you but I do know him and I keep his word. Abraham your father was glad to see my day. He saw it and exulted."

So the Jews said "You're not yet fifty and you've seen Abraham?"

Jesus said to them "Amen amen I tell you before Abraham was I am."

They took up stones then to throw at him but Jesus was hid and went out of the Temple.

Going on he saw a man blind from birth.

His disciples asked him "Rabbi, who went wrong—this man or his parents that he was born blind?"

Jesus answered "Neither this man went wrong nor his parents but so the deeds of God might be shown in him. We must do the deeds of the one who sent me while it's day; the night's coming when no one can work. While I'm in the world I'm the light of the world." That said he spat on the ground and made clay out of the spit, put the clay on his eyes and said to him "Go wash in the pool of Siloam" which is translated *Sent*.

So he left, washed and came back seeing.

Then his neighbors and those that saw him before as a beggar said "Isn't this the man that sat and begged?" Some said "This is he." Others said "No but he's like him."

The man said "I'm he."

So they said to him "How were your eyes opened?"

He answered "The man named Jesus made clay, anointed my eyes and told me 'Go to Siloam and wash' so going and washing I saw."

They said to him "Where is he?"

He said "I don't know."

They led him to the Pharisees the once blind man. Now it was Sabbath on the day when Jesus made clay and opened his eyes. So again the Pharisees asked him how he saw.

He said to them "He put clay on my eyes. I washed and I see."

Some of the Pharisees said "This man's not from God since he doesn't keep the Sabbath." But others said "How can a wrongful man do such signs?" and there was a split among them. So they said to the blind man again "What do you say about him now since he opened your eyes?"

He said "He's a prophet."

But the Jews didn't trust him that he was blind and saw till they called the parents of the one that had seen and asked them "Is this your son whom you say was born blind? How is he seeing now?"

His parents answered "We know that this is our son and that he was born blind but how he's seeing now we don't know or who opened his eyes we don't know. Ask him—he's of age; he'll speak for himself." His parents said that because they feared the Jews for the Jews had already agreed that if anyone should declare him Messiah he would be put out of the synagogue so his parents said "He's of age; ask him."

So they called the man a second time who was blind and said to him "Give glory to God. We know that this man's a wrongdoer."

The man answered "If he's a wrongdoer I don't know it. One thing I know that being blind now I see."

They said to him then "What did he do to you? How did he open your eyes?"

He answered them "I told you already and you didn't hear. Why do you want to hear again? You want to become his disciples too?"

They insulted him and said "You're a disciple of that

man but we're disciples of Moses. We know that God spoke to Moses but this man—we don't know where he's from."

The man answered them "The wonderful thing is this then that you don't know where he's from yet he opened my eyes. We know that God doesn't hear wrongdoers but if anyone is God-fearing and does his will he hears that person. From eternity it was never heard of that anybody opened the eyes of a man born blind. If this man weren't from God he couldn't do anything."

They answered him "You were born wholly in wrong and you're teaching us?" and they threw him out.

Jesus heard that they'd thrown him out and finding him said "Do you trust in the Son of Man?"

He answered "Who is he, sir, so I may trust in him?"

Jesus said to him "You've seen him and the one speaking to you is he."

He said "I trust, sir" and bowed down to him.

Jesus said "For judgment I came into this world so the ones not seeing may see and the ones seeing may go blind."

Some of the Pharisees who were with him heard this and said to him "Are we blind too?"

Jesus said to them "If you were blind you'd have done no wrong but since you say 'We see' your wrong remains. Amen amen I tell you the one not entering through the door into the sheepfold but climbing in another way that one's a thief and a robber. But the one entering through the door is the shepherd of the sheep. To him the doorkeeper opens, the sheep hear his voice, he calls his own sheep by name and leads them out. When he lets out all his own sheep he goes in front of them and the sheep follow him since they know his voice. No way will they follow a stranger but will run from him since they don't know the stranger's voice."

Jesus told them this metaphor but they knew nothing about what he was saying to them.

So Jesus said again "Amen amen I tell you that I'm the

door for the sheep. Those who came before me are thieves and robbers but the sheep didn't hear them. I'm the door. If anyone enters through me he'll be saved and will go in and out and find pasture. The thief comes only to steal, kill and ruin. I came so they might have life and have it richly. I'm the good shepherd. The good shepherd lays down his life for the sheep. The hired man who isn't a shepherd and doesn't own the sheep sees the wolf coming, leaves the sheep and runs. The wolf seizes and scatters them because he's a hired man and cares nothing for the sheep.

"I'm the good shepherd and I know mine and mine know me as the Father knows me and I know the Father. I lay down my life for the sheep. And I have other sheep which aren't from this fold. I must bring them too. They'll hear my voice and there'll be one flock, one shepherd. So the Father loves me because I lay down my life to take it up again. No one took it from me but I laid it down by myself. I have the right to lay it down and the right to take it up again. I got this command from my Father."

Again there was a split among the Jews because of these words. Many of them said "He has a demon and is raving. Why hear him?" Others said "These aren't the words of a demoniac. Can a demon open the eyes of the blind?"

Then there was the feast of Dedication in Jerusalem. It was winter and Jesus walked in the Temple in Solomon's porch.

So the Jews surrounded him and said to him "How long will you hold our soul suspended? If you're Messiah tell us plainly."

Jesus answered them "I told you and you don't trust me. The deeds I do in my Father's name witness to me. But you don't trust because you're not my sheep. My sheep hear my voice, I know them, they follow me and I give them eternal life. No way will they be lost for eternity and no one shall seize them out of my hand. My Father who gave them to me is greater than all and no one can seize them out of the Father's hand. I and the Father are one."

The Jews took up stones again to stone him.

Jesus answered them "I showed you many good deeds from the Father. For which of the deeds do you stone me?"

The Jews answered him "We don't stone you for good deeds but for blasphemy and because you're a man who's making yourself God."

Jesus answered them "Isn't it written in your law '*I said you are gods*'? If he called them gods to whom he'd sent his word—and scripture can't be revoked—then to him whom the Father consecrated and sent into the world you're saying 'You blaspheme' because I said 'I'm the Son of God.' If I'm not doing my Father's deeds don't trust me but if I do, even if you don't trust me, trust the deeds so you know and go on knowing that the Father's in me and I in the Father."

They tried again to seize him.

But he got out of their hands, went away again across the Jordan to the place where John first baptized and he stayed there.

Many came to him and said "John actually did no sign but however many things John said about this man were true" and many trusted in him there.

Now a certain man was sick, Lazarus from Bethany from Mary's village and Martha's her sister. Mary was the one who anointed the Lord with ointment wiping off his feet with her hair whose brother Lazarus was sick. So the sisters sent to him saying "Lord, look, the one you love is sick."

Hearing Jesus said "This sickness is not to death but for God's glory so the Son of God may be glorified through it." Now Jesus loved Martha, her sister and Lazarus. When he heard then that he was sick he stayed in the place where he was two days. After that he said to the disciples "Let's go to Judea again."

The disciples said to him "Rabbi, just now the Jews were trying to stone you and again you're going there?"

Jesus answered "Aren't there twelve hours to the day? If someone walks in the day he doesn't stumble because he sees the light of this world but if someone walks at night he stumbles because there's no light in him." He said these things and after that he said to them "Lazarus our friend has gone to sleep but I'm going to wake him."

The disciples said to him "Lord, if he's gone to sleep he'll be cured."

Now Jesus had spoken about his death but they thought that he'd spoken of restful sleep.

So Jesus told them plainly "Lazarus died and I'm glad for you that I was not there so you may trust but let's go to him."

Thomas who was called the Twin said to his fellow disciples "Let's go too so we may die with him."

Coming then Jesus found him already four days in the tomb. Now Bethany was near Jerusalem about two miles away and many of the Jews had come to Martha and Mary so they might console them about their brother.

So when Martha heard that Jesus was coming she met him but Mary sat in the house.

Martha said to Jesus "Lord, if you'd been here my brother wouldn't have died. Yet I still know that whatever you ask God, God gives you."

Jesus said to her "Your brother will rise again."

Martha said to him "I know he'll rise again in the resurrection on the last day."

Jesus said to her "I'm the resurrection and the life. Who trusts in me even if he should die will live and everyone living and trusting in me shall no way die through eternity. Do you trust this?"

She said to him "Yes, Lord. I trust that you're Messiah the Son of God that's coming into the world." Saying this she went off and called her sister Mary secretly saying "The teacher's here and asks for you."

When she heard she got up quickly and came to him.

Now Jesus hadn't yet come into the town but was still at the place where Martha met him.

So the Jews who'd been with her in the house consoling her, seeing that Mary rose up quickly and went out, followed her thinking "She's going to the tomb to weep there."

Mary came to where Jesus was and seeing him fell at his feet saying to him "Lord, if you'd been here my brother wouldn't have died."

When Jesus saw her weeping and the Jews weeping around her he groaned in spirit, harrowed himself and said "Where have you put him?"

They said "Lord, come and see."

Jesus wept.

So the Jews said "Look how he loved him." But some of them said "Couldn't this man who opened the eyes of the blind man have kept this man from dying?"

Jesus again groaning in himself came to the tomb.

It was a cave and a stone was lying on it.

Jesus said "Lift the stone."

The sister of the one who'd died Martha said "Lord, by now he stinks; it's the fourth day."

Jesus said to her "Didn't I tell you that if you trust me you'll see God's glory?"

So they lifted the stone.

Jesus lifted his eyes up and said "Father, I thank you that you heard me. I knew that you always hear me but because of the crowd standing round I spoke so they may trust that you sent me." Saying these things in a loud voice he cried, "Lazarus, come out."

The one who'd died came out bound feet and hands with wrappings and his face bound round with a napkin.

Jesus said to them "Loose him and let him go."

So many of the Jews who'd come to Mary seeing what he did trusted in him but some of them went off to the Pharisees and told them the things Jesus had done.

The chief priests and Pharisees gathered a council and said to them "What do we do since this man's doing many signs? If we leave him like this everyone will trust in him and the Romans will come and take our place and our nation."

But one of them Caiaphas the High Priest that year said to them "You know nothing and haven't reckoned that it's better for us that one man die for the people and all the nation not be lost." He said this not from himself but being High Priest that year he prophesied that Jesus was about to die for the nation and not only for the nation but so he might gather the scattered children of God into one. From that day on then they made plans to kill him.

So Jesus no longer openly walked among the Jews but went off from there to the country near the desert to a town called Ephraim and stayed there with the disciples.

Now the Passover of the Jews was near and many went up to Jerusalem out of the country before Passover so they might cleanse themselves. They hunted Jesus and said to one another standing in the Temple "How does it seem to you — that he's no way coming to the feast?"

The chief priests and Pharisees had given orders that if anyone knew where he was he should tell so they could arrest him.

Six days before Passover then Jesus came to Bethany where Lazarus was whom Jesus raised from the dead.

They made a dinner for him there and Martha served — Lazarus was one of those lying back with him. So Mary took a pound of expensive pure nard ointment and anointed Jesus' feet and with her hair wiped his feet off. The house was filled with the fragrance of the ointment.

Judas Iscariot one of his disciples the one about to betray him said "Why wasn't this ointment sold for three hundred denars and given to the poor?" He said this not because the poor mattered to him but because he was a thief and carried the cash bag and lifted what was put into it.

Jesus said "Leave her be so she may keep it for the day of my burial. The poor you'll always have with you but you won't always have me."

So the big crowd of Jews knew that he was there and they came not just because of Jesus only but so they could see Lazarus whom he'd raised from the dead.

But the chief priests made plans to kill Lazarus too since because of him many of the Jews went off and trusted in Jesus.

Next day the big crowd that came to the feast, hearing that Jesus was coming to Jerusalem, took branches from palm trees, went out to meet him and cried

"Hosanna!
*Blessed is the one coming in the name of the Lord,
the king of Israel.*"

Finding a young ass Jesus sat on it as it was written

*Fear not, daughter of Zion.
Look, your king comes
Sitting on an ass's foal.*

His disciples didn't understand these things at first but when Jesus was glorified then they recalled that these things had been written about him and that they'd done these things to him.

The crowd that had been with him when he called Lazarus from the tomb and raised him from the dead witnessed. So another crowd met him because they heard that he'd done this sign.

The Pharisees said among themselves "See, you're not gaining anything here. Look, the world's gone after him."

Now there were some Greeks going up to worship at the feast. They approached Philip the one from Bethsaida of Galilee and said "Sir, we want to see Jesus."

Philip came and told Andrew.

Andrew and Philip told Jesus.

And Jesus answered them "The hour has come when the

Son of Man is glorified. Amen amen I tell you unless the grain of wheat falling into the earth dies it stays single but if it dies it bears much fruit. The one loving his life loses it. The one hating his life in this world will keep it to eternal life. If anyone serves me let him follow and where I am there too my servant will be. If anyone serves me the Father will honor him. Now my soul is harrowed and what can I say 'Father, save me from this hour'? But I came for this hour. Father, glorify your name."

There came a voice from heaven "I have glorified it and will glorify it again."

The crowd standing and hearing said that it had thundered. Others said "An angel has spoken to him."

Jesus answered "Not for me did this voice come but because of you. Now is the judgment of this world; now the ruler of this world shall be thrown out and I if I'm lifted up from the Earth will draw everyone to me." He said this showing what kind of death he was going to die.

So the crowd answered him "We heard from the law that Messiah stays for eternity. How can you say that the Son of Man must be lifted up? Who is this Son of Man?"

Jesus said to them "Still a short time the light is among you. Walk while you have the light or darkness overtakes you and the one walking in darkness doesn't know where he's going. While you have the light trust the light so you may be children of light." Jesus said these things and going off was hid from them.

But having done so many signs before them they didn't trust in him so the word of Isaiah the prophet might be fulfilled which said

Lord, who trusted our report

And to whom was the arm of the Lord revealed?

So they couldn't trust since Isaiah said again

He has blinded their eyes

And hardened their heart

> *So they might not see through their eyes*
> > *And understand with the heart and turn*
> *And I would heal them.*

Isaiah said these things since he saw his glory and spoke of him. Still even among the leaders many trusted in him but because of the Pharisees they didn't admit it or they'd be put out of the synagogue for they loved men's glory more than God's glory.

Jesus cried out though and said "The one trusting in me doesn't trust in me but in the one who sent me. The one seeing me sees the one who sent me. I've come as a light into the world so everyone trusting in me may not stay in darkness. And if anyone hears my words and fails to keep them I don't judge him for I came not to judge the world but that I might save the world. The one refusing me and not accepting my words has one that judges him—the word which I spoke, that will judge him in the last day. For I didn't speak of myself but the Father who sent me gave me a command of what to say and what I may speak and I know that his command is eternal life. Whatever I speak then I speak as the Father told me to speak."

Now before the feast of Passover Jesus knowing that his hour had come when he should leave this world for the Father, loving his own in the world he loved them to the end. During supper since the Devil now had put into the heart of Judas son of Simon Iscariot that he should hand him over, Jesus—knowing that the Father had given all into his hands and that he came from God and was going to God—got up from supper, took off his clothes, took a towel and covered himself. Then he put water into a basin and started washing the disciples' feet and wiping them off with the towel he was wearing. So he came to Simon Peter.

Peter said to him "Lord, you're washing my feet?"

Jesus answered him "What I'm doing you don't know yet but you'll know after this."

Peter said to him "No way will you wash my feet not till eternity."

Jesus answered him "Unless I wash you you have no part in me."

Simon Peter said to him "Lord, not just my feet but also my hands and head."

Jesus said "The one that's bathed needs only to wash his feet and is wholly clean. You're clean but not all" for he knew the one handing him over so he said "You're not all clean." When he'd washed their feet then, put on his clothes and lain back again he said to them "Do you know what I've done to you? You call me teacher and lord and well you say it for I am. If then I your lord and teacher washed your feet you ought also to wash each other's feet. I've given you an example so as I did to you so you may do. Amen amen I tell you a slave is not greater than his lord nor one who's sent greater than the one sending him. If you know these things then you're blessed if you do them. I'm not speaking of all of you. I know whom I chose but so the scripture be fulfilled, *'The one eating my bread lifted his heel against me.'* Now I tell you before it happens so you may trust it when it happens—that I am. Amen amen I tell you the one accepting whomever I send accepts me and the one accepting me accepts the one who sent me." Saying these things Jesus was harrowed in his soul, witnessed and said "Amen amen I tell you that one of you will hand me over."

The disciples looked at each other baffled as to whom he spoke of.

One of the disciples was lying back on Jesus' chest, the one whom Jesus loved.

So Simon Peter nodded to him and said "Ask who it is he's talking about."

Leaning back like this on Jesus' chest he said to him "Lord, who is it?"

Jesus answered "It's the one I'll give a sop to when I've

dipped it." So dipping the sop he took and gave it to Judas son of Simon Iscariot.

After the sop then Satan entered into him.

Jesus said to him "What you're doing do quickly."

No one lying back at the table knew why he'd told him this. Some thought it was because Judas kept the cash bag that Jesus was telling him "Buy what we need for the feast" or that he should give something to the poor.

Taking that sop then he went out at once and it was night.

When he left Jesus said "Now the Son of Man is glorified and God is glorified in him. If God is glorified in him God will also glorify him in himself and at once glorify him. Children, just a short while I'm with you; then you'll hunt me and as I told the Jews 'Where I go you can't come' so I tell you now. A new command I give you that you love each other. As I loved you so you love each other. By this everyone will know that you're my disciples if you love each other."

Simon Peter said to him "Lord, where are you going?"

Jesus answered "Where I'm going you can't follow me now but you will follow later."

Peter said to him "Lord, why can't I follow you yet? I'd lay down my life for you."

Jesus answered "You'd lay down your life for me? Amen amen I tell you no way will the cock crow till you've denied me three times. Don't harrow your heart. Trust in God; trust in me too. In my Father's house there are many resting places. Otherwise I'd have told you since I go to ready a place for you and if I go and ready a place for you I'll come back and take you to myself so where I am you may be too. Where I'm going you know the way to."

Thomas said to him "Lord, we don't know where you're going. How can we know the way?"

Jesus said to him "I'm the way, the truth and the life. No one comes to the Father but through me. If you'd known me you'd have also known the Father. From now on you know him and have seen him."

Philip said "Lord, show us the Father. That's enough for us."

Jesus said to him "Have I been with you so long and you still don't know me, Philip? The one who's seen me has seen the Father. How can you say 'Show us the Father'? Don't you trust that I'm in the Father and the Father is in me? The words which I say to you I don't speak from myself but the Father dwelling in me does his deeds. Trust me that I am in the Father and the Father in me or trust because of the deeds themselves. Amen amen I tell you the one trusting in me, the deeds that I do that one will do too and greater than these he'll do since I'm going to the Father and whatever you ask in my name that I'll do so the Father may be glorified in the Son.

"If you ask me anything in my name I'll do it. If you love me you'll keep my commandments and I'll ask the Father and another Advocate he'll give you who'll be with you to eternity—the Spirit of truth which the world can't receive since it fails to see him or understand. You know it since it dwells with you and will be in you. I won't leave you orphans; I'm coming to you. Just a while and the world no longer sees me but you see me; since I live you'll live too. On that day you'll know that I'm in my Father and you in me and I in you. The one who has my commands and keeps them that one is loving me and the one that loves me will be loved by my Father and I'll love him and show myself to him."

Judas (not Iscariot) said to him "Lord, what's happened that you'll show yourself to us and not to the world?"

Jesus answered him "If anyone loves me he'll keep my word and my Father will love him and we'll come to him and make a home with him. The one who doesn't love me fails to keep my words. The word which you hear isn't mine but the Father's who sent me. These things I've told you while I'm still with you but the Advocate, the Holy Spirit which the Father will send in my name that one will teach you everything and remind you of everything which I told you. Peace I'm leaving you; my peace I'm giving you. Not as the world gives do I give you. Don't let your heart be harrowed nor fearful. You heard what I told you—I'm going and coming back to you.

"If you loved me you'd have been glad that I'm going to the Father since the Father is greater than I. And now I've told you before it happens so when it happens you'll trust. From now on I won't speak much with you for the ruler of the world is coming and he has no part in me. But so the world knows I love the Father and as the Father gave me commands so I do. Get up; let's go out.

"I'm the true vine and my father is the grower. Every branch on me that bears no fruit he takes and each that bears fruit he prunes so it bears more fruit. Now you're clean because of the word I've spoken to you; dwell in me and I in you. As the branch can't bear fruit by itself unless it stays on the vine so you can't unless you dwell in me. I'm the vine, you the branches. The one dwelling in me and I in him, that one bears much fruit since away from me you can't do anything. Unless one dwells in me he's thrown out and withers; they gather them, throw them into the fire and they're burned. If you dwell in me and my words dwell in you, ask whatever you want and it will come to you. So my Father is glorified that you bear much fruit and so you'll be my disciples. As the Father loved me I also loved you—dwell in my love.

"If you keep my commands you'll dwell in my love for I've kept the commands of my Father and dwell in his love. These things I've said to you so my joy may be in you and your joy be full. This is my command that you love each other as I loved you. Greater love than this no one has, that one should lay down his life for his friends. You're my friends if you do what I command you. No more will I call you slaves since the slave doesn't know what his lord does but I've called you friends since everything I heard from my Father I made known to you.

"You didn't choose me but I chose you and appointed you to go and bear fruit and that your fruit should last so whatever you ask the Father in my name he'll give you. This I command you that you love each other. If the world hates you you know that before you it hated me. If you were from the world the world would love its own but since you're not from the world and I chose you out of the world so the world hates you.

"Remember the word I told you — no slave is greater than his lord. If they persecuted me they'll persecute you too. If they kept my word they'll keep yours too. But they'll do all these things to you because of my name since they don't know the one who sent me. Unless I came and spoke to them they'd have had no wrong but now they have no pretext for their wrong. The one hating me also hates my Father. If I hadn't done among them the deeds no other man did they'd have had no wrong but now they've both seen and hated me and my Father. This happened though so the word of their law might be fulfilled 'They hated me freely.'

"But when the Advocate comes whom I'll send you from the Father — the Spirit of truth which comes out of the Father — that one will witness to me and you too shall witness since you were with me from the start. I've said these things to you so you won't stumble. They'll put you out of the synagogue and an hour's coming when anyone killing you thinks he's offering a service to God. They'll do these things because they don't know the Father or me. But I've said these things to you so when their hour comes you remember that I told you.

"I didn't say these things from the start since I was with you but now I'm going to the one who sent me and not one of you is asking me 'Where are you going?' Because I've said these things to you grief has filled your heart but I tell the truth — it's better for you that I go away for if I don't go the Advocate can no way come to you but if I go I'll send him to you and coming he'll rebuke the world for wrong as to justice and judgment—for wrong because they didn't trust me, for justice because I'm going to the Father and you'll no longer see me, for judgment since the ruler of this world has been judged.

"I've still got many things to tell you but you can't bear them now. When the Spirit of truth comes he'll guide you into all the truth for he won't speak from himself but what he hears he'll speak and he'll declare the coming things to you. That one will glorify me for he'll take what's mine and declare it to you. Everything the Father has is mine so I said that he takes what's mine and declares it to you. In a little you'll no longer see me and another little while and you'll see me."

Then some of the disciples said to each other "What's this he tells us 'A little and you won't see me and another little and you'll see me' and 'Because I'm going to the Father'?" They said "What's this he calls 'a little while'? We don't know what he's talking about."

Jesus knew they wanted to question him and he said to them "You're searching with each other because I said 'A little and you won't see me and another little and you'll see me'? Amen amen I tell you that you'll weep and mourn but the world will exult. You'll be grieved but your grief will become joy. When a woman gives birth she grieves because her hour came but when she delivers the child she no longer recalls the trial because of her joy that a child is born into the world. So you grieve now but again I'll see you and your heart will gladden and no one can take that gladness from you.

"On that day you'll ask me nothing. Amen amen I tell you whatever you ask the Father he'll give you in my name. Till now you've asked nothing in my name; ask and you'll receive so your joy may be full. I've said these things to you in metaphors; an hour's coming when I'll no longer speak to you in metaphors but plainly I'll declare the Father to you. On that day you'll ask in my name and I don't say to you that

I'll ask the Father for you for the Father himself loves you since you've loved me and have trusted that I came out from God. I came out from the Father and came into the world; again I leave the world and go to the Father."

His disciples said "Look, now you're speaking plainly and aren't speaking metaphors. Now we know that you know everything and don't need anyone to question you. So we trust that you came out from God."

Jesus answered them "Now you trust? Look, an hour's coming—and has come—when you're scattered each to his own and you'll leave me alone but I'm not alone since the Father is with me. I've said these things to you so in me you may have peace. In the world you'll have pain but, courage, I've overcome the world."

Jesus said these things and lifting his eyes to Heaven he said "Father, the hour has come. Glorify your Son so the Son may glorify you as you gave him rights over all flesh so he might give eternal life to all you've given him. This is eternal life that they know you as the only true God and him whom you sent Jesus Christ. I glorified you on Earth finishing the deed you'd given me to do. Now glorify me, Father, along with yourself with the glory I had with you before the world was. I showed your name to those you gave me from the world. They were yours and you gave them to me. They've kept your word. Now they've learned that everything you've given me is from you because the words you gave me I've given them; they received them and knew truly that I came out from you and they trusted that you sent me.

"I pray for them—not for the world am I praying but for them whom you gave me since they're yours and all my things are yours and your things mine and I've been glorified in them. I'm no longer in the world but they're in the world and I'm coming to you. Holy Father, keep them whom you've given me in your name so they may be one as we are. When I was with them I kept them you've given me in your name. I guarded them and not one of them was lost except the son of loss so scripture be fulfilled. But now I'm coming to you and I say these things in the world so they may have my joy ripened in themselves. I've given them your word and the world hated them because they're not of the world as I'm not of the world.

"I don't ask that you take them out of the world but that you keep them from evil. They're not of the world as I'm not of the world. Consecrate them in the truth—your word is the truth. As you sent me into the world I also sent them into the world and for them I consecrate myself so they too may be consecrated in truth. I don't ask for these alone but for those trusting in me through their word that all may be one as you Father are in me and I in you so they may be in us that the world may trust that you sent me.

"The glory you've given me I've given them so they may be one as we're one—I in them and you in me—so they may be perfected in one so the world may know you sent me and loved them as you loved me. Father, I want those you've given me to be with me where I am so they may see my glory which you've given me since you loved me before the founding of the world. Just Father, the world doesn't know you but I know you and these you sent me know you. I declared to them your name and will declare it so the love with which you've loved me may be in them and I in them."

Saying these things Jesus went out with his disciples across the Kidron ravine where there was a garden which he entered with his disciples.

Now Judas the one handing him over also knew the place since Jesus had often met there with his disciples. So Judas taking the Roman cohort and guards from the chief priests and the Pharisees came there with lanterns, lamps and weapons.

Jesus knowing everything coming down on him went forward and said to them "Whom are you hunting?"

They answered him "Jesus the Nazarene."

He told them "I am."

Now Judas the one betraying him also stood with them.

So when he told them "I am" they stepped back and fell on the ground.

Again he asked them "Whom are you hunting?"

And they said "Jesus the Nazarene."

Jesus answered "I told you that I am. If you're hunting me let these go" (so the word be fulfilled which he'd said "Of those you gave me I have not lost one").

Then Simon Peter having a knife drew it, struck the High Priest's slave and cut off his right ear—the slave's name was Malchus.

Jesus said to Peter "Put the knife in its sheath. The cup the Father has given me shouldn't I drink it?"

So the cohort, the captain and the guards from the Jews took Jesus, bound him and led him to Annas first since he was father-in-law of Caiaphas who was High Priest that year. It was Caiaphas who'd advised the Jews that it was better one man die for the people.

Simon Peter and another disciple followed Jesus. That disciple was known to the High Priest and went with Jesus into the courtyard of the High Priest but Peter stayed at the door outside. So the other disciple known to the High Priest came out, spoke with the girl at the door and brought Peter in.

The girl at the door said to Peter "Aren't you one of this man's disciples?"

He said "I'm not."

The slaves and guards who stood there had made a charcoal fire since it was cold and they were warming themselves.

Peter was standing with them warming himself.

So the High Priest questioned Jesus about his disciples and his teaching.

Jesus answered him "I spoke plainly to the world. I always taught in the synagogue and in the Temple where all the Jews gather; in secret I said nothing. Why question me? Question the ones who heard what I said to them. Look, they know what I said."

As he said these things one of the guards standing struck Jesus a blow saying "You're answering the High Priest like that?"

Jesus answered him "If I spoke wrongly witness to my wrong but if well why hit me?"

So Annas sent him bound to Caiaphas the High Priest.

Now Simon Peter was standing and warming himself.

They said to him "Aren't you too one of his disciples?"

He denied it and said "I'm not."

One of the High Priest's slaves, a relative of the one whose ear Peter cut off, said "Didn't I see you in the garden with him?"

Again Peter denied it and at once a cock crowed.

They led Jesus from Caiaphas to the Pretorium. It was early and they didn't enter the Pretorium or they'd be defiled and couldn't eat the Passover.

So Pilate went out to them and said "What charge do you bring against this man?"

They answered him "Unless he was a criminal would we have delivered him to you?"

Pilate said to them "Take him and judge him according to your law."

The Jews said to him "For us it's not legal to kill anyone" so Jesus' word might be fulfilled which signified what death he was about to die.

Pilate entered the Pretorium again, called Jesus and said to him "You're the king of the Jews?"

Jesus answered "On your own you're saying this or others have told you about me?"

Pilate answered "Am I a Jew? Your nation and your chief priests handed you over to me. What have you done?"

Jesus answered "My reign is not of this world. If my reign

was of this world my servants would have fought so I wouldn't be delivered to the Jews but now my reign is not here."

Pilate said to him "Are you really a king?"

Jesus answered "You say that I'm a king. I was born for this and for this I came into the world so I might witness to the truth. Everyone who belongs to the truth hears my voice."

Pilate said to him "What is truth?" And saying this he went out again to the Jews and told them "I find no blame in him but you have a custom that I should release someone to you at the Passover. Do you want me then to release you the king of the Jews?"

They cried out again "Not this man but Barabbas"—now Barabbas was a robber.

So Pilate took Jesus and scourged him. And when the soldiers had plaited a wreath of thorns they put it on his head, threw a purple robe round him, came to him, said "Hail, king of the Jews!" and struck him.

Then Pilate went out again and said to them "Look, I bring him out to you so you may know that I find no wrong in him."

Jesus came out wearing the thorny wreath and the purple robe.

He said to them "Look, the man."

When the chief priests and guards saw him then they shouted "Crucify, crucify!"

Pilate said to them "You take him and crucify him; I find no blame in him."

The Jews answered him "We have a law and according to the law he ought to die because he made himself Son of God."

When Pilate heard that word he was even more afraid. He went into the Pretorium again and said to Jesus "Where are you from?"

But Jesus didn't give him an answer.

So Pilate said to him "You're not speaking to me? Don't you know that I have the right to release you and the right to crucify you?"

Jesus answered "You'd have no right over me unless it was given you from above. So the one handing me over to you has the greater wrong."

From there on Pilate tried to free him but the Jews shouted "If you free this man you're no friend of Caesar! Anyone making himself a king speaks against Caesar."

Pilate hearing these words brought Jesus out and sat on the bench in a place called the Pavement (in Hebrew *Gabbatha*). Now it was the Preparation for Passover about noon and he said to the Jews "Look, your king."

They shouted "Take him, take him and crucify him!"

Pilate said to them "Shall I crucify your king?"

The chief priests answered "We have no king but Caesar."

So he delivered him to them to be crucified.

They took Jesus and he bearing his own cross went out to what was called Skull Place which is called in Hebrew *Golgotha* where they crucified him and with him two others on this side and that and in the middle Jesus.

Pilate also wrote a placard and put it on the cross. It was written "Jesus the Nazarene the King of the Jews."

Many Jews read the placard since the place where Jesus was crucified was near the city and it was written in Hebrew, Latin and Greek.

So the chief priests of the Jews said to Pilate "Don't write 'The King of the Jews' but that the man said 'I'm king of the Jews.' "

Pilate answered "What I've written I've written."

The soldiers when they'd crucified Jesus took his clothes and made four parts, to each soldier a part, and his coat—now the coat was seamless woven from the top straight through. They said to each other then "Let's don't tear it but cast lots for it whose it shall be" so the scripture be fulfilled

> They parted my clothes among themselves
> And for my clothing cast lots.

The soldiers did those things.

But near the cross stood Jesus' mother and his mother's sister Mary of Klopas and Mary the Magdalene.

Jesus seeing his mother and the disciple he loved standing near said to his mother "Woman, look, your son."

Then he said to the disciple "Look, your mother."

And from that hour the disciple took her to his home.

After that Jesus knowing how everything had been done so the scripture was fulfilled said "I'm thirsty."

A jar was there full of sour wine. Putting a sponge full of the wine on a hyssop they brought it to his mouth.

When he'd taken the wine Jesus said "It's done" and bowing his head handed over his spirit.

So the Jews—since it was Preparation and bodies shouldn't stay on the cross for the Sabbath (that Sabbath was a great day)—asked Pilate that their legs be broken and they be taken down.

The soldiers came then and broke the legs of the first man and the other crucified with him but coming to Jesus when they saw he'd already died they didn't break his legs though one of the soldiers pierced his side with his spear.

At once there came out blood and water and the one who saw this has witnessed. His witness is true and he knows he speaks truly so you too may trust for these things happened so the scripture be fulfilled 'A *bone shall not be broken in him*' and again another scripture says '*They'll look at him whom they pierced.*'

After these things Joseph from Arimathea being a disciple of Jesus hidden out of fear of the Jews asked Pilate that he might take Jesus' body.

Pilate allowed it.

So he came and took his body.

Nicodemus came too, the one who'd come to him by night at first, bringing a mixture of myrrh and aloes about a hundred pounds. They took Jesus' body then and bound it in wrappings with the spices as it's the Jews' custom to bury. Now there was in the place where he was crucified a garden and in the garden a new tomb in which no one had yet been put. There then because of the Jews' Preparation and because the tomb was near they put Jesus.

On the first day of the week Mary the Magdalene came early while it was still dark to the tomb and saw the stone taken off the tomb. She ran and came to Simon Peter and to the other disciple whom Jesus loved and said to them "They've taken the Lord out of the tomb and we don't know where they put him."

So Peter and the other disciple went out and came to the tomb. The two ran together.

The other disciple ran ahead quicker than Peter, came first to the tomb and stooping he saw the wrappings lying but he didn't enter.

Then Simon Peter came following him, entered the tomb and saw the wrappings lying and the kerchief which was on his head not lying with the wrappings but apart folded up in one place.

So the other disciple who'd come first to the tomb entered and saw and trusted. They didn't yet know the scripture that he must rise from the dead.

The disciples went off again by themselves.

But Mary stood near the tomb outside weeping. As she was weeping she stooped into the tomb and saw two angels in white sitting one at the head and one at the feet where the body of Jesus had lain.

These said to her "Woman, why are you weeping?"

She said to them "They took my lord and I don't know where they put him." Saying that she turned back and saw Jesus standing, not that she knew it was Jesus.

Jesus said to her "Woman, why are you weeping? Whom are you hunting?"

She thinking it was the gardener said to him "Sir, if you carried him off tell me where you put him and I'll take him."

Jesus said to her "Mary."

Turning she said to him in Hebrew "*Rabboni!*" which means "Teacher!"

Jesus said to her "Don't hold me for I haven't yet gone up to the Father but go to my brothers and tell them 'I'm going up to my Father and your Father, my God and your God.' "

Mary the Magdalene came declaring to the disciples "I've seen the Lord" and that he'd said these things to her.

So when it was early evening on that first day of the week and the doors had been shut where the disciples were out of fear of the Jews, Jesus came and stood in the midst and said to them "Peace to you." Saying this he showed both his hands and his side to them.

The disciples exulted seeing the Lord.

Jesus said to them again "Peace to you. As the Father sent me I also send you." Saying this he breathed on them and said to them "Receive the Holy Spirit. Whosoever wrongs you forgive they've been forgiven them; whosoever you keep they've been kept."

But Thomas one of the Twelve called Twin was not with them when Jesus came.

So the other disciples said to him "We've seen the Lord."

But he said to them "Unless I see in his hands the mark of the nails and put my finger in the mark of the nails and put my hand in his side no way will I trust."

After eight days his disciples were again inside and Thomas with them.

Jesus came, the doors being shut, and stood in the midst and said "Peace to you." Then he said to Thomas "Bring your finger here and see my hands and bring your hand and put it into my side and don't be doubting but trusting."

Thomas answered him "My Lord and my God."

Jesus said to him "You trust because you've seen me? Lucky the ones not seeing yet trusting."

Jesus did many other signs before his disciples which are not written in this book but these have been written so you may trust that Jesus is Messiah the Son of God and that trusting you may have life in his name.

After these things he showed himself again to his disciples on the sea of Tiberias and showed himself this way. Simon Peter, Thomas called Twin, Nathanael from Cana in Galilee, Zebedee's sons and two other disciples were together.

Simon Peter said to them "I'm going fishing."

They said to him "We're coming with you."

They went out, got into the boat and all that night caught nothing.

But when it was early morning Jesus stood on the shore, not that the disciples knew it was Jesus.

So Jesus said to them "Boys, nothing to eat?"

They answered "No."

He said "Cast the net to starboard and you'll find some."

They cast and they couldn't drag it in because of the swarm of fish.

So the disciple whom Jesus loved said to Peter "It's the Lord."

Simon Peter hearing that it was the Lord tucked his coat up for he was naked and threw himself into the sea.

But the other disciples came on in the little boat hauling the net of fish since they were only about a hundred yards from land. When they got out on land they saw a charcoal fire laid, a fish lying on it and bread.

Jesus said to them "Bring some of the fish you just caught."

Simon Peter got up and dragged the net to land full of a

great many fish—a hundred fifty-three—and with so many still the net wasn't torn.

Jesus said to them "Come eat."

None of the disciples dared question him "Who are you?" knowing it was the Lord.

Jesus came, took the bread and gave it to them, also the fish.

This was the third time Jesus was shown to the disciples raised from the dead.

So when they'd eaten Jesus said to Simon Peter "Simon son of John, do you love me more than these?"

He said "Yes Lord, you know I care for you."

He said to him "Tend my lambs." He said to him again a second time "Simon son of John, do you love me?"

He said to him "Yes Lord, you know I care for you."

He said "Guide my sheep." He said to him a third time "Simon son of John, do you really care for me?"

Peter was saddened that he said to him a third time "Do you care for me?" and he said to him "Lord, you know everything. You know I care for you."

Jesus said to him "Tend my sheep. Amen I tell you when you were younger you dressed yourself and walked where you wished but when you age you'll stretch out your hands and another will dress you and carry you where you don't want to go." He said this showing by what death he'd glorify God. Saying this he told him "Follow me."

Turning Peter saw the disciple whom Jesus loved following, the one who also leaned on his chest at supper and said "Lord, who's handing you over?" Seeing this one Peter said to Jesus "Lord, and what about this one?"

Jesus said to him "If I want him to stay till I come what's it to you? You follow me."

So word went out to the brothers that this disciple wouldn't die but Jesus didn't say to him that he wouldn't die, only "If I want him to stay till I come what's it to you?"

This is the disciple witnessing to these things and writing these things and we know that his witness is true. There were many other things Jesus did which if each were written I think the world couldn't hold the books written.

A MODERN
APOCRYPHAL GOSPEL

A PREFACE TO
AN HONEST ACCOUNT OF
A MEMORABLE LIFE

AT Duke University twice in recent years, I have led a seminar in the study of the gospels of Mark and John. All the students have been undergraduates, a few of them with considerable prior awareness of New Testament literature but most with virtually none—my only suggestion to them on the question of their eligibility for the seminar is that they bring to it minds not shut by the blinders of an unquestioning religious fundamentalism. Through the first two months of the term—line by line in my own plain translations—we discuss the historical, narrative, and religious connotations of Mark (the oldest life of Jesus) and John (the most mysterious and unaccountable for, once we conceive it as a problem). Despite the fact that a great weight of recent scholarship denies that we can look to the gospels for an experience comparable to that we find in works of modern biography, I nonetheless call the two gospels *lives*.

And I call them *lives* since, whatever their theological aims, Mark and John are first of all brief attempts to record the crucial events in a certain order, and the meaning within those events, of a single temporal earthly existence. Their human subject led, to be sure, an existence that Mark and John thought of indispensable meaning for the transformation of human life; and the nature of that imperative transformation is central to what their two books thrust toward us so powerfully, for all their elliptical strangeness. Modern attempts to deny that the actual events of a particular human life—arranged in a meaningful narrative order—are the bedrock of all the gospel stories are ignorant of the universal motive and history of narrative.

Next in the seminar's work, we pass briskly through the gospels of Matthew and Luke, with their long detours into ethical discourse; and the students are encouraged to read the remainder of the canonical New Testament—the Acts of the Apostles, Paul's letters, and the other letters and tracts. Then we read the major surviving uncanonical or apocryphal gospels (*apochruphos* in Greek means *hidden away*; that is, not read in public, not widely accepted). Most interesting among them are *The Protogospel of James*, *The Gospel of Thomas*, and several less cogent early documents pertaining to Jesus and the Jesus sect.

At midterm as we prepare to write substantial seminar papers, the students and I agree upon a common set of sources for our ground plans—as a general rule, we are free to use Matthew, Mark, Luke, John, Acts (the one other surviving lengthy first-century narrative concerned with the effects of Jesus' life), the undisputed letters of Paul, and those other canonized documents which may at least have originated in the first generation of men and women who knew Jesus of Nazareth—The Letter to the Hebrews, The Letter of James, The First Letter of Peter, The Three Letters of John, and The Revelation to John.

A reader may wonder why I set the students and myself such a task when we already have four impressive gospels, two of which stand an excellent chance of proceeding directly or at only second hand from eyewitnesses of Jesus' acts and teaching. The simplest justification for the effort, and one that has lain behind the thousands of attempts on Jesus that have burdened libraries for the past two millennia, is that the career of a particular Palestinian Jew of the first century and the effects of that life on world history have proved so magnetic in their mystery as to demand ceaseless watch and question by human beings whose minds have ranged from the caliber of Augustine, Aquinas, Luther, and Calvin through numerous lunatics, sadists, masochists, plain readers, and selfless ministers to the sufferings of others.

A more precise explanation of why I set my seminar to work on further attempts would center on a feeling that I share with most students of Matthew, Mark, Luke, and John—each one of the four offers a balance of readily credible acts and speeches that are found in no other early source and that beg to be shuffled together in one account which offers all the crucial acts and sayings of one impressive man. The famous lost *Diatesseron* or *Through the Four*, which Tatian composed in the Syriac language in the second century, was only the most widely circulated of such attempts at compiling a satisfying single Jesus story, a harmony of all known gospel themes. Anyone aware of the contents of the four will have long since shuffled their unique findings into at least a mental harmony—the familiar Christmas story, for instance, which underlies so much of the art and ongoing devotion of the West is a shuffling of Matthew's and Luke's special strands.

With similar aims then, and on that common base of evidence, the students and I begin to write our individual apocryphal gospels. In the first two rounds of the seminar, students have produced the most surprisingly excellent sets of papers I have received in nearly four decades of teaching; and as I have learned to expect, the student gospels generally prove to be a good deal freer than mine in arranging, discarding, or elaborating the oldest evidence and hints. A number of them, for instance, write from the points of view of women mentioned in canonical accounts—Mary the mother of Jesus, Mary of Magdala, the nameless woman cured of a hemorrhage.

My gospel, on the contrary, hews closely to Mark's generally convincing chronology for the life, work, and death of Jesus—an outline that seems to come from Mark's main informant, who was almost surely Peter: Simon son of Jonah, the fisherman from Bethsaida whom Jesus named *Kepha* or

Rock. It is fashionable now, as indeed it was with Papias in the second century, to deny that Mark preserves a trustworthy outline for Jesus' career; but I feel, with many older scholars as learned and discerning as Albert Schweitzer and C. H. Dodd, that a thoroughly credible (if hardly exhaustive) temporal, geographic, and psychic progress can be inferred from Mark's bare account.

Into Mark's loose-limbed itinerary then, I've inserted certain events and speeches which seem genuine to me from Matthew, Luke, and John; and I've added as well the apparently genuine but unattached episode of Jesus' response to the woman taken in adultery (it is not a part of the oldest manuscripts of any one of the canonical gospels, though it is often placed for convenience in John). I have made such inclusions into Mark's outline only when they seem indispensable for the fullest understanding of Jesus that we can hope to reach if we try to keep faith with the oldest witnesses and with the dim but likely outline they provide for his short career (with all the dozens of contradictions in the details of their stories, the ultimate arc of Jesus' career remains the same throughout). I set the additions to Mark's outline at points where they serve both a narrative and an emotional logic and do part-justice to at least two aspects of Jesus' nature—his apparently inexhaustible compassion for human wrongdoing and suffering and his ferocious anger at the intractable presence of evil in the world and the agonies it produces in creatures, good and bad.

Such a shuffling of narrative and teaching sources is frowned upon by many New Testament scholars as being disruptive of what they take to be the mutually exclusive narrative and theological errands of the four gospel writers. I dissent, with no sense of error, from their prohibition. Most early writers in the Jesus sect dissented likewise and for one large reason. The first three gospels were quite surely built by just such a process of conflation and interleaving of multiple sources, oral and written, historical and legendary. And since the most inexplicable acts, the most astounding claims, of Jesus are described by the oldest writers with a flat-footed refusal to heighten their marvels, most of those events mix well with one another. From whichever gospel we draw them, they seem so starkly matter-of-fact that in general they lie together easily. Mark's rushed and secretive man Jesus finally stands with no necessary adjustment of focus beside John's divine Son of God announcing his blazing transcendence in the daylight of Yahweh's Temple Mount in the presence of enemies.

Where I rearrange the order of incidents in Mark or, rarely, where I invent a piece of bridgework between incidents—moving Jesus from place to place in Palestine, say, or linking separate acts in what seem possible ways or implying certain evolutions through time in Jesus' own sense of his nature and his meaning—I do so in the manner sketched by my originals in the few moments when they enter Jesus' mind; they proceed with sober speculation and a minimum of narrative embroidery. Faced with imposing memories that may often have reached the canonical writers devoid of geographical or chronological context, those writers built the best homes they could manage with such detached timbers; and I do not hope to better the poetic fidelity of their well-informed inventions.

When I imagine the conception and birth of Jesus, for instance, and when I set three invented speeches into the mouths of his family and pupils (Joseph at the birth, Peter at the Transfiguration, Mary of Magdala at the tomb—each invention set in italics), I do so with guidance from those few apocryphal stories which seem profound in their guesswork or, just conceivably, some scrap of tradition which may have reached them. My main hints come from the impressive first-person nativity speech of Joseph and the geography of the birth, both contained in the second-century *Protogospel of James*. I rely on the reader's native wit to note that in places

237

my history is metaphoric. The solemn dance and the song in which Jesus leads his pupils after the last supper come directly from *The Acts of John*, a second-century narrative of real fascination.

I likewise add the odd reliable-sounding detail from other early sources. From Justin Martyr in the mid-second century, for instance, I take the detail of a fire in the Jordan at Jesus' baptism. I note Paul's claim in The First Letter to the Corinthians, chapter 15, that the risen Jesus appeared to James, who was Jesus' brother; and from Paul's claim that Jesus appeared also to "the Twelve," I deduce an appearance to Judas his traitor. An occasional speech of Jesus derives from the impressive and quite early *Gospel of Thomas*, discovered whole in the Egyptian desert as recently as 1945; and from scattered other early sources I employ a few sayings that ring true—I've invented no single important saying from whole cloth.

From other early accounts that may well preserve fact, I suggest that Jesus in his early manhood had worked at the blacksmith's forge and that Zebedee's son John sold fish to the High Priest in Jerusalem; and when a modern archaeological finding has seemed relevant, or a topographical or climatic observation from my own two visits to Israel, I have included it. Throughout I emulate the original first-century Greek in avoiding punctuation except where confusion might result. It is a virtue of such clean prose to keep a reader watchful and to drive off the inattentive.

My hope is that a discerning reader will recognize and register my few inventions as careful meditations on a quantity of bedrock history that exceeds the facts we possess for any other ancient life whose force survives in our civilization. We after all know as much or more of the life of Jesus of Nazareth as we know of such clamorous lives as Ramses II's, Alexander the Great's, or even Augustus Caesar's; and we maim our good luck in having so much, and our common sense in gauging its worth, when we fail to grant the wealth of our sources.

As Mark, John, Matthew, and Luke all transform speech and act into story with the purpose of discovering both the path of a life and that life's meaning, so my own mosaic finds a figure deep in its surface. That figure is of course shaped and colored by my own predilections, as Schweitzer showed the hero of most nineteenth-century lives of Jesus to be the Jesus wanted or needed by their individual authors. But a brief summary will, I hope, show my bias as sane at least and justified by the ancient evidence. I have represented fairly, I hope, even those strands of Jesus' teaching which condemn important parts of my own life; but I trust that no reader will conclude that I have any pretensions for my work other than a lifelong concern with the material, a keen seriousness of purpose, and a sense of the unparalleled value of the life described. Any thought of creating a new text for dogmatic scrutiny or for anyone to lean on as the primary source of personal enlightenment is far from my intention.

My version of the life and meaning has a spine like this. *In the reign of the Roman emperor Augustus, a young man named Jesus—intended by God as his Son—grows up obscurely in a village in northern Palestine. From early years he ponders the aim of his life and then confirms his sense of unique Sonship in the revelatory moment of his baptism by John, a desert prophet. Jesus ratifies that Sonship, to his own amazement and doubt, in a crowded tour of teaching and healing through the towns and farms of his home district, Galilee. That early teaching declares the coming reign of God on Earth and the necessity that people must turn, in preparation, from their accustomed ways. Jesus' apparent doubts of his own mission, and of the nature of the coming reign, are resolved and profoundly altered when he learns, in a moment of inexplicable exaltation on the heights of Mount Hermon, that his fated mission is the largest in history—the blood redemp-*

tion of humankind from its willful fall into self and greed. Confirmed in his surety of purpose, Jesus then descends with his baffled pupils to Jerusalem, challenges both the Temple authorities and the Roman overlords; and after an hour of terrible fear and doubt in Gethsemane, he dies at his enemies' joined hands, is buried late on a Friday afternoon, and rises bodily from the dead two mornings later. In uncanny but convincing appearances, he rallies his frightened and scattered pupils for a campaign of mercy, warning, and hope to all human creatures—a campaign that continues today.

The evidence seems to me to permit that one legible pattern among almost innumerable others—the sight of a single human life lived nearer to the Maker's mind than any other life yet heard of, west of the Jordan river at least and through all Western history till now. My simplest hope here is to have clarified, from the earliest witnesses, one at least of the credible shapes of that life as it cut its lines on the eyes and minds of men and women no more receptive or retentive than ourselves yet who nonetheless brought him onward through time—as large a gift as words have to give us and as heavy a freight.

AN HONEST ACCOUNT OF
A MEMORABLE LIFE

AN APOCRYPHAL GOSPEL

BY REYNOLDS PRICE

AN HONEST ACCOUNT OF
A MEMORABLE LIFE

It began with a girl who was loved by God. The girl was named Mary and was aged fourteen. She had been promised in childhood to the builder Joseph but her mother Anna was wasting with sickness and Mary had Joseph's leave to stay home till her mother was walking again or dead. So the girl lived on in her mother's house which was one dry room that backed on a cave. Her father had been a priest of the Temple but died years back in the battering sun as he walked from Jerusalem down to Bethlehem, a town of six hundred souls, the home of King David dead a long thousand years.

On a spring afternoon in the year before King Herod died in filth and worms, Mary brought water in from the well and was kneeling beside her sleeping mother to wipe the feverish face and arms when a silent voice gripped the girl's strong hand. She'd heard the voice twice before but only in music, a keen distant chanting.

Now the chant was distant words so high that the girl looked down to see if fear had waked her mother.

Anna lay still on her clean pallet.

The first words again and again were a name *Sweet Mary*.

The girl went on soothing her mother. Mary had known her own beauty for two years but this was a prideful demon to shun.

The next high words were separate but clear. *You—God's choice—your son—his son.*

Baffled but calm as she'd never been, Mary faced the door to the world and said *Yes* with a single nod. When her hand came back to her mother's brow, her mother was dead.

Mary spent an hour washing the body and wrapping it in the linen they had saved for this last purpose. Then she stood and walked toward Joseph's shop.

Joseph lived in the back and slept on boards. But at dark that day he moved in beside young Mary at last—the law allowed it after betrothal—and they were married by midsummer though only in law. Near her there in her old home, Joseph slowly learned of the terror planted in her womb and growing daily. Through the long wait his pallet lay apart from Mary's by the reach of his arm, and there were days that summer and fall when Joseph pressed iron nails deep into his hands to let out part of the pain he felt but never told. This girl had been taken and used to the dregs before he touched her.

*

So early that winter—a freezing night when Mary called Joseph's name in the dark before the pain broke from her in groans—Joseph brought the lamp, saw she was wet but clean of blood, then ran uphill to the midwife's house.

As the midwife stepped out onto the path she gave him her own jar to fill at David's spring.

Long after they moved to Nazareth in Galilee where Joseph's brother Clopas owned land and a building business, when Joseph would stop to watch Mary's boy—with Mary's likeness in the lean dark face—he recalled the strangeness that came down on him as he trotted home that night with water. *My heart had seized up in my chest. A nighthawk hung in the air beyond me all but in reach. Through the open door of a house in lamplight, I saw three men and a dwarfish girl stalled in the cold—*

bread in their fingers aimed at their lips but still as bones. Yet when I looked the stars were wheeling. Then suddenly blood roared again in my ears, and I went toward home.

At home the midwife had led Mary back to the cave that served as a stable and pen. The colt and the hens had warmed the space; and when Joseph bent to look in the door, the boy was already born and dugging his mother's breast.

Her eyes had found their lifelong sight, but she looked to Joseph and told him the boy would be named Jesus.

*

Joseph raised the boy, the first in a line of five sons and three daughters. He led the sons to the synagogue school where they each surpassed him by learning their letters and reading the law and prophets on sight. He found good husbands for the girls.

And the eldest boy, the one from Bethlehem, repaid the training Joseph gave him. After he and his brothers left school for work in the family trade, Jesus would go to the rabbi at night and read the law and prophets till late. Before he was grown he knew them well; and many nights while his kinsmen slept, Jesus walked alone in the hills. He could look down on the plain of Jezreel where God and his armies had fought Israel's enemies and where the great battle of the last days would rage. He could look to the lights of Herod Antipas's capital Sepphoris three miles from Nazareth—a marble city with a palace, a theater, baths and a temple to the deified man Augustus Caesar. The boy learned the story of all he saw.

Every spring he went up with his family to eat the Passover feast in Jerusalem, honoring the night when God's mercy spared the slave hovels where Hebrews lived in Pharaoh's Egypt but killed the firstborn in their masters' homes. Old King Herod's new Temple in Jerusalem, built on the site of Solomon's Temple, was all but finished after decades of work. There among its ivory and gold, young Jesus talked with any priest or lawyer who would hear his questions. He was already asking if God was truly the Father of all and if so then who could watch the world of blood and hate and think God was loving?

Back in Nazareth Jesus showed keen skill at the smithing forge among his four brothers who were masons and carvers. And from the day when Joseph died, young Jesus bore the first son's duty to tend his mother who at forty was hunched with all she'd borne as God's choice—the lean girl Mary who was bent now and worn.

*

But when Jesus passed his thirtieth year, he turned his back on the home he'd known. His mother and all his brothers and sisters stayed in Nazareth, but in the spring Jesus walked south through Galilee and on down the banks of the Jordan through country held by Rome now and ruled at the will of Tiberius Caesar by the puppet sons of old Herod the Great. Their moves were watched by the merciless eye of Pontius Pilate, Caesar's prefect in Palestine. When Jesus reached a bend in the river near Jericho, he saw the man he'd come to find—a man whose fame had reached even Nazareth.

It was near sundown and the mob who daily came from Jerusalem—lawyers, priests, rich women, whores, wretches— had ridden southwest back up through hills toward the golden Temple or were cooking over their fires on the east bank. The famous man that Jesus had come for was John the Baptizer. John had cried out here since the winter solstice against all evil hearts around him.

John warned of God's taut patience and wrath, the imminent coming down of God's last plan in fire and terror. He would say "One stronger than I is coming whose sandal I'm not fit to loosen. The winnowing fan is in his hand. He'll utterly sweep his threshing floor and gather the good wheat into his barn. He'll burn the chaff in roaring fire. Take shelter now. Thresh your own grain."

John offered a ritual washing from error, for readiness. Near dusk as it was, John was still at the edge of the river this day, still waiting in his camel skins. To the eye he made a believable image of the prophet Elijah whose return was expected as the near forerunner of God's anointed. Many hoped that the longed-for man, God's son Messiah, would roll Rome into the Roman sea, mount Israel's throne and open souls to God's whirlwind—God's hand in history redeeming time. What John was waiting to welcome had come. Jesus beyond him was surely the man. John sensed him on sight, beckoned the younger man toward him, then forded the river to the waist-deep midst.

Jesus stripped and waded to meet John.

John met Jesus' eyes with half the blaze of recognition; but when Jesus gave no nod or sign, then John's eyes faltered. So he seized Jesus by the hair and buried him backward in the stream.

When he drew Jesus up, John's eyes still questioned him.

But Jesus faced the dusky zenith. Whatever John or the cooking stragglers saw or heard, Jesus watched the sky torn open above, a white dove sifting down through the air and what he heard was that same voice his mother heard but kept in secret. It said *You are my only Son.*

A fire blazed in the actual water.

*

For more than a month Jesus walked alone in the desert past Jericho, the crags and wastes by the hot Dead Sea, Earth's deepest pit. He thought his way the best he could through what he'd seen and heard that dusk with John above him in the cold brown river, God's meaning for him and the time he'd have before the great coming. In the early days he thought he heard God's voice again "My Son, I waited the ages for you through all the prophets, that you come at last and I might rest." For a while after that the time felt short.

Then vipers, jackals, a starved lion, and swarms of flies crossed Jesus' path in the sunstruck gullies. A flock of ravens circled his head too famished to caw; but even when his own hunger sapped him and he was sleeping nights in gullies with no more cover than his seamless coat, no creature more than sniffed his hand or licked the dry soles of his feet.

What came nearer to harming Jesus in those days was the tempting spirit that crossed his path in numerous forms. One form wore his mother's face and led a child by the hand toward him saying "This is my son"—the child was himself. Another form likewise wore Jesus' face but was old and smiling with sons and daughters that bore his traits and tended his age. A third was all the human beauty he'd known till now, all the hair he'd touched.

Eventually on the fortieth day Jesus fended the spirit off. By then he was high on a peak above Jericho. When the final tempter melted in air, Jesus howled to the rocks, gnawed thorny weeds and turned his lean face back to the north but not toward home. What he thought he'd understood in the desert burned to be told. God was a father who yearned toward his children and would come to them soon in flaming justice and then a long mercy. So Jesus went toward the harp-shaped lake of Kinnereth set in the hills of south Galilee though he hardly knew what his mind or hands, his power or weakness, would do once there.

*

As he walked the lake's broad shore and hills, he told whomever would pause to listen the news he'd learned alone in the desert—that the reign of God would break in on them any day, that they must turn from waste and hatred to ready themselves for a fierce coming judgment and then for the endless reign of love. His hearers were farmers and fishermen, their wives and children, the occasional rabbi and village crank, the whores, cheats and scapegoats.

From among them he chose two pairs of brothers. The first were Simon son of Jonah and his brother Andrew, then John the son of Zebedee and his brother James—all four were fishermen. The sons of Zebedee were heirs to their father's thriving business which sold dried fish to prosperous households as far south as Jericho and Jerusalem, a two-day trek. Even the High Priest bought their fish at his back door downhill from the Temple.

The way Jesus called them was the first strange thing. One late spring evening he came along the strand near their town Capernaum and as he saw them beaching boats and mending nets he told them "Come. We'll fish for humans."

For reasons they never plumbed, the four men dropped their work and followed him. Where he led them first was to Simon and Andrew's house. He was weak with hunger.

But Simon's mother-in-law was down with a lingering fever and not till Jesus went to her pallet, crouched beside her whispering, then took her hand and raised her up did she have the strength to cook a supper for the five men newly bound together as teacher and pupils.

In that small town word leaked at once that the teacher Jesus had brought Simon's mother from the edge of death and by the time the men finished eating, a crowd had gathered at the narrow door.

Among them was a leper too grim to watch. The crowd stood back when the leper pressed through Simon's door to stand above where Jesus sat. He said to Jesus "You can heal me if you want to."

Jesus stayed in place but met the man's eyes, managed a smile and said "I want to."

The leper was healed. By the time he'd run out into the street, his open sores were sealing and fading.

Then the crowd rushed to enter the house—there was only room for a dozen people.

But Jesus made his way out through them. The synagogue was twenty yards north. He led the way there and was trying to pray when a man in the milling crowd behind him was flung to the floor by a demon seizure.

The man writhed, foamed, then stretched out rigid with his eyes rolled back and his hands clenched so hard the blood leaked from them.

Jesus tried to go on praying but he finally turned and seeing the man, he called out loudly to the demon that held him "Come out now!"

The demon cringed hard and howled. "Have mercy, Jesus. We know who you are—"

Jesus stopped it from telling the truth by saying "Silence! Come out now!"

With a last shudder the demon obeyed and soon the man was upright and thankful.

So Jesus had no choice but to go back out to the street and heal whomever brought him their bodies. He failed no one and was white with exhaustion when the last man, woman and child were gone and he could rest on Simon's packed floor. Till now the demons had not obeyed him, and the new power shook him in dreams all night. He could see his own face again, his own strong body tall and throned in the reign of God with the pit of demons scattered beneath him.

✳

Word of that night swept the whole lakeshore and the hills behind. And while Jesus meant to go on telling people of the imminent breaking in of God and the need for love and mercy meanwhile, he was met in every town and field by mobs of the sick who silenced his teaching. Even healthy people brought him their cripples in carts and barrows.

Balked as he was he felt real anguish and pity at the sight of the power of demons on Earth and he healed when he could, when he knew he was trusted. Even back home in Capernaum he could hardly rest.

One day he was inside teaching his pupils and a few of the lawyers who'd come from Jerusalem to check on rumors. The door was shut on the crowd outside, but a pair of desperate men from the hills climbed onto the house with their paralyzed brother and broke through the mud and straw roof with poles. Then they lowered their brother's pallet near the spot where Jesus sat and they begged him for healing.

At once the lawyers reminded Jesus that this was the Sabbath and work was forbidden.

So Jesus faced the cripple and said "Son, your wrongs are forgiven."

The cripple had hardly come for that but he nodded thanks.

The lawyers were amused, then appalled. "No one forgives real error but God."

The cripple likewise nodded at that.

But Jesus faced him smiling and said "So you know the Son of Man has power to forgive all wrongs—" He raised his hand and the cripple was amazed. Jesus said "Stand, take your cot and go."

The man walked out on two sound legs toward his brothers bawling for joy outside.

But the lawyers were scandalized and left. By their lights this man was not only breaking the laws of God but was dangerously attracting mobs that might yet boil into one more round of the common bloody quarrels with Rome. From that day they and Herod's henchmen all plotted to silence Jesus or end him. This was Herod Antipas, Rome's puppet in Galilee, Samaria and Perea—a man whom Jesus called "the

Fox." Herod had stopped John the Baptizer for now—John was jailed for denouncing Herod's marriage to his living brother's wife.

So Jesus stayed on the restless move, choosing pupils to add to the four from Capernaum. In the final body of Twelve were Simon who was later called Peter, Andrew his brother, John and James the sons of Zebedee whom Jesus called the Sons of Thunder, Philip, Bartholomew, Matthew, Thomas, James son of Alpheus, Thaddeus, Simon the Zealot and Judas Iscariot. There were also women who followed his wanderings providing for him out of their belongings. Among them was Mary from the town of Magdala on the lake. Jesus had flushed seven demons from her body and her thanks were endless.

*

As they walked through the towns of Galilee, Jesus healed where he could and tried to make people hear the heat of his call to change. God's reign was near, maybe on them already. How could they know of the fullness of time, of God's impatience to love them again—they with their lives still strapped in harness and their eyes on the ground? They must love God above all and each of their neighbors in complete fairness with minds pure of pride or greed. Then they would be ripe to welcome the reign.

Once when he sat in a boat offshore to speak to a crowd without being mobbed, Jesus felt God's nearness beating so hard that he cried "Look, I've come to set fire to the world. See how my hands are bound till it blazes!"

But some of the sickest plunged into the water and started toward him.

The pupils oared the boat farther out, set sail and went toward the eastern shore where towns were sparse and wilderness stretched. Toward evening a storm broke. The boat was swamping but Jesus was sleeping curled in the stern. The pupils shook him—"Can't you see we're drowning? Do something now."

Jesus looked at the waves, smiled and said "Be still."

The water was calm long before the pupils could trust their safety.

But as they landed near sunset, Jesus saw first thing a man on the brow of the rise ahead.

The man was naked and foul with wild hair. His hands and legs were locked in shackles, but he'd broken the chains.

A boy on the strand said the man had been crazy all the boy's life, that he lived in the graves, cut at himself with flints and shells and ate raw fish which he caught by hand.

The pupils wanted to put back out—a graveyard dweller was impure to touch.

But Jesus jumped from the boat and walked in a straight line toward the man.

The man held still but when Jesus neared, the man cried "Back! Stay back, oh God!"

Jesus came to him and held out a hand. When the man recoiled Jesus asked him his name.

An entire tribe of demons was in him refusing to answer. But when Jesus raised his voice to press them, they finally said "Our name is Legion." They spoke like a chorus of bats in the dark that was rushing in.

But Jesus kept saying "Out, come out" in a steady voice.

When the demons knew they had to obey, they spoke again and begged to be sent into some young pigs that were rooting nearby.

Jesus nodded.

The demons flew straight into the pigs.

The pigs shied, then stampeded over a ledge to drown in the darkening water below.

But the man that had been the Legion stood peaceful. For the first time in his memory he was clean.

Jesus took off his own head cloth, gave it to the man and he wrapped himself.

Then the man fell forward to worship Jesus, pleading to serve him any way.

But Jesus raised him, said he should find his people now and show what God had done for him. Then Jesus walked ahead into darkness, leaving the man and the baffled pupils on the strand below.

When he didn't return the pupils gave up and sailed toward home. Past midnight the wind rose and midway out they were bailing water when one of them looked, and there was Jesus walking on the surface toward them. They thought he'd somehow died and was coming back as a ghost, so even drowning felt preferable. They cried out for him to leave them be.

But he called across the water "I am." In their own language his words amounted to the name God gave from the burning bush when Moses asked, the name *I Am*.

That hardly calmed their terror.

But Jesus walked on into the boat and again curled up and slept in the stern. In the hours he'd spent alone in the hills, he'd prayed again for light on the matter of who he was and what God meant for his Son to do if God had truly called him Son as he rose from the Jordan in John's hands.

*

The following day a synagogue leader in Capernaum tracked Jesus down, told him his little daughter was dead—the child of his heart—and begged for Jesus to hurry and call her back from sleep.

Jesus said that the leader was right "She's asleep." But the man kept begging so Jesus followed the man toward his fine house.

In the stragglers behind them was a woman who had followed Jesus for days. She had suffered unstanchable menstrual blood for twelve years, had been broke by doctors and was now too wretched in her uncleanness to speak to Jesus. So she came up behind him in silence and knowing she only needed to touch him, she reached and touched the hem of his coat. At once the hemorrhage stopped inside her.

Jesus had felt the power leave him. He turned and said "Who touched me then?"

The pupils said "In all this mob you expect us to know?"

By now the woman was on her knees in tears of thanks and mingled fear—would he grudge her the health?

But Jesus only touched her again and said her trust had made her well.

Then they were at the leader's door. The sound of hired mourners was strong and the women were howling above the flutes.

Jesus took only Peter, James and John and pushed past the mourners to the room where the girl lay still on her mat.

She was white and cold in the dark chill room.

Again Jesus bent and took her hand. *"Talitha koum"* he said in their language—"Lamb, get up."

The girl's eyes opened. She slowly rose on unsure legs— she was twelve years old.

Her parents were speechless.

She entered their arms.

Then still to the sound of useless mourners, Jesus said "Give her something to eat" and left them.

*

News of that traveled far and fast. All sorts wondered who this man was or would turn out to be.

Soon John the Baptizer sent messengers from prison and asked for a simple answer from Jesus "Are you really the one to come or not?"

Jesus waited all night, then called the messengers to him at dawn and said "Tell John this. The blind see, the lame walk, lepers are clean, the deaf hear and speak, the dead are raised and the poor learn the news of God's coming reign. Bless him who trusts me." It was all he said.

But when John's messengers nodded and left, Jesus turned to the pupils stunned beside him and said one more thing "Foxes have holes, the birds have nests but the Son of Man has nowhere to lay his head."

Peter and Andrew at least were offended. They'd given him room and board for weeks.

Others thought he was crazy. Some turned back home abandoning hope in what they thought he'd meant and offered—rest, power and glory in God's coming reign.

But after a troubled while the Twelve held firm around him stumped as they were.

So Jesus called them apart in secret. He gave them power over foul demons and to heal the sick. He said that they were to go through all the towns and farms of Galilee, telling the hearers of God's coming reign. "Go two by two with no gold or silver, no extra shirt, just sandals and a stick and announce to Israel the good news that God is at hand. Bless the house that receives you. When a town won't receive you shake its dust from your feet. Amen I tell you it will be far better for Sodom and Gomorrah on Judgment Day than for that town.

"I'm sending you out like sheep among wolves. Be wise as snakes and guileless as doves and when they attack you here run there but never rest from telling God's news to the lost and wicked—they're welcome too just as they are in the midst of their lives. Both God and the angels welcome wrongdoers more gladly than the good. Amen I tell you, you won't have gone through the towns of Israel before the Son of Man comes in glory."

The pupils were amazed at his expectation, but they tried to obey him and they went off in pairs.

While the Twelve were gone Jesus heard that Herod the Fox had killed John the Baptizer—this Fox had teeth and would use them at will. So Jesus moved on alone through Galilee, continuing the work that was dogged by menace from friends and haters. Yet his power worked wherever he was trusted. In Bethsaida he met a completely blind man.

The man begged to touch him.

Jesus led the man by the hand out of town and when they were apart, he spat on the man's eyes. "Do you see anything?"

The man said "I see men that look like trees walking."

Again Jesus laid his hands on the eyes.

And the man saw clearly.

Jesus sent him home and warned him "Don't even pass back through town."

Then while Jesus still traveled alone his mother and brothers came from Nazareth to take him home—Joseph the builder had recently died. They'd heard the news of Jesus' wandering and thought he was crazy. When they reached where he was, he was in a house talking with serious men and women from the district. The family sent word for him to come out.

But Jesus refused and gestured around him. "Who's my mother and who are my brothers? Amen I tell you that my family is all who hear and trust me. Don't think I come to bring peace on Earth. I bring a great sword. I set a son against his father, a daughter against her mother and a man's worst enemies will be his own household. Remember I've come to set fire to the world and oh I long to see it blaze!"

The brothers took his mother back to Nazareth. She was bowed with sadness but had also seen in the eyes seated round him a reflected glare she recalled from his childhood and the distant sound of his voice had brought back the words she heard in Bethlehem when she learned of his coming, *God's choice—your son.*

*

Then the Twelve returned from their separate travels on a day like any other day. No one could see that the reign of God had come or was closer.

Jesus saw their bafflement and said "Let's go to the wilderness and rest." Any thoughts of his own were inward and secret.

They got in the boat, sailed east again on the lake and found a secluded place where Jesus could pray a little apart even from them and they could rest with no sad mobs of the sick and idle.

After a while though someone found them and a crowd gathered in the wilderness with no food or shelter.

Many violent and outcast men and women were among them. There was nothing to do but face the mob so Jesus told them this story about the Father's thirst for their souls. He said "A man had two sons. The younger one said to his father 'Father, give me my share of all that will come to me.' So the father divided his belongings between them. A few days later the younger son packed all he had and traveled far off. There he wasted his share in wild living and when he had spent everything a hard famine struck that place. The son was desperate so he hired himself to a man who sent him out to pasture his swine.

"The son would gladly have eaten the roots the swine ate—no one gave him anything. But once he finally came to himself, he said 'My father's slaves have food to spare but I'm starving here. I'll go to my father and tell him "Father, I've erred against Heaven and you. I'm not worthy to be called your son. Treat me like one of your hired hands." ' Then he went homeward toward his father.

"But while the son was still at a distance his father saw him and had pity. He ran and kissed him. The son said 'Father, I've erred against Heaven and you. I'm not worthy to be called your son.' But the father said to his slaves 'Quick, bring the best coat and put it on him. Put a ring on his hand, shoes on his feet and kill the fat calf. We'll eat and be glad for this son of mine was dead and is now alive. He was lost and we've found him.' They began to be glad.

"Now the elder son was out in the field and as he got near the house he heard music and dancing. He called one of the slaves and asked what this meant and the slave told him 'Your brother is home and your father has killed the fat calf because he's got him back safe and whole.' But the elder son was angry and refused to go in.

"His father came out and begged the elder son but he answered his father 'Look, all these years I've served you and never disobeyed your orders yet you never gave me even a kid so I might celebrate with my friends. But when this son of yours returned—the one that squandered your money on whores—you killed the fat calf for him.' So the father said to him 'Son, you're always with me and all that's mine is yours. It's fitting now to be grateful and glad for your younger brother was dead and is back alive. He was lost and is found.' "

When Jesus had taught them about God's hunger for their souls, evening was coming and he took pity on them. He said to Philip "How are we going to feed these people?"

Philip said "We aren't. Two hundred denars wouldn't buy bread for them."

But Andrew, Simon's brother, said "There's a boy here with five barley rolls and two fish."

So Jesus said "Make the people sit down"—there was deep green grass where they were.

The people sat down. With women and children there were some five thousand.

Jesus took the boy's rolls and fish. He thanked God for them, then passed them out to the seated crowd as much as they wanted.

When all were full the pupils picked up twelve baskets of uneaten scraps.

And when the men took the meal as a sign that God's anointed had truly come and his reign was at hand, they talked of seizing Jesus on the spot and making him king.

Jesus left quickly and the pupils followed.

*

For lack of any safe destination, he led them north into Gentile country, the towns around Tyre and Sidon in Phoenicia. They tried to move without being stopped but even that far north Jesus wasn't entirely unknown and couldn't be hid. His power was evident even when muffled.

So a Gentile woman found him—a Greek. She fell at his feet and begged him to heal her little daughter of a foul spirit.

Jesus said "Let the children of Israel be fed first. It's not right to take the children's bread and throw it to pups."

The woman said to him "Yes sir but pups under the table eat the children's crumbs."

Jesus smiled and told her "For that you can go home with something for your pains. The demon is gone from your daughter."

When the woman got home her daughter was well.

*

From there Jesus led the Twelve northeast to the flanks of Mount Hermon and the hamlets near Caesarea Philippi. More and more he was walking ahead of them or praying apart. But once on a lonely stretch of road he stopped, turned back and asked the pupils "Who do people say I am?" He had never told them outright whatever he thought.

They could see that now he needed to know. So they told him "Some say you're Elijah, some John the Baptizer, some say you're a prophet."

Jesus pressed them. "But you—who do you say I am?"

There was silence till Simon spoke out. "You're Messiah." The Jews had long awaited Messiah, a man whose Hebrew title means *Anointed*. Again some thought he was meant to free them and repair their pride in God's chosen people. Some thought he would come as a warrior chief. Some thought he'd be an eternal priest.

But as soon as Simon spoke Jesus warned the pupils to say nothing of this. Then as they walked he began to tell them that now the Son of Man must suffer many things, be refused by the lawyers and priests and be killed. "Then I will rise on the third day" he said. He spoke quite plainly.

Simon took him aside and began to warn him of such wild words—he thought Messiah was meant to reign in painless eternity.

But Jesus wouldn't take the rebuke. It defied his growing sense of his fate. He turned on Simon saying "Get behind me, Satan. You're thinking of human things, not God's." But after a while he said to Simon "Simon son of Jonah, now I'll call you Peter" (*Peter* means *Rock*). And to the other pupils he said "This is Peter and on his shoulders I'll lay my whole plan. The gates of Hell itself won't shake it." Then he went on talking about his fate—pain and death and rising again.

The pupils and even Peter were baffled. They'd waited for places in God's coming reign but now they said nothing.

*

Then after six days Jesus took Peter, James and John apart from the others and led them on to the heights of Mount Hermon. He barely spoke through the arduous climb. Then near the peak and alone in their presence, he was changed in form. His clothes turned a very shining white like nothing a human can make on Earth. His face was gleaming and Elijah and Moses were talking with him, one at each side.

Peter was cold with fright so he said "Rabbi, it's fine to be here! Let's pitch three tents—one for you, one for Moses and one for Elijah." He didn't know what he was saying. They were terrified.

A cloud came down and covered them; a voice from the cloud said "This is my Son, the one I love. Hear him."

Peter's arms and legs were frozen; and he said to himself *I've given too much to this one man, and now he shows me this wild sight—me with a home and a hungry family I've left to chase what's either Messiah or the shrewdest demon I've yet known. Should I run for my life or fling myself off this high rock? My family might starve but no one would see my dead shamed face.*

Then suddenly Peter and the others looked round and saw themselves alone with Jesus.

As they came down the mountain, Jesus ordered them to tell no one what they'd seen till the Son of Man should die and rise alive from the dead.

The pupils were baffled but asked him nothing.

As they reached the foot of the mountain they saw a big crowd around the nine other pupils and the usual lawyers were arguing with them.

When the crowd saw Jesus they rushed to greet him. One of them said "Teacher, I've brought you my son who has a dumb spirit. It seizes and flings him. He foams and gnashes his teeth and goes stiff. I told your pupils to help him but they couldn't."

Jesus was angry. He said to the pupils "Disbelievers! How long must I bear you?" But he told the father to bring the son forward.

They brought the boy forward and that near Jesus the

spirit shook the boy so hard he fell to the ground and wallowed foaming.

Jesus asked the father how long this had gone on.

The man said "Since childhood. It often throws him into fire or water to kill him. If you can do anything, sir, take pity on us."

Jesus said " 'If you *can*'? Everything *can* be for a believer."

The father cried out "Sir, I believe. Help my unbelief!"

The crowd was pressing closer on them so Jesus hurried and said to the demon "Dumb and deaf spirit, I order you to come out and leave him for good."

Screaming and tearing him hard the demon came out.

The boy looked lifeless.

Many thought he was dead.

But Jesus took his hand, pulled him up and he stood.

When the crowd had scattered, the nine pupils asked Jesus why they'd failed to expel the demon.

He said "That kind will only come out for hard prayers."

But when they asked him to teach them a secret powerful prayer, he only said what he'd told them before "Our Father in Heaven, your kingdom come. Your will be done on Earth as in Heaven. Give us today the bread we need, forgive us our debts as we forgive our debtors, and lead us not to trial but free us from the evil one. Amen."

They said "Sir, we prayed as hard as we've ever seen you pray."

Jesus said "Try harder. If your son asks for bread, will you give him a stone? If he asks for a fish, will you give him a snake? If he asks for an egg, will you give him a scorpion?"

So one of them asked if God would ever refuse to hear Jesus.

Jesus said "You don't understand at all, do you?" And though he half smiled he walked far ahead till they were in sight of Nazareth where he'd grown up.

On the Sabbath he went to the synagogue there and stood to read. A scroll he'd known since childhood, a text of the prophet Isaiah, was handed to him. Unrolling it Jesus found the place he wanted and read to the crowd,

> *The spirit of the Lord is on me*
> *Because he anointed me*
> *To cheer the poor.*
> *He has sent me announcing release to captives,*
> *Sight to the blind,*
> *Balm to the bruised,*
> *Announcing the welcome year of the Lord.*

Rolling up the scroll and giving it to the rabbi, Jesus sat and the eyes of all were fixed on him. He began to tell them "Today this scripture is fulfilled in your eyes—"

At first many commended him and wondered at the graceful words from his mouth. They said "Isn't this the builder, Mary's son and the brother of James, Joses, Judas and Simon and aren't his sisters here with us?"

But when he couldn't heal there because some people doubted him, Jesus said "Surely you'll tell me 'Do here what you've done in Capernaum.' But I tell you honestly there were many lepers in Israel under Elisha the prophet, and not one was healed but Naaman the Syrian. For a prophet is dishonored only in his own town among his own people and in his own house."

All who heard that were filled with rage and rising they led him out of town to the brow of a hill and meant to pitch him over.

But Jesus managed to pass straight through them and go his way.

Behind him the pupils argued among themselves.

When they were back in Capernaum, Jesus asked them "What were you arguing on the road?"

They kept silent not wanting him to know that they'd argued who would be first in God's coming reign.

But Jesus knew. He said "If anyone wishes to be first he shall be last of all and the slave of all."

After that he taught them secretly the thing he knew now. He said to all the Twelve that "The Son of Man is betrayed into men's hands. They'll kill him and being killed after three days he'll rise." He told them many times but they couldn't understand. Then though he kept the Twelve with him, he sent out seventy other pupils saying that they must go through all Judea at once announcing God's coming in every town he meant to visit when he moved south.

The seventy went.

Jesus waited alone on the hills in prayer and hope.

And when they returned they were full of their victory. They said "Sir, even the demons fly from us when we use your name."

Jesus said "Amen then I've seen Satan fall like lightning from Heaven!" For once he exulted.

And those around him watched for the sky to burst with God's full justice and glory. They'd fallen far back of Jesus in understanding his path.

By now it was winter.

*

So Jesus set his face toward Jerusalem.

The loyal baffled Twelve came behind him—he had that power still.

Behind the Twelve came the loyal women who'd helped him according to the little they had.

On the way a young man ran up and knelt to Jesus saying "Kind teacher, what must I do to win eternal life?"

Jesus said "Why call me kind? No one is kind but God. You know the commandments—'*Do not kill, do not commit adultery, do not steal, do not give false witness, honor your father and mother.*'"

The man said "Teacher, I've done all that."

Gazing at him Jesus loved him and said "One thing's lacking then. Go sell all you own and give it to the poor. You'll have treasure in Heaven. Then follow me."

But the young man was shocked.

Jesus said "Look, your miserable brothers and sisters—all of them children of Abraham too—live in filthy rags and starve. Your house is stocked with all good things."

So the young man went away grieving. He had great possessions.

Looking round at the pupils, Jesus said "It's easier for a camel to go through the eye of a needle than for a rich man to enter God's reign."

They were poor but puzzled and said among themselves "Then who can be saved?"

Jesus said "With humankind it's impossible but not with God—everything's possible with God."

Peter started saying "Look, we gave up everything for you—"

But Jesus stopped him. "Amen I tell you there's no one who left home or brothers or sisters or mother or father or children or farms for my sake and the sake of the good news but shall get a hundredfold back in the age to come and eternal life." Again he told them of the Son of Man's fate. Then he turned to walk on.

They were coming to see that by *Son of Man* he somehow meant himself, so they let him precede them by considerable distance. They were stunned and afraid but still they came on.

*

It was the feast of Dedication and Jerusalem was mobbed with pilgrims to the Temple. Jesus and the pupils stayed east of the city on the Mount of Olives but daily he walked in the porches of the Temple and announced his news to all, Jew or Greek.

Some trusted him at once from the news they'd heard. Others hounded his steps in the hope of trapping him in some blasphemous or seditious claim—everyone in power feared his hold on the poor and outcast.

One group asked him by what right he did his work, who gave him his power?

Jesus said "Answer me one thing and I'll tell you by what right I do my work—John's baptism, was it from God or humankind?"

They reasoned among themselves "If we say 'From God' he'll say 'Then why didn't you obey him?' but if we say 'From men' "—they were slow to say that, knowing how the people had honored John. So they said "We don't know."

Jesus said "Then I won't tell you where I get my power."

One of the lawyers, knowing he'd answered them well, said "Sir, what commandment stands first of all?"

Jesus said "First is '*Hear, Israel, the Lord our God is one Lord and you shall love the Lord your God with all your heart, with all your soul and with all your strength.*' Second is this '*You shall love your neighbor like yourself.*' There's no commandment greater than these."

The lawyer said "True, teacher. There's no other beside God and to love one's neighbor like oneself is more than all burnt offerings and sacrifices."

Jesus told the man "You're not far from the reign of God. Remember God's word when he said '*Amen I will have mercy and not sacrifice.*' "

Then they brought him a woman caught in the very act of adultery. They stood her before him and said "Moses ordered us to stone such a woman. What do you say?"

Jesus stooped and wrote on the ground with his finger as if he hadn't heard them.

So they asked him again.

He stood and said "The one that's pure among you, let him throw the first stone." Again he stooped and wrote on the ground.

One by one, from the oldest to the youngest, the men walked off and left Jesus alone with the woman.

Jesus said to her "Woman, where are your accusers? Is no one condemning you?"

She said "No sir."

He said "Neither do I. Go and wrong no more."

Later in Solomon's Porch in the Temple, he told this story. "A man planted a vineyard, put a fence around it, dug a wine vat and built a watchtower. Then he leased it to tenants and went away. In the summer he sent a slave to the tenants to get some grapes. They beat the slave and sent him away empty-handed. The owner sent another slave. They beat his head and insulted him. The owner sent a third. They killed that one and many more—beating some, killing others.

"He had one left, a much-loved son. Finally he sent him to the tenants, saying to himself 'They'll honor my son.' But the tenants said to themselves 'Here's the heir. Let's kill him and all the inheritance is ours.' Then they killed the son and flung his body out of the vineyard. What will the owner do? He'll come, kill the tenants and give the vineyard to others."

Some saw that Jesus was speaking of himself and some of them loved him for it, some meant to arrest him, some to stone him. But they knew he'd told the story on them too. They feared his mob and waited in silence.

So Jesus and the pupils withdrew from Jerusalem and crossed the Jordan beyond the place where John had baptized not two years before.

Many came to Jesus there and trusted in him.

*

Then in Bethany on the Mount of Olives in sight of the Temple a man named Lazarus fell sick. He was Jesus' friend and the brother of Jesus' friends Mary and Martha. The sisters sent word to Jesus beyond the Jordan and though he loved Lazarus and the sisters he waited two days before saying he'd go to Bethany.

At once the pupils tried to dissuade him. They said "Rabbi, you're in trouble there so near Jerusalem."

Only Thomas was eager. He said "I'm ready to die beside him."

Jesus set out, the others fell in and when they'd passed the Dead Sea and Jericho and climbed the long rise to Bethany, Lazarus had been in the grave four days.

Meeting Jesus on the road Martha even said "Sir, if you'd come sooner he wouldn't have died."

When Mary met him she said the same.

But Jesus walked straight past them to the grave where his friend lay wrapped and cold. When he got there he could not conceal his grief. It made him shudder hard and weep.

Many had come from Jerusalem to mourn. They all watched Jesus.

And at last he said "Take the stone off the grave."

Martha said "But sir, he'll stink by now."

They rolled the stone off the dark grave shaft.

Then groaning again and in a loud voice Jesus cried "Lazarus, come out!"

The man who was dead four days came out still wrapped in grave linen.

Jesus kissed him and said "Untie him. Let him live."

All who'd stood by watching were startled. Many trusted in Jesus.

But others went back to Jerusalem and told the chief priests and the ruling council.

Among themselves the council said that if they let Jesus work among them then all the people would follow him and soon the Romans would come and crush them—Jesus, his rabble, the nation around them, the priests and the Temple.

Caiaphas the High Priest finally said "It's better that one man die for the people than that we and all the nation be slaughtered." And from that day the priests and the council searched for a way to catch him on safe ground apart from his mob and kill him quickly.

Before they could act Jesus withdrew again, this time to a town named Ephraim north of Jerusalem near the wilderness. He understood that his time was near and more and more he walked out alone and slept apart. Again and again he asked himself if he'd been wrong about God's love—could any father who presided over the demons of sickness and pain, want, hate and loss be rightly called *loving* by his lone afflicted creatures?

But the Twelve were still with him waiting still.

*

Then the time for Passover came in early April. Pilgrims moved toward the Temple from all the nation and from foreign lands and the city swelled many times over.

By the first day of Passover week Jesus thought he had answered his awful question—how could it matter if the Father loved his creatures? The Father was the only God; if Jesus was his Son then the question was meaningless—God's will was sovereign for joy or pain. So he led the pupils back along the eastern approach to the crest of the Mount of Olives. Looking down on the city and the nearby hamlet of Bethphage he called two of the pupils and said "Go to that hamlet there and you'll find a tethered colt on which no one's ever sat. Untie it and bring it here. If anyone asks what you're doing say 'The teacher needs it and will send it right back.' "

Just as he said they found a colt tied to a door outside in the street and they brought it to Jesus, throwing their coats across its back.

Jesus sat on it, rode down the Mount to the depth of the valley and began the steep climb to the Temple.

Many spread their coats in the road and others spread leafy branches from the fields. The ones in front and those behind cried out " 'Hosanna! Blessed is he who comes in the Lord's name!' " Few of them recalled what the prophet Zechariah had said long ago,

> *Rejoice greatly, O daughter Jerusalem!*
> *Look, your king comes to you.*
> *Triumphant and glorious is he,*
> *Humble and riding on an ass,*
> *On a colt the foal of an ass.*

Even the pupils didn't understand though some of the lawyers said to him "Teacher, calm your pupils."

Jesus answered "Amen I tell you if they were silent the stones themselves would cry out."

The priests were only biding their time. Herod was watching. The Romans were watching.

Jesus dismounted at the Temple doors, looked round the courts that were sparsely filled so late in the day, then went back out.

That night Jesus led his pupils again uphill to Bethany where they dined with Lazarus and his sisters Martha and Mary.

At the end of the meal, Mary came forward with a pound of expensive perfumed ointment. She wiped Jesus' feet with it and dried them with her hair. The splendid odor filled the whole house.

Judas who kept the common purse for Jesus and the pupils was plainly indignant and said "Why wasn't this ointment sold for three hundred denars and the money given to the poor?"

But Jesus said "You'll have the poor with you always but not me. Let Mary be. She'll keep the remainder to sweeten my corpse."

No one but Jesus smiled.

*

On the following morning he entered the Temple courts. He'd brought a stout cord which served as a whip and with it he drove out the merchants, their sacrificial livestock and the money handlers who defiled the place by exchanging coins for the Temple tax. As they ran he cried out "Remember it's written '*My house shall be called a house of prayer for all nations.*' But you have made it a bandits' cave."

The priests were watching.

The rest of that day and the next three days as Jesus taught and argued in the Temple his enemies worked to lure him into their trap. They even tried to catch him in sedition. Some lawyers approached him and said "Teacher, we know you're honest and that no one counts heavily with you since you aren't partial to appearances but teach God's way. So tell us is it right to pay tribute to Caesar? Should we pay or not?"

Jesus said "Why tempt me? Show me a coin."

They showed him one.

And he said "Whose picture is this and whose inscription?"

They said "Caesar's."

So he told them "Give Caesar's things back to Caesar. Give God's things to God."

Later to the crowd he denounced the lawyers. "Beware these lawyers. They love to parade in long robes, be bowed to in the market, take the best seats in synagogue and at banquets. Yet they likewise eat up widows' houses under cover of prayer. They'll get the reward of their pride and their lies." Then turning on the lawyers at hand Jesus said "Great sorrow to you, false teachers. You're like whitewashed tombs that shine in the light but inside are full of dead bones and filth. You're a nest of vipers—who'll save you now? Those who trust me are saved by God's truth. Truth sets them free."

The lawyers said "Look, we're sons of Abraham just like you and have never been slaves. How can you say we're not free?"

Jesus said "Amen I tell you that anyone erring and erring again is the slave of error. I know you claim to be sons of Abraham but you're trying to kill me because I'm bearing the Father's news."

The lawyers said "Our father is Abraham."

Jesus said "Abraham's children do God's will. You're doing the will of your father Satan."

The lawyers laughed. "What's to keep us from saying you're gripped by a demon and mad as a lunatic?"

Jesus said calmly "I know no demons. I honor my Father. You dishonor me. Amen I tell you a final time that anyone hearing and trusting my news will never see death."

The lawyers said "Now we know you're mad. Abraham died, all the prophets died but you're saying 'If anyone trusts me he'll live forever'?"

Jesus nodded and said "Your father Abraham foresaw my day, saw it and delighted."

They laughed again. "You're not even forty and you've seen Abraham?"

Jesus said "Amen amen I tell you before Abraham was I am."

There was rubble handy from the work on the Temple. Many took up stones to throw at Jesus, but he managed to leave.

At last though, taking God's name as he had, he'd insured his death.

Jesus well knew that. He believed himself. He was on the verge of the fate he'd glimpsed as a boy in school, not to be the glorious warrior chief who'd vanquish the Romans but the sacrificial slave of God whom he'd found foreseen in the prophet Isaiah—the slave who was somehow God's own self.

> He was pierced for our trespasses,
> Crushed for our wrongs,
> He bore the strokes that left us whole
> And by his bruises we are healed.

On the Wednesday Jesus sat with the pupils on the Mount of Olives and looked toward the Temple porches and courts. White marble and gold dazzled in sunlight. Giant hewn stones braced it stronger than any building on Earth. Yet Jesus told the pupils plainly "See those great buildings? There'll be no stone left standing on stone which shall not be toppled."

When the pupils were baffled his feeling deepened and he cried toward the city "O Jerusalem, Jerusalem, killing the prophets and stoning the messengers. How often I'd have gathered your children as a hen gathers her brood to her wings but you wouldn't come. And now the days are strictly numbered till the sun goes dark, the moon fades and all the powers of Heaven quake with the coming trial. For then you'll see the Son of Man coming on clouds with power and glory, sending his angels to gather the chosen from pole to pole. He'll separate the souls as a shepherd parts his sheep from the goats—the sheep on his right hand, goats on his left.

"Then the Son will say to those at his right hand 'Come O blessed by my Father. Inherit the kingdom readied for you from the start of the world. For I was hungry and you fed me, thirsty and you gave me drink, I was a stranger and you welcomed me, naked and you clothed me, sick and you visited me, in prison and you came to me.'

"The righteous will say to him 'Lord, when did we see you hungry or thirsty or a stranger or naked and serve you or sick or in prison and visit you?' And the Son will answer them

'Amen I tell you when you did that to the least of my children you did it to me.'

"Those on his left hand will say 'Lord, Lord, haven't we cast out demons in your name and done many wonders? Haven't we kept the law?' But the Son will tell them 'I never knew you. Leave me and enter eternal fire prepared for Satan and his angels for I was hungry and you gave me no food, thirsty and you gave me no drink, a stranger and you never welcomed me, naked and you failed to clothe me, sick and in prison and you never visited me. When you did it to the least of my kin, you did it to me.' They'll depart from there into lasting fire but the just will enter eternal life."

Thomas asked him when this trial would be.

Jesus said "Amen I tell you that no way shall this generation pass till all these things come down upon you. Heaven and Earth shall pass to dust. My words won't pass. But as to the hour and day none knows, not the angels in Heaven nor even the Son but only the Father. Stay wakeful and watch both day and dark or the Lord may come and find you sleeping."

Peter said "But teacher, who can face the Son? We're common men."

Jesus said "Be perfect like your Father in Heaven."

It made Peter angry the rest of that day.

And late that same night Judas Iscariot who was one of the Twelve went to the priests and offered to betray Jesus' nighttime whereabouts. No one ever knew why he made that choice.

But as the priests heard Judas's offer, they were glad and promised him money if he found an occasion to lead them to Jesus when he was alone apart from the mob.

*

On Thursday which was the first day of unleavened bread when they sacrificed the Passover lamb, the pupils said to Jesus "Where do you want us to go and arrange for you to eat the feast?"

He sent two of them saying "Go into the city. You'll be met by a man with a water jug. Follow him. Wherever he enters tell the owner 'The teacher says "Where is my guest room so I can eat the Passover with my pupils?" ' He'll show you a big room upstairs spread and ready. Prepare for us there."

The pupils went out and found the room as he told them.

So as evening fell Jesus came with the Twelve. When they'd taken their places around the table Jesus took off his shirt, wrapped a towel around himself, poured water into a bowl and began to wash the pupils' feet, drying them with the towel at his waist.

He got to Peter but Peter protested "Lord, you'll never wash my feet."

Jesus said to him "If I don't wash you, you'll have no part in me."

Peter said "Then not just my feet but my hands and head too."

Jesus washed them all, even Judas who was set on his course now.

As they were eating Jesus said "Amen I tell you one of you will betray me, one eating with me here."

The pupils were distressed and said to one another "Surely not me."

Jesus said "One of you who dips bread into the dish with me—better for that man if he'd not been born."

Then Judas left on his errand. He knew where Jesus would go after this to be apart.

As they finished eating Jesus took a last loaf and blessing it he broke and gave it to them saying "Take. This is my body." Then lifting a cup and giving thanks, he gave wine to them.

All drank it.

He said to them "This is my blood of the promise poured out for many. Amen I tell you never in any way will I drink of the fruit of the vine till that day when I drink it new in the reign of God." Then when all had drunk, he led them in a final solemn joyous dance—a rite that mirrored the course of the stars, the currents of time, during which they sang the truth he'd told them only now,

> A *light I am to you who see,*
> A *glass I am to you who look,*
> A *door I am to you who knock,*
> A *road I am to you who walk.*

When that was done Jesus said a last thing "You have seen your brother, you have seen your God."

And after singing the final hymn they walked down the side of Zion and up the dry bed of the Kidron brook to a garden at the foot of the Mount of Olives where they'd stayed that week. And Jesus said to them "All of you shall stumble tonight for it's written

> *I'll strike down the shepherd*
> *And the sheep shall be scattered.*

But after I'm raised I'll go ahead of you to Galilee."

They'd still never understood his word *raised.*

But Peter told him "Even if everybody stumbles not I."

Jesus said to Peter "Simon, Simon—look—Satan begged hard to have you to thresh like harvest wheat. I've prayed for you that your faith won't fail."

Peter said "Oh Lord, no way, no way."

Jesus said to him "Amen I tell you—you, today, tonight before the cock crows twice—you'll deny me three times."

But Peter just kept saying "If I must die with you no way would I deny you."

All the others said likewise.

*

They came to a plot of land called Gethsemane or *Oil Press*. Jesus told the pupils "Sit here while I pray." Taking Peter, James and John with him he went on farther under the olive trees and began to be deeply appalled and harrowed. He said to the three men "My soul is anguished to death. Stay here and watch." It was ripe in his mind now—the Father might here require the Son to throw his own life in the press of time to ease the coming down of the reign. The prospect scalded.

So going on a little, Jesus fell to the ground and prayed that if it were possible the hour of sacrifice might turn away. He said "*Abba*, Father, everything is possible to you. Take this cup from me—still not what I want but you." He came, found the three pupils sleeping and said to Peter "Simon, are you sleeping? Couldn't you watch with me one hour? Watch and pray so you don't come to testing. Oh the spirit is ready but the flesh is weak."

They didn't know how to answer him.

Going back alone Jesus prayed the same words. But then the wrongs of all humanity were laid on his head, and at last he felt the weight of the ransom he'd vowed to pay.

This time Peter heard the prayer and saw great drops of sweat like blood on Jesus' face. He meant to stand and go toward Jesus but his legs were weak from the long day.

So Jesus came again and found them sleeping since they didn't know how to answer his need.

Once more Jesus pled alone with the Father. Then he came back a third time and said to the three men "Sleep now and rest. It's over. I paid. The hour came. But look, the Son of Man is betrayed into wrongdoers' hands. Get up. Let's go. See, the one who betrays me is nearing."

At once while Jesus was still speaking, Judas Iscariot appeared and with him a cohort of Roman soldiers and a squad with swords and sticks from the chief priests, lawyers and elders. The traitor had given them a signal—"Whomever I kiss is he. Seize him and take him off securely." Coming up to Jesus then, Judas said "Rabbi!" and kissed him lovingly.

The men got their hands on Jesus and bound him.

Peter drew his knife, struck the High Priest's slave and cut off his ear. The man's name was Malchus.

Jesus said to the men "Did you come out armed to arrest a rebel? I was with you every day in the Temple and you didn't seize me."

Deserting him then all the pupils ran.

Only Judas stayed to get his reward.

And one young man who had followed Jesus was dressed in a linen shirt over his nakedness. The men seized him too but leaving the shirt behind he fled naked.

Then they took Jesus off to the High Priest.

All the chief priests, elders and lawyers gathered.

Peter and John had followed at a distance. They got right into the High Priest's courtyard.

Again John's family sold salt fish to the Priest so he was known here and could move farther in.

Peter stayed in the courtyard with several slaves and warmed himself by a blaze in the chill night.

*

Now the priests and the council took testimony from many liars that Jesus had said "I'll tear down this Temple made by hand and after three days I'll build another that's not handmade." Even so the witnesses were not consistent.

Rising in the center of the chamber the High Priest said to Jesus "Won't you answer to what these men testify?"

But Jesus was silent standing there.

So the High Priest said "Then you are Messiah, the Son of the Blessed?"

Jesus said "I am and you shall see the Son of Man sitting at the right hand of power and coming with clouds of Heaven."

The High Priest tore his robe at that, meaning Jesus had finally sealed his doom.

All the council likewise condemned him to death. Some spat on him, covered his eyes, struck him and said "Now prophesy!"

Even the slaves treated him to blows.

And while Peter was down in the courtyard one of the High Priest's maids saw him warming himself. She said to him "You're with the Nazarene Jesus."

But Peter denied it saying "I don't know him. What are you talking about?" Then he went out to the porch and a cock crowed.

Seeing him the maid said to those standing round "This man is one of them."

Again Peter denied it.

After a little those standing round said to Peter "Surely you're one of them. Anybody can hear you're a Galilean."

Peter began to curse and swear. "I don't even know this man you mention." Then a second time the cock crowed and Peter remembered Jesus saying "Before the cock crows twice you'll deny me three times." Dwelling on that he wept bitterly.

In the morning the priests, the lawyers, the elders and all the council handed Jesus over to Pilate at Roman headquarters in the former palace of Herod the Great by the western gate. For fear of defiling themselves that day and being unfit to eat the Passover they stayed outside while the soldiers led Jesus.

Pilate asked him "You're the King of the Jews?"

Jesus said "You say."

Pilate asked him "Then what have you done? Are you some zealot?"

Jesus said "My reign is not here and now. If it were my friends would fight for me."

Pilate said "So you're a king?"

Jesus said again "You know the truth."

Pilate said "What's the truth?"

Jesus said no more.

Then Pilate went out to the waiting accusers and said "You have your custom that I free one prisoner at every Passover. Do you want me to free the King of the Jews?"

They all cried "Barabbas! No, give us Barabbas." Barabbas was a jailed bandit.

Pilate said "Then what must I do with Jesus?"

They cried "Crucify him!"

So Pilate had the soldiers take Jesus and whip him. Then they dressed him in a royal purple robe, plaited a crown of thorns for his head, saluted him as King of the Jews, mocked and spat on him and returned him to Pilate.

Pilate led Jesus back outside. To the waiting accusers he said "Here's the man."

They only cried again "Crucify him!"

Pilate handed Jesus to a squad of soldiers who stripped him of his robe, laid the armpiece of his cross on his shoulders and led him north through the city to die. When Jesus stumbled under the weight, they forced one Simon from Cyrene to bear it.

So they went north through the Gennath gate and came to the hill Golgotha, *Skull Place,* in a limestone quarry long since worked out. They gave Jesus wine that was drugged with myrrh, a token mercy. Then they stripped him naked, nailed his arms at the wrist to the armpiece, then hoisted that upright onto the stake and nailed his feet. At his head they posted the charge against him written in Latin, Hebrew and Greek. It said "Jesus of Nazareth King of the Jews."

Below him, as was their privilege, the soldiers divided his clothes. His coat was woven in a single piece so rather than tear it they cast lots for it. Then at Jesus' right and left they crucified two thieves.

It was about noon.

The passersby insulted Jesus by wagging their heads and

saying "So!—the man who'd destroy the Temple and build it in three days. Save yourself. Step down from the cross."

The chief priests also watched and mocked him.

Even the thieves beside him cursed him.

None of his friends were near at hand. Only the women who had followed from Galilee stood at a distance watching in grief. Among them were Mary from Magdala, Mary the mother of the younger James and Joses, and Salome. They tried to console his mother who was with them.

The blank sky gave no sign whatever of angels on clouds proclaiming the reign.

At last a great darkness settled on the place and at three in the afternoon Jesus shouted in a loud voice " *'Eloi Eloi lema sabachthani?'* " It means "My God, my God why did you desert me?"

Some of the bystanders thought he was calling Elijah. One of them ran, filled a sponge with vinegar, put it on a stick and held it up to his mouth to drink, saying "Let's see now if Elijah saves him."

No one saved him.

So Jesus cried out loud again and breathed his last.

Since the priests had a rule against leaving dead men on their crosses after sundown, above all on the Sabbath, the soldiers came in late afternoon to break the legs of Jesus and the thieves. It would speed their deaths since, broken, they could not press up on their feet to breathe. When the soldiers reached Jesus, he seemed to be dead. For certainty one soldier pierced his side with a spear.

Blood and water poured out. He was long since dead.

Sundown Friday was coming fast—the preparation for the Sabbath—so Joseph from Arimathea, an important member of the council who likewise expected God's coming reign, went boldly to Pilate and asked for Jesus' body.

Pilate wondered if he was already dead and called the captain of the hanging party.

The captain confirmed it.

So Pilate presented the corpse to Joseph.

Quickly buying new linen and hauling Jesus down from the cross Joseph hurried to wrap him in the linen with spices. Near the cross was a garden where Joseph's own rock tomb was waiting—it had never been used. They laid Jesus there and rolled a heavy stone to the entrance.

The two younger Marys watched where he was put. They would come back after the Sabbath to finish washing the body. With all the rules against work on the Sabbath, that could be no sooner than dark on Saturday or Sunday dawn.

*

At daylight Sunday morning the two Marys and Salome returned to the tomb with cloths and spices to wash and anoint Jesus' body. All the way they asked themselves "Who'll roll back the stone?"—the stone was huge. But when they reached the actual tomb the stone was rolled back. The entrance was open. Two of the women balked in fear.

Mary from Magdala walked forward though, telling herself at every step *The world is frozen now in death. At last the demons have fouled his body. Even my hand that would wash his corpse is helpless in chill air before me. All my life has passed by useless.* When she took the last step she saw a young man on the right of the tomb where the corpse had lain.

The man wore a white coat; and when he saw Mary near he said "Don't be afraid. Are you hunting Jesus the dead Nazarene? He was raised. He's gone. Go tell all his pupils and Peter that he's going ahead to Galilee. You'll see him there as he told you before."

Going out again the women fled. They were shuddering and wild with shock and for a cold hour they told no one nothing.

When the women finally broke their story the pupils doubted and feared a trap.

But Peter and John ran toward the tomb.

John got there first, stopped at the entrance and bent to look in. He saw the linen lying empty.

Peter went straight in, saw the linen and also the face cloth apart from the linen folded neatly.

John went in then, examined the linen and believed. Then he and Peter returned to where the pupils had hid for fear of their enemies.

But Mary from Magdala had followed them back to the tomb and now she stood alone weeping at the entrance.

A man behind her said "Woman, why weep?"

Mary turned but did not know him as Jesus. She thought he was a gardener. She said "Sir, if you've taken him show me where."

The man said "Mary—"

Then she knew. She cried out "Rabbi!" and knelt to clasp his knees.

Jesus said "Stop holding me" and raised her upright. Then he told her plainly what to tell the pupils—he was risen indeed.

After that he went to the High Priest's servant and gave him part of the linen shroud that had covered his own dead body in darkness.

*

When Mary got to the pupils with her news they were even more amazed. They stayed in hiding afraid and uncertain. But that night when they'd finished eating Jesus suddenly stood in their midst—the door had been locked. They were terrified and thought he was a ghost.

He said "No fear. I am—look." He showed them the holes in his wrists and feet and the wound in his side. Then he asked for something to eat. They brought him part of a broiled fish and a comb of honey and he ate in plain view. Then he told them again he was bound for Galilee.

After that Jesus showed himself unmistakably to James his brother. James had sworn that he would never eat or drink again till he had seen the risen Lord so Jesus came to him, took bread and wine, blessed them and said "Eat, brother, and drink your fill for the Son of Man is risen from among them that sleep."

He also came to Judas the traitor, touched him firmly and ringed his wrist though he said no words and left still silent.

Then Judas went out to the field he'd bought with his blood money and hanged himself.

Jesus likewise appeared unquestionably to upward of five hundred people who'd known him. It was later in Galilee that he left the remaining pupils.

*

Peter and Andrew, James and John sons of Zebedee, Thomas, a man named Nathanael and two more pupils returned to Capernaum to wait for his coming as the Son in glory. One night Simon said "I'm going fishing."

The others said "We're coming with you."

They went out, got into the boat and all that night caught nothing.

But when it was dawn Jesus stood on the shore, not that the pupils knew it was Jesus.

Jesus called to them "Boys, nothing to eat?"

They called back "No."

He said "Cast to starboard. You'll find some."

They cast the net and then could barely drag it, there were so many fish.

John said to Peter "It's the Lord."

Peter hearing that tucked his coat up—under it he was naked—and threw himself into the lake.

But even in sight of Jesus again the other pupils came on in the boat hauling the lucky net of fish. They were only a hundred yards from shore. When they landed they saw a charcoal fire laid, a fish lying on it and bread.

Jesus said to them "Bring some of your fish."

Peter got up—he'd been panting in the shallows—and helped beach the net. They'd caught a hundred fifty-three fish but the net wasn't torn.

Jesus said "Come eat."

None of the pupils dared ask him "Who are you?" knowing it was Jesus raised from the dead.

When they'd eaten in silence Jesus pointed to all the men and said to Peter "Simon son of Jonah, do you love me more than these?"

He said "Yes Lord, I love you."

Jesus said "Feed my lambs." Then a second time he said "Simon son of Jonah, do you love me?"

Peter said "Yes Lord, you know I love you."

Jesus said "Tend my young sheep." A third time he said "Simon son of Jonah, do you love me?"

Not understanding that Jesus was letting him cancel each of his three denials, Peter was grieved that he'd asked him a third time. He said "Lord, you know everything. You know I love you."

Jesus said again "Tend my young sheep."

Peter nodded yes and took more bread.

The other pupils watched in silence.

Then Jesus rose and walked away to the east in the new light of that last day.

It had been two years since they first met him and they'd never see him again on Earth. It would only be slowly that they came to see how, in the time they shared his life, his hard ordeal and calm return had ended things as they'd been from the start. He'd reconciled an outraged God to them and their kind, all human creatures till the end of time.

And whatever they lacked that final dawn, they gave the rest of their lives to his other task, the task he failed—to make all people know that God is at hand with his flaming love, comprehensible at last—and they never lost hope to see him come again on clouds in the Father's power to claim them. One of their cries in their own language was "*Maranatha*"—"Lord, come now!" They thought he had promised that.

In other lives their cry has lasted near two thousand years.

REYNOLDS PRICE

Reynolds Price was born in Macon, North Carolina, in 1933. Educated in the public schools of his native state, he earned an A.B. summa cum laude *from Duke University. In 1955 he traveled as a Rhodes Scholar to Merton College, Oxford University, to study English literature. After three years and the B.Litt. degree, he returned to Duke where he continues teaching as James B. Duke Professor of English.*

With his novel A Long and Happy Life *in 1962, he began a career which has resulted in numerous volumes of fiction, poetry, plays, essays, and memoir. His* A Palpable God—*which appeared in 1978 and provided translations from the Old and New Testaments, with an essay on the origins and aims of narrative—was the first outcome of his study of sacred story.*

He is a member of the American Academy of Arts and Letters, and his work has appeared in sixteen languages.